Praise for The HappyCow Cookbook

"For so many years, HappyCow has given vegans the ability to access vegan food anywhere we go, which is crucial to the vegan lifestyle and sense of belonging. This book takes that mission to the next level, bringing the fantastic food we seek out into our homes and kitchens. What a brilliant addition to any chef's library!"

—Mayim Bialik, actress on *The Big Bang Theory* and author of *Mayim's Vegan Table*

"*The HappyCow Cookbook* is the next best thing to sitting at the table of the best chefs in the world."

—Howard F. Lyman, author of *Mad Cowboy*

"Well done, HappyCow! Here's your chance to enjoy delectable, health-promoting, plant-based cuisine from some of the finest restaurants in the world—without leaving home."

—J. Morris Hicks, author of *Healthy Eating, Healthy World*
and international blogger at hpjmh.com

"HappyCow, the amazing website and indispensable app, has directed me toward delicious vegan cuisine in my travels and even at home for years. Their new cookbook brings exciting, exotic, and extraordinary plant-based cuisine to your own home, enabling you to re-create the masterpieces from some of the most talented chefs around the world. I highly recommend this gorgeous, inspiring collection for anyone who appreciates the art of cooking and/or just enjoys eating delicious, health-promoting food."

—Julieanna Hever, MS, RD, CPT, author of *The Complete Idiot's Guide to Plant-Based Nutrition* and host of Veria's wellness talk show, *What Would Julieanna Do?*

"These chefs are the go-to connoisseurs of great vegan food, and now they're making it possible for us to eat at home what we would have had to travel the globe to find! These dishes are going to make you so happy!"

—Kathy Freston, *New York Times* best-selling author
of *Veganist, The Lean,* and *Quantum Wellness*

"*The HappyCow Cookbook* is long overdue! I love that I can revisit all my favorite vegan restaurants from my travels from the comfort of my own kitchen! For vegan foodies who crave these delicious dishes but don't have the luxury of hopping on a plane every weekend to visit these great locales, *The HappyCow Cookbook* is the perfect addition to your collection so you can dine at a different restaurant every day!"

—Carolyn Scott-Hamilton, "The Healthy Voyager" and author
of *The Healthy Voyager's Global Kitchen Cookbook*

THE
HappyCow Cookbook

Recipes from Top-Rated
Vegan Restaurants around the World

EDITED BY

ERIC BRENT
AND
GLEN MERZER

BenBella

BenBella Books
Dallas, Texas

BenBella Books, Inc.
10300 N. Central Expressway
Suite #530
Dallas, TX 75231
www.benbellabooks.com
Send feedback to feedback@benbellabooks.com

Printed in the United States of America
10 9 8 7 6 5 4 3 2

Library of Congress Cataloging-in-Publication Data
The happycow cookbook : recipes from top-rated vegan restaurants around the world / edited by Eric Brent and Glen Merzer.
      p. cm.
   Includes bibliographical references and index.
   ISBN 978-1-939529-66-4 (trade paper : alk. paper) — ISBN 978-1-939529-67-1 (electronic) 1. Vegan cooking. 2. International cooking. I. Brent, Eric, editor of compilation. II. Merzer, Glen editor of compilation. III. Title: The happy cow cookbook.
   TX837.H37 2014
   641.5'636—dc23   2013041820

Editors: Eric Brent and Glen Merzer
Senior Editor: Maria Teresa Hart
Associate Editors: Evelyn Hays and
      Christy Morgan
Assistant Editors: Jessika Rieck and Vy Tran

Copyeditor: Shannon Kelly
Proofreaders: Kim Marini and Kristin Vorce
Cover Designer: Faceout Studio
Text design and composition by Kit Sweeney
Printed by Versa Press

Distributed by Perseus Distribution
www.perseusdistribution.com

To place orders through
Perseus Distribution:
Tel: (800) 343-4499
Fax: (800) 351-5073
E-mail: orderentry@perseusbooks.com

Significant discounts for bulk sales are available.
Please contact Glenn Yeffeth at glenn@benbellabooks.com or (214) 750-3628.

THE
HappyCow Cookbook

Contents

Foreword　　　　　　　　7

Introduction　　　　　　8

Restaurants

42°Raw　　　　　　　　13

222 Veggie Vegan　　　　19

Ain Soph. Ginza　　　　　25

Blackbird Pizzeria　　　　29

Buddha Burgers　　　　　35

Café Blossom　　　　　　43

Candle Café　　　　　　49

Chaco Canyon　　　　　55

Choices Café　　　　　　61

Coox and Candy　　　　　67

Cornbread Café　　　　　73

Counter Culture　　　　　79

El Piano　　　　　　　　85

Evolution　　　　　　　91

Funky Pies　　　　　　　97

G-Zen　　　　　　　　103

Green Cuisine　　　　　109

Green New American
　　Vegetarian Restaurant　115

Hangawi Restaurant　　　121

Karyn's On Green　　　　127

Lettuce Love Café   131
Loving Hut   137
Lovin' Spoonfuls   143
Lucky Leek   147
Luna's Living Kitchen   153
Millennium   161
Mi Vida   167
Mudra Café   171
Native Foods Café   177
Peacefood Café   183
Plant   189
Portobello   197
Rawlicious   203
Real Food Daily   209
Sage's Café and Vertical Diner 215
Souley Vegan   221
Stuff I Eat   225
Sublime   231
SunCafé Organic   237
True Bistro   241
Vegetarian Haven   247
Veggie Grill   253
Veggies on Fire   259
Wayward Café   265
ZenKitchen   269

Index   277
Acknowledgments   281
About the Editors   282
About HappyCow   282

Foreword

I've been vegan for more than twenty years. I was vegan throughout my pregnancy, and now I'm raising a healthy vegan baby boy. I am proud to be vegan and to know that no animal has to suffer or die for my sustenance. Like millions of my fellow vegans around the world, I know that the diet we've chosen is the one that reduces greenhouse gases and water pollution so that our planet can have the best chance to heal.

There are many millions of vegans, and our numbers are growing by the day, but in a world of seven billion people, clearly we are still outnumbered virtually everywhere we go. We are surrounded by friends, family, colleagues, and strangers who have not yet made the switch. They have not yet registered how much cruelty is involved in an animal-based diet, and how entirely unnecessary that cruelty is. They have not yet registered how badly our oceans, rivers, farmland, and air are polluted and plundered by the collective madness known as the animal-based diet. They have not yet registered that their diet isn't as natural as they might have thought.

It's crucial that we vegans have a way of reaching out to one another in common purpose. There is a natural bond between all people who cannot imagine seeing animals as food. We feel the need to create a community—a welcoming one that others are encouraged to join. No single entity has done more to create an international veg community than HappyCow, the world's premiere website for all things veg.

I love HappyCow. I couldn't imagine traveling around the country or the world without it. And now there's something else I couldn't imagine being without—*The HappyCow Cookbook*. Use it as a resource for your travels or for your kitchen, and you will be even more a part of this community than you were before.

—Emily Deschanel

In 1984, at the age of eighteen, I did a three-month trip through Europe, hitchhiking with a backpack from Finland to Greece. I had such a good time bouncing around with my backpack that, at twenty-one, after graduating from college, I traveled with my trusty backpack for another fifteen years, never living anywhere for more than five or six months at a time. I spent most of that time in Europe and Asia, but also traveled through North and Central America, Australia and the South Pacific, and the Caribbean. My habit was to spend a few months at a time teaching English, often in Taiwan, to earn and save money, and then resume my shoestring travels. I traveled to over fifty countries, and I managed to live on just a few thousand dollars for nine months a year. I loved changing my environment so that each day was an adventure. I was introduced to new people, new culture, and new cuisine everywhere I went.

But increasingly, the cuisine became a problem for me as a traveler because I had become a vegetarian as a college student. While I was attending the University of California at Santa Cruz, a friend brought me to a small, popular local restaurant, then called McDharma's Natural Fast

Foods (now Dharma's). I ordered a Brahma Burger, made of beans, nuts, seeds, and grains. After I ate it, I began thinking hard about the source of meat burgers, my mind churning with images of the blood and suffering associated with it. I decided then and there to never eat red meat again.

When I returned to my travels after graduation, traveling as a vegetarian—or near-vegetarian—became challenging for me, especially in parts of the world where meat and fish are ubiquitous in the cuisine and vegetarianism is almost unknown. If I was unlikely to find a vegan or vegetarian restaurant, I asked locals where I could at least find a veg-friendly place so that I could eat and stay healthy and live in accordance with my beliefs. It was always a struggle.

Unfortunately, I continued to eat eggs and shrimp for a while, since I somehow didn't see that as the same thing as eating animals. But when I informed a Buddhist master in Taiwan, with whom I studied privately, of my diet, he asked me in turn, "What is the difference between a shrimp and a cow?" There was no need to respond. The question answered itself profoundly. I gave up shrimp in that moment. For some reason, the master didn't ask me the difference between an egg and a cow, so I continued to eat eggs a little while longer, until I came in contact with another spiritual teacher, Master Ching Hai, who helped me see that it was time to stop consuming eggs as well as honey and to stop wearing leather.

As hard as it was to travel as a vegetarian, it was harder still to travel as a vegan. When I took a trip on the Yangtze River in China, I didn't eat anything but white rice for a week. Seeing the inhumane way the animals were treated in China (animals were sold in markets still half-alive, hearts barely beating) further convinced me that I could never again eat them. But there were few options for me besides rice. At the time, there were no useful guides to vegetarian restaurants, and asking locals for suggestions rarely worked out. Traveling in Malaysia in 1991, after walking all day in the hot sun searching for vegan food, I nearly passed out from hunger and heat exhaustion, and had to be rescued by locals.

On a subsequent trip from Taiwan to India in 1999, accompanied by my then-partner, Irene Andersson, I was inspired to create the HappyCow website to help the world's veg travelers find "safe" food. I often lamented aloud about my food woes while we were living in Rishikesh, in northern India at the base of the Himalayas. After hearing me complain again and again, Irene challenged me to take action. So within a few weeks I taught myself HTML. When I was ready to upload the very primitive, basic website, it took me a full two days to do so because the dial-up Internet connection was so bad. After various improvements and conversion to a dynamic database, HappyCow.net finally began to gain traction, and it really began to flourish a couple of years later when we added the ability for users to write their own reviews and upload photos.

In the past several years, the site has taken off with the help of new partnerships and the hard work of numerous contributors. HappyCow.net has grown into a worldwide community and has improved countless lives. People who used to complain about the painfully difficult search for veg food in foreign cities now

I loved changing my environment so that each day was an adventure. I was introduced to new people, new culture, and new cuisine everywhere I went.

can check out the innumerable restaurants listed on HappyCow, which are reviewed by their fellow travelers. They can even get the information via our mobile app. I'm always gratified to hear stories from our community about how HappyCow transformed traveling from a burden to a pleasure.

HappyCow is a user-generated-content website; its content is contributed by members and other contributors worldwide. Its success has been achieved by a selfless international community of vegetarians and vegans who want to help others like themselves find up-to-date information on veg restaurants or health food stores. Presently, we feature over 25,000 veg and veg-friendly listings of restaurants and stores with upwards of 60,000 reviews. HappyCow has become an indispensable resource for veg travelers all over the world, and those travelers are in turn an indispensable resource for the site, updating it with information on a daily basis, sending in reviews, and participating in forum discussions.

But there's more to the site than that. There's listings of veg shops and bakeries, veg B&Bs, veg catering companies, veg organizations, and farmers' markets. There are articles on how to eat veg and stay healthy while traveling, addressing such matters as veg airplane meals and veg camping. There are articles on nutritional topics. There are links to all kinds of veg travel resources, such as guided veg travel or veg retreats. There are spotlights on different cities. There are blogs on wide-ranging subjects and there's an incredibly long list of famous vegetarians—a list that is growing by the day. Visitors to HappyCow can find recipes, interactive maps to guide users to veg destinations, a VegIQ test, a shopping site, a live chat room, a veg humor page, our *MooZine* newsletter, and more.

We offer HappyCow apps for iPhones and Android phones. And there's an evolving mobile web version for all other smartphones, too.

We strive to maintain the integrity of the site and to thereby help veg*ns (vegetarians and vegans) maintain the integrity of their diets. Our listings are defined by the level of "veg-ness" (vegan/vegetarian/veg-friendly). Each restaurant submission is reviewed and investigated. In order to get a listing on our site, a veg-friendly place has to demonstrate that it makes serious efforts to accommodate veg*ns and is not simply willing to leave out the meat. In addition, HappyCow volunteers moderate member reviews for adherence to our rules. I like to think that HappyCow's emphasis on integrity is responsible for our good reputation and loyal following, and it's why we've been voted favorite vegetarian website for seven consecutive years in the *VegNews* survey. The majority of HappyCow members are veg*ns themselves, so the contributions from our members are more attuned to the concerns of the veg*n community, and more accurate, than reviews one could find from mainstream sites like Yelp, OpenTable, or Google+ Local. When I say that veg*ns trust HappyCow, it's just another way of saying that we trust our own community.

Yes, it's possible to get a vegetarian meal, and sometimes a vegan meal, in a "regular" restaurant, and that's why HappyCow includes veg-friendly listings. Veg-friendly listings on the site are decided on a case-by-case basis, allowing for such factors as the size of the town where the restaurant is located. But I personally like to eat at and support vegetarian, and preferably vegan, restaurants. That's why we at HappyCow decided to create this cookbook to celebrate purely vegan restaurants. The restaurants selected for this volume have earned our support with their commitment to purely vegan food and with their high ratings from our members.

While these restaurants make an important contribution to the environment simply by shunning foods created by animal agriculture—an industry whose impact on greenhouse gases and climate change, according to a 2006 United Nations report, is greater than all forms of transportation combined—they also demonstrate a concern for the planet that goes above and beyond just being vegan. Maybe I'm biased, but I doubt

> The restaurants selected for this volume have earned our support with their commitment to purely vegan food and with their high ratings from our members.

HappyCow has grown consistently since its founding in 1999, but the most explosive growth has been in the last few years, coinciding with the explosive growth in the plant-food movement.

you'd find such environmental awareness and sensitivity in restaurants that serve meat. I think we veg*ns just care more about the planet. After all, that's one reason why many people turn to the veg diet in the first place.

The restaurants in this volume range from upscale, gourmet vegan dining establishments, like Sublime in Fort Lauderdale, to small, fast-but-healthy-food joints like Buddha Burgers in Tel Aviv, which makes food deliveries by bicycle. What they have in common, beyond their commitment to vegan food and a healthy planet, is the enthusiastic support of members of the HappyCow community.

HappyCow has grown consistently since its founding in 1999, but the most explosive growth has been in the last few years, coinciding with the explosive growth in the plant-food movement. Maybe we'll one day approach a tipping point, a time when veg*n concerns become mainstream concerns, when even vegan restaurants become commonplace, and when vegan world travelers will find a plethora of dining options everywhere they turn. We're not there yet. In the meantime, let's celebrate these remarkable vegan restaurants that someday may be hailed as pioneers. Try their recipes, and by all means visit their establishments and enjoy!

—Eric Brent

founder and director of HappyCow

42°Raw

COPENHAGEN, DENMARK

Pilestræde 32
1112 Copenhagen, Denmark
+45-3212-3210

(Second location in Hellerup, Denmark)

www.42raw.com

Jesper Rydahl, owner

42°Raw is a contemporary interpretation of plant-based eating, committed to changing the way people think about food and to serving food in its most natural state.

Is this your first restaurant?
Yes.

When did it open?
November 2009.

You currently have two locations in, and near, Copenhagen. Do you have plans for further expansion?
Yes, I hope to open a new location in London in 2014.

What's your favorite dish on the menu?
The lasagna; it's creamy and filling. It resembles a traditional lasagna, just in a healthier version.

What's your most popular appetizer?
Hummus—one of our recipes in this cookbook. Served with vegetable sticks, it constitutes a great healthy snack for adults and kids alike.

What's the most popular entrée on the menu?
Tapas—a selection of lasagna, Thai noodles, and avocado sandwich.

What's your most popular dessert?
Cupcakes, in all different flavors and colors.

What do you feel is special about your restaurant?
We are a one-hundred-percent plant-based fast-food concept in a contemporary setting—our ambition is to make plant-based eating desirable to a mainstream audience. Actually, only five percent of our guests are vegan or vegetarian; everyone else is just looking for a delicious and healthy meal.

How often do you change your menu items? Do you have daily or weekly specials?
We experiment all the time and continually introduce new dishes, drinks, and desserts.

Do you have gluten-free, soy-free, and sugar-free options on your menu?
Everything is gluten-free and sugar-free—that is, free from cane sugar—we

use agave syrup and coconut palm sugar. We are also soy-free except for our coffee, chai latte, and hot chocolate, where the guests have a choice between organic soy milk or homemade organic almond milk.

What do you do to reduce your environmental impact?

We are one-hundred-percent plant-based, which is a very important environmental contribution. We also use sustainable packaging for our takeout and energy-saving lightbulbs in our lamps.

What are the most important lessons you've learned as owner or chef of this restaurant?

That a mainstream audience will eat one-hundred-percent plant-based if presented with delicious food and drinks in an inviting space.

What led you to want to open a vegan restaurant, and/or what led you to the vegan diet yourself?

I started eating more plant-based for health reasons. My journey started six years ago when I quit sugar and experienced immediate relief from blood-sugar rushes and daily headaches. A year later I quit dairy and gluten and my lifelong allergy symptoms such as an often stuffed nose, breathing difficulties, and an itching throat disappeared almost overnight.

Three-and-a-half years ago I heard about raw food for the first time. I opened 42°Raw six months later and since then my diet has continued to become even more plant-based.

I am actually not a vegan myself, but I eat primarily plant-based. I represent a level of plant-based eating that a wide audience of conventional eaters can relate to. They see what I'm doing and say, "I could do that." It is important for people to find the level of plant-based eating they are comfortable with. Otherwise they will become discouraged and feel alienated.

In the time since your restaurant first opened, how has the plant-based food movement changed? Do you find more demand now for vegan food?

Yes, absolutely—raw food was basically unknown in Denmark when we opened. Now the whole nation

knows about it, which has helped shine light on plant-based eating and brought in a whole new audience. Women's magazines often have articles on raw food and green juices. It's becoming more mainstream—even fashionable.

A walk across a continent starts with taking the first steps in the right direction. Eventually you'll reach your destination if you keep walking. It's a transition that can take years.

Society at large still makes eating a plant-based diet challenging when you're on the go. We need more mainstream initiatives such as 42°Raw to build large chains and make delicious plant-based foods readily available in our cities, train stations, and airports. For now, there is still often a negative trade-off when trying to eat vegan in many places, because the options you're presented with aren't attractive enough. If delicious plant-based options are readily available, many people will be encouraged and go for it.

Since your restaurant first opened, has your view of what constitutes healthy or delicious food changed? Have you changed the types of foods you offer?

Yes, we are now moving from having only raw food into serving warm dishes with quinoa and whole-grain rice. People need warm food in the winter months in northern Europe.

Where do you see the plant-based food movement going in coming years?

It is going mainstream. I am one-hundred-percent convinced. 🐾

Thai Noodles

Serves 4

For the sauce:
1   medium mango
1½ teaspoons garlic
1½ teaspoons fresh ginger
1½ teaspoons red chili pepper
2   tablespoons red onion
4   dates
1½ teaspoons chopped fresh basil
3   tablespoons coconut oil or
    vegan butter
1½ teaspoons curry powder
2   teaspoons salt, or to taste
½   teaspoon ground black pepper
1   tablespoon sesame oil*
2   tablespoons tamari sauce
2   tablespoons lime juice
½   cup cashews
1   cup water

For the noodles:
4   zucchini or yellow squash
8   carrots

For the garnish:
4   tablespoons chopped spring
    onions
4   teaspoons black sesame seeds
Pinch red chili, to taste**

* Quality of sesame oils varies. If using a pure sesame oil, use 3 tablespoons in the recipe. If using a sesame oil blend, use 6 tablespoons in the recipe.

** Ideally fresh sliced chili, but chili powder will do.

> **Equipment needed:** *spiralizer*

In a blender, add all sauce ingredients except cashews and water. Blend on high until smooth. Add cashews and water and blend on high until smooth. Make noodles from the squash and carrots using a spiralizer, and mix with sauce just before serving. Top with chopped spring onions, black sesame seeds, and a few tiny pieces of red chili.

Zucchini Hummus

Serves 6–8

½   cup sunflower seeds
2½ cups sesame seeds
½   cup olive oil
1   tablespoon plus 1 teaspoon
    lime juice
1¼ cups red onion
1   teaspoon garlic
1   teaspoon salt
2   teaspoons paprika
1½ teaspoons ground cumin
    seeds
1½ teaspoons mustard seeds
1   teaspoon ground black
    pepper
1¾ cups chopped zucchini

First, grind the sunflower seeds and set aside. Then grind sesame seeds in blender until fine. Add oil, lime juice, onion, garlic, salt, paprika, cumin seeds, mustard seeds, and black pepper and blend until smooth, about 30 seconds. Add ground sunflower seeds and chopped zucchini. Blend until smooth. Use the blender plunger to help push zucchini pieces downward to the blade.

Serve with vegetable stalks and your favorite crackers.

222 Veggie Vegan

LONDON, ENGLAND

222 North End Rd.
West Kensington, London W14 9NU England
+44-020-7381-2322

www.222veggievegan.com

See HappyCow reviews at
www.happycow.net/book/222-veggie-vegan

Elegant and relaxed, with a menu as diverse as it is delicious, 222 Veggie Vegan is London's top spot to enjoy hearty food that happens to be very good for you.

Ben Asamani, owner and chef

Is this your first restaurant?
It's the first restaurant that I also own. Previously, I was head chef at a couple of vegan restaurants in the West End of London.

When did 222 Veggie Vegan open?
2004.

Do you want to have more than one restaurant?
Yes, I'd love to open some accessible take-away cafés in London to bring affordable healthy food to lots more people.

What's your favorite dish on the menu?
When I want something creamy, it's the stroganoff; when I feel like something heartier, it's the raclette.

What's your most popular appetizer?
Heart's Desire, which is sautéed artichoke hearts on rocket (arugula) leaves with a roasted red-pepper sauce.

What's the most popular entrée on the menu?
Probably the baked pumpkin and pine nut risotto.

What's your most popular dessert?
Spice Island Pie, one of our raw dishes, made from cashew and almond cream and sweetened with agave syrup.

What do you feel is special about your restaurant?
I think we have a real warmth—we always try to make everyone who comes here feel cared for. We are committed to helping people live a healthier life. Our regular customers become like family.

How often do you change your menu items? Do you have daily or weekly specials?
We change the menu about once a year and have daily specials every evening.

Do you have gluten-free, soy-free, and sugar-free options on your menu?
Yes, we want everyone to feel that they have lots of options, regardless of their dietary restrictions.

What do you do to reduce your environmental impact?
We try to minimize our environmental impact both in the materials used in the restaurant (the paint, the furniture, etc.) as well as our everyday actions (recycling and using green cleaning products). We would also like to use only organic ingredients and are working toward this.

What are the most important lessons you've learned as owner or chef of this restaurant?
Running a restaurant is hard work and takes a lot of energy. If you don't love the reason behind your restaurant, it will come across. If you can connect to a greater good like this, then you'll have lots of energy!

What led you to want to open a vegan restaurant, and/or what led you to the vegan diet yourself?

When I was fifteen, I went to a health talk organized by my local church, which changed my life. I realized that we don't need to eat animal products, and since that day I never have!

In the time since your restaurant first opened, how has the plant-based food movement changed? Do you find more demand now for vegan food?
The demand is really growing. These days we're busy all the time and not just with strict vegans or vegetarians. More and more people are realizing that healthy food can be delicious and satisfying, so they forget about whether it's labeled vegan or not.

Since your restaurant first opened, has your view of what constitutes healthy or delicious food changed? Have you changed the types of foods you offer?
People have become more open-minded. We don't have to create dishes anymore that look like "normal" nonvegan recipes. Raw vegan food is a completely original culinary art.

Where do you see the plant-based food movement going in coming years?
I think as more people experience vegan food and realize that it has the most wonderful flavors and gives you energy, rather than making you feel tired, they will naturally want to eat it more frequently. In addition, they will realize that by doing so they are making a big, positive difference to the planet. How can you argue with that? 🐮

An easy and delicious raw dish to fill you with energy.

Pumpkin Noodle Salad

Serves 4 (as a side dish)

¼ *medium-size pumpkin or
    ½ medium-size butternut
    squash, peeled*
1   *zucchini*
1   *medium cucumber*
¼ *cup chopped fresh basil*

For the dressing:
1   *cup mixed bean sprouts*
1   *clove garlic*
2   *tablespoons extra-virgin olive oil*
Juice of ½ lemon
½ *teaspoon sea salt*

For the garnish:
¼ *cup sunflower seeds*
¼ *cup pumpkin seeds*
¼ *cup freshly grated coconut**

** As a shortcut, you can use
the ready-to-eat freshly grated
coconut (not dried) found in some
supermarkets.*

Grate the pumpkin or squash, zucchini, and cucumber lengthwise into long noodles, using a julienne peeler if possible (or a spiralizer). Mix together in a bowl.

Combine all the dressing ingredients in a blender until the mixture has the texture of hummus.

Stir in the basil, adding more salt if necessary. Carefully mix the dressing with the noodles, divide onto serving plates, and sprinkle with garnish.

An original reinterpretation of the classic hearty and warming Swiss dish.

Oyster Mushroom and Spinach Raclette

Serves 4

2   *medium potatoes*
4   *cups vegan cottage cheese (see below)*
2   *cups sliced spinach*
¼   *cup diced onion*
2   *tablespoons chopped garlic*
1   *cup vegan béchamel sauce (see below)*
2   *cups oyster mushrooms*
2   *tablespoons toasted sesame oil*
¼   *cup roughly chopped fresh basil*

For the vegan cottage cheese:
⅓   *cup soy milk**
⅓   *cup cold-pressed sunflower oil*
¼   *teaspoon chopped garlic*
½   *tablespoon sea salt*
1   *teaspoon fresh lemon juice*
3   *cups firm tofu, drained and mashed*
2   *teaspoons dried parsley*

For the vegan béchamel sauce:
¼   *cup raw cashews*
½   *cup water*
¼   *cup soy milk**
Pinch sea salt
Pinch chopped garlic
½   *teaspoon brown rice flour*

For the garnish (optional):
Salad leaves
Cherry tomatoes

* Almond or rice milk may be substituted for soy milk.

Preheat the oven to 375 degrees. Cut the potatoes in half lengthwise and then cut two ⅓" slices from each half. (For these thin slices, you can use a mandoline, if you have one.) These will serve as the bases for the raclette portions. Cook the slices in a pan of boiling water until soft but still firm—about 6 minutes.

To make the vegan cottage cheese, first blend the soy milk, sunflower oil, garlic, and sea salt in a blender on high for 7 minutes. Pour into a bowl and stir in the remaining cottage cheese ingredients.

Add the spinach, onion, and remaining garlic to the cottage cheese and mix well. Place the cooked potato slices on an oiled baking tray and divide the spinach–cottage cheese mixture in even mounds over the 8 slices. Bake at 375 degrees for 15 minutes.

Meanwhile, prepare the vegan béchamel sauce. Process the cashews and water in a blender for 5 minutes. Heat the soy milk to a simmer in a pan with the salt and garlic. Mix the rice flour with a little water, enough to form a smooth paste, and stir it into the milk until the sauce thickens. Remove from heat and stir into the blended cashews.

Sauté the oyster mushrooms in the sesame oil over medium-high heat until soft, then stir in the basil. Place 2 potato slices on each serving plate, pour the béchamel sauce around the potatoes, and pile on the sautéed mushrooms. Garnish with salad leaves and cherry tomatoes, if using.

Ain Soph. Ginza

TOKYO, JAPAN

4-12-1 Ginza, Chuo-Ku
Tokyo, Japan
+81-3-6228-4241

(Other locations in Tokyo)

www.ain-soph.jp/pg185.html

"Returning to your true self" is the concept behind Ain Soph. Ginza, and to diners that means handmade, innovative Western-style cuisine with a Japanese twist, served in a pleasant atmosphere.

Yuki Shirai, owner

Is this your first restaurant?
Yes.

When did it open?
December 3, 2009.

You currently have two restaurants, Ain Soph. Ginza and Ain Soph. Journey. How many do you hope to have in the future? Will you expand further?
Yes. I'm planning to own more than five restaurants within three years.

What's your favorite dish on the menu?
I love our tomato soup. It always makes me happy and relaxed.

What's your most popular appetizer?
I would say the Today's Fresh Salad with fresh lettuce with cured leaves and potherb mustard as the base and seasonal vegetables. It's served with our original dressing made from rapeseed oil, organic mustard, soy sauce, and other ingredients. The dressing has a rich taste and it draws out the delicious flavors of the fresh vegetables.

What's the most popular entrée on the menu?
The two most popular dishes are the *Hayashi* Rice (a vegan take on a Western-influenced stewed beef dish) and the tortilla roll with fresh green leaves, hummus, avocado, paprika, and mock soy meat.

What's your most popular dessert?
Our customers love our brownie with carob chips.

What do you feel is special about your restaurant?
Although we serve only vegan dishes, most of our customers are not vegetarians and yet they enjoy our dishes.

How often do you change your menu items? Do you have daily or weekly specials?
It depends on the item, but we change our lunch menu every day. We change the desserts every season. One of our newest and most popular offerings is our vegan pancake.

Do you have gluten-free, soy-free, and sugar-free options on your menu?
Some dishes have no gluten, soy, or sugar. We use beet sugar and agave syrup instead of refined sugar.

What do you do to reduce your environmental impact?
We do not waste gas, water, electric power, or paper. We try not to make too much garbage, and we always try to order sustainably grown vegetables and to consider the sustainability of any other product [we use].

What are the most important lessons you've learned as owner or chef of this restaurant?
The concept of Ain Soph. is returning to our true selves through vegan diet.

I think choosing the vegan diet is one of the most effective ways for us to be connected to the universe. I believe vegetarianism helps us to be awakened spiritually and to expand our consciousness.

Essentially, if we are connected to the energy of love, it's easier for us to realize which direction we should take in our lives. And when we are in such a state, we are more powerful and creative. We are our true selves when we're connected to the energy of love.

Running this restaurant encouraged me—in a natural way—to follow my own path in life.

What led you to want to open a vegan restaurant, and/or what led you to the vegan diet yourself?
In the beginning, I never thought I would run a vegan restaurant. It all started when I understood that everything is made out of love, and that we can choose and create any path in our lives. Also, I realized we have the power to restart our lives anytime

at any age, whatever the circumstances are; we are the creators of our own world.

I really wanted to give to the world all the things I received, mainly, the greatness of being our true selves.

In the time since your restaurant first opened, how has the plant-based food movement changed? Do you find more demand now for vegan food?
When our restaurant opened in December 2009, there were very few vegan restaurants. In Japan, we still find such restaurants are quite limited, even in downtown Tokyo neighborhoods like Ginza and Shinjuku, where our restaurants are located. But the number of customers coming to Ain Soph. has increased in the past few years. And we've noticed that plant-based food has been acknowledged by more people since our restaurant first opened. Also, a wider variety of vegan ingredients have become available in recent years, like vegan cheese and vegan cream.

Since your restaurant first opened, has your view of what constitutes healthy or delicious food changed? Have you changed the types of foods you offer?
I think plant-based food has gathered more attention in the past few years. At first most of our customers were vegetarians or people who were very plant-based-food focused.

But now almost all of our customers are non-vegetarians. They're drawn in by beauty, health, and dietary concerns. We welcome this change. We'd like to suggest that everyone try a plant-based meal once or twice a week. The more people turn to this food for beauty, health, and environmental concerns, the more people will see it as healthy and delicious food.

Where do you see the plant-based food movement going in coming years?
I think the plant-based food movement will become much more popular and people will find plant-based options at any store or restaurant. It'll no longer require a special explanation ("Do you have plant-based food?"/"What is included in this food?"), and it'll grow in popularity.

Hayashi Rice

Serves 4

2   tablespoons rapeseed oil
⅔   cup chopped onion
½   cup chopped carrot
2   bay leaves
1   tablespoon plus 1 teaspoon
     flour
½   cup thickly sliced mushrooms
     (a variety)
1½   teaspoons red wine
1½   cups crushed canned tomatoes
⅓   cup water
1   tablespoon Hatcho miso (or
     regular miso, if not available)
2   teaspoons soy sauce
1   tablespoon beet sugar*
1   pack of vegetable bouillon
Salt, to taste

*You can substitute regular sugar if
beet sugar cannot be found.

Heat 1 tablespoon of rapeseed oil in a pan over medium heat. Add the onion and carrot and cook and stir until they are tender. Add bay leaves and flour. Stir until thoroughly combined but not burned. Remove from heat.

In another larger pan, heat 1 tablespoon of rapeseed oil over medium heat; sauté mushrooms until tender; add red wine and boil for 5 minutes over low heat.

Add the carrot and onion mixture from the first pan into the second. Add canned tomatoes, water, miso, soy sauce, beet sugar, and vegetable bullion. Boil for 20 minutes over low heat and then remove, add salt to taste, and serve.

Blackbird
-ALL ITEMS ARE VEGAN-

SANDWICHES

CUBANO	8.5
MEDITERRANEAN	7.5
CHICKPEA 'TUNA' WRAP	7
ROAST PORTOBELLO	8
GRILLED VEGGIE	7
SEITAN CHEESESTEAK	9
PICNIC	8

SALADS

MUSHROOM	8
GREEN	7
CAESAR	7
BEET	7.5

SIDES

HAND CUT FRIES	3/4
SIDE SALAD	4
POTATO SALAD	4
SAUTEED GREENS	4

TEMPEH CHILI   5

Blackbird Pizzeria

PHILADELPHIA, PA

507 S. 6th St.
Philadelphia, PA 19147
(215) 625-6660

www.blackbirdpizzeria.com

Opened by a devoted group of pizza and sandwich enthusiasts, Blackbird strives to prepare the most enjoyable vegan food possible—and succeeds, much to the delight of the denizens of the City of Brotherly Love.

Mark Mebus, owner and chef

Is this your first restaurant?
Yes, it's my first, as an owner. I have been working in the vegan/vegetarian food community for over ten years, though.

When did it open?
September 30, 2010.

Do you want to have more than one restaurant?
Possibly. My co-owner Ryan and I do talk about expansion.

What's your favorite dish on the menu?
Probably the Haymaker Pizza (with seitan sausage, red onions, garlic butter, and vegan cheese) or the smoked tofu Cubano sandwich.

What's the most popular entrée on the menu?
The Haymaker Pizza. It's a crowd favorite.

What's your most popular appetizer?
House-made seitan wings. They come in either habañero-citrus Buffalo sauce or a root beer BBQ sauce.

What's your most popular dessert?
All our desserts seem equally popular. We currently get desserts from Vegan Treats, a bakery in Bethlehem, Pennsylvania.

What do you feel is special about your restaurant?
Pretty much everything. I generally try to give everything on the menu a little bit of a twist to make it more interesting and stand out. My goal isn't just to make a vegan version of a pizza place; it is to make the best food I can that just happens to be vegan. I think the feel of the restaurant is different: We try to do more than

your average pizza/sandwich shop. We make an effort to make as many items from scratch as possible, and to change the menu semi-frequently. And we embrace the punk/hardcore community more than most establishments.

How often do you change your menu items? Do you have daily or weekly specials?
Every six months or so we tweak the menu a little bit. For the most part, it stays the same, though. I do specials here and there, but it isn't a constant thing.

Do you have gluten-free, soy-free, and sugar-free options on your menu?
Gluten-free is difficult because there is so much flour around and because we make seitan on premises. It's hard to guarantee that something didn't come into contact with gluten. We do have plenty of items without soy or added sugar.

What do you do to reduce your environmental impact?
We compost all the food waste through a local composting company. All the packaging we use is compostable and primarily made from post-consumer waste. All of our used cooking oil gets turned into biodiesel fuel. Pretty soon we should be switching to using only solar and wind power for electricity through an alternative energy supplier in the area. I'm actually just waiting for them to make the service available to commercial customers.

What are the most important lessons you've learned as owner or chef of this restaurant?
Probably that drinking lots of coffee solves most day-to-day problems.

What led you to want to open a vegan restaurant, and/or what led you to the vegan diet yourself?
Well, I always wanted to go into cooking, and once I did, I wanted to open my own restaurant. I have been vegan since my eighteenth birthday, so naturally I wanted to open a vegan restaurant. I went vegan primarily due to a moral obligation I felt, and still feel, the need to abstain from things contributing to animal abuse. I grew up going to hardcore shows, and the hardcore music scene is greatly influenced by the vegan straight-edge movement. So there were a lot of great bands and people that supplied me with information [about veganism] during my teenage years.

In the time since your restaurant first opened, how has the plant-based food movement changed? Do you find more demand now for vegan food?
I think that interest in vegan food is booming. I'm sure there are many reasons for this happening, but it is definitely on an upswing.

Since your restaurant first opened, has your view of what constitutes healthy or delicious food changed? Have you changed the types of foods you offer?
Neither of these things has really changed for me. I've been in the vegan/natural food community for a while now, so for the most part I've formed my opinions on a lot of these matters. I'm always open to new information, though; I just haven't come across much new info in the past few years.

Where do you see the plant-based food movement going in coming years?
Hopefully it will continue to grow. My first job in a restaurant was at [vegan restaurant] Candle 79 in New York back in 2004. Since then I have worked at many vegetarian and vegan places and from what I can tell, it has been constantly growing. I really don't see any reason for it to slow down. 🐾

Beet Salad

Serves 2

4 tablespoons coarse kosher salt
1 large red beet
1 large golden beet
1 large leek, green parts removed

1 tablespoon olive oil
Pinch salt and pepper
¼ cup raw pumpkin seeds
1 large navel orange

2 cups baby arugula
Shallot-Thyme Dressing (recipe follows)

Preheat the oven to 350 degrees. Cut 2 square pieces of foil (each large enough to cover a beet completely). Place 2 tablespoons of kosher salt on each sheet of foil. Place the red beet on one foil square and the golden beet on the other and wrap them completely. Bake until the beets are very soft and easily pierced with a knife, about an hour or longer. Allow to cool completely, then unwrap and peel the beets. Roughly dice the beets into 6 pieces ¾" thick. Refrigerate before using in the salad.

Clean the leek by slicing it vertically down the middle and running it under cool water to remove any dirt from the inside. Cut the leek into thin slices and place in a mixing bowl. Toss the sliced leeks, olive oil, salt, and pepper and bake for 10 to 12 minutes, or until the leeks are beginning to brown. Allow to cool completely before using in the salad.

Keeping the oven heated to 350 degrees, place the raw pumpkin seeds on a baking sheet and bake until deeply toasted but not burned (approximately 10 minutes).

To assemble: Using a sharp knife, cut all the peel off the orange. Carefully cut out segments of orange, slicing on either side of each segment to extract just the flesh of the orange. Place the baby arugula, orange segments, roasted leeks, and dressing in a mixing bowl. Toss in the bowl until the salad is fully dressed. Place the contents of the bowl into the middle of a large plate. Arrange the roasted beets around the salad, and top it off with the toasted pumpkin seeds.

Shallot-Thyme Dressing

Juice of ½ lemon
1 tablespoon whole-grain mustard
1 tablespoon apple cider vinegar
½ large shallot, chopped
¼ cup water
¼ teaspoon caraway seeds
⅛ teaspoon fennel seed
½ teaspoon salt
⅛ teaspoon black pepper
1 teaspoon agave syrup
½ cup olive oil
2 tablespoons fresh thyme

In a blender, add all the ingredients except the olive oil and the thyme and blend them at high speed. While blending, slowly add in the olive oil in a thin stream. Add the thyme leaves and pulse in the blender so that the thyme is dispersed and the dressing has green flecks throughout. Once the oil is incorporated and the dressing is emulsified, it's ready to serve.

Nacho Pizza

Makes 1 pizza

For the pizza sauce:
1   12-ounce can crushed tomatoes
1   teaspoon minced garlic
2   tablespoons chopped fresh
    basil
1   teaspoon dried oregano
Juice of 1 lemon

For the pizza crust:
Cornmeal or flour (for dusting the
    pizza peel)
1   11-ounce ball pizza dough
    (recipe follows)

For the toppings:
⅓   cup shredded cheddar-style
    vegan cheese (preferably
    Daiya)
¼   avocado, thinly sliced
10 Pickled Jalapeños (recipe
    follows)
¼   cup Caramelized Onions
    (recipe follows)

Timing: Pizza dough must be made at least 12 hours in advance.

Equipment needed: pizza stone, pizza peel

Add all pizza sauce ingredients together in a bowl; stir and set aside.

Place a pizza stone in the oven and preheat to 500 degrees. Allow the oven to maintain this temperature for at least 1 hour to make sure the stone has absorbed the heat properly. Spread a light dusting of cornmeal or flour onto a pizza peel. Pick up the dough ball and lightly press it to flatten it slightly without pushing any air out. Using your knuckles, gently stretch the dough ball, working around the edge. Slowly move hand over hand until the pizza has reached 10" to 12" in diameter. Transfer the stretched pizza dough onto the pizza peel.

Spread the pizza sauce in an even layer over the surface of the dough, working from the middle out in a circular motion.

recipe continued next page

Sprinkle the vegan cheddar cheese over the pizza. Place the sliced avocado and pickled jalapeño slices evenly around the surface of the pizza. Drape the caramelized onions on top of the avocado and jalapeño slices. Slide the pizza onto the preheated stone in the oven and bake until golden brown (approximately 6 to 12 minutes, depending on the oven).

Pizza Dough

5   cups bread flour
1¼ cups semolina flour
2   tablespoons olive oil
1   tablespoon agave syrup
1   tablespoon kosher salt
1½ teaspoons yeast
1⅞ cups cold water (55 degrees)

Equipment needed: standing mixer with a dough hook

Place all ingredients in a standing mixer fitted with a dough hook and mix on low speed for 5 minutes. Allow the dough to rest for 15 to 20 minutes in the bowl of the mixer. Resume mixing the dough on low speed for another 5 minutes. Remove and place the dough on a floured counter. Divide the dough into 4 equal pieces, approximately 11 ounces each. Cupping your hands and moving in a circular motion, shape each piece of dough into a tight, smooth ball. Coat each dough ball lightly with oil and place them on a sheet tray. Cover the dough balls loosely with plastic wrap and refrigerate for at least 12 hours before using.

Pickled Jalapeños

1   cup sliced fresh jalapeño peppers
1   cup apple cider vinegar
1   tablespoon kosher salt
1   tablespoon sugar
1   teaspoon black peppercorns
1   teaspoon juniper berries
½   teaspoon fennel seed
2   cloves garlic, smashed

Place jalapeño pepper slices into a jar or bowl. Combine all other ingredients in a small saucepan and bring to a boil. Let the mixture boil for 2 minutes and then pour it over the jalapeño slices. Allow the mixture to cool to room temperature and then refrigerate until needed.

Caramelized Onions

4   large yellow onions, very thinly sliced
1   teaspoon kosher salt
1   tablespoon olive oil

Combine all ingredients in a medium saucepan over the lowest possible heat. Cook slowly, stirring semi-frequently, until the onions are dark brown and very sweet (at least 1 to 2 hours).

Buddha Burgers

TEL AVIV, ISRAEL

Yehuda HaLevy 21
Tel Aviv, Israel
+972 3-510-1333

(Other locations in Tel Aviv, Haifa, Ra'anana, and Eilat)

www.buddhaburgers.co.il

See HappyCow reviews at
www.happycow.net/book/buddha-burgers

Buddha Burgers lives by a simple but meaningful philosophy: healthy vegan food should be available to everybody.

Arie Rave, co-owner and chef

Is this your first restaurant?
Yes. I started Buddha Burgers seven years ago with no prior experience in the restaurant business. It's in a small venue, in the backyard of a central Tel Aviv shopping mall, with only ten seats around a bar. To my surprise, within one month the place was basically booked solid from lunch to evening.

When did it open?
The first location, at Yehuda HaLevy 21, opened in December 2007.

How many do you hope to have in the future? Will you expand further?
I'm focused on our current locations. I want to create places with good, inexpensive dishes that are as well-regarded as our flagship restaurant in Tel Aviv, so I won't strive to open more branches. We have branches in central Tel Aviv and Ra'anana [a suburb of Tel Aviv], as well as the Haifa branch that opened in May 2013, that are independent franchises.

What's your favorite dish on the menu?
I personally eat almost exclusively raw, and I can say if it weren't for my regular intake of sprouted lentils, and all the energy and physical and mental strength I gain from them, the restaurant never would have come into creation. So my favorite dish would be sprouted lentil salad with greens and bell peppers, and for this reason we have quite a large salad bar with about thirty-four different vegetables, as well as tofu and seitan products.

What's your most popular appetizer?

Our Seitan Fingers, which is seitan cut into sticks, covered with a mixture of bread crumbs, nutritional yeast flakes, salt, and pepper, then fried. It'll take care of any meat cravings.

What's the most popular entrée on the menu?

One very popular entrée is our stuffed peppers; the traditional stuffing is a mixture of meat and rice; we make ours with seitan and brown rice, plus greens and dried cranberries.

What's your most popular dessert?

Because I'm originally from Vienna, and I remember the desserts in those coffeehouses, I put a lot of effort behind my desserts here, and many nonvegetarians are astonished by our capabilities. Two popular desserts are our Un-Cheese Cake and our tiramisu.

What do you feel is special about your restaurant?

Our customers, who are incredibly intelligent, and our team. I'm always trying to find team players who are vegan or at least will be capable of understanding our mission. And with them, I know that we maintain a very high standard.

How often do you change your menu items? Do you have daily or weekly specials?

We do offer seasonal dishes; for example, when apricots are in season, we make apricot balls (a sweet dough ball with an apricot in the center) for dessert. Daily specials were dropped some years ago, but maybe they'll return again.

Do you have gluten-free, soy-free, and sugar-free options on your menu?

The awareness of gluten intolerance has risen in Israel over the last few years, so many of our dishes are made and marked as gluten-free. We also have soy-free options, but we didn't label them as such, since not many customers request it. And we also serve sugar-free desserts made with maltitol and stevia.

What do you do to reduce your environmental impact?

All of our deliveries are done by bicycle, [and have been] since day one. We were the first in Tel Aviv, maybe in the whole of Israel, to do this, and others copied us since then. We do this mainly to emphasize the environmental advantages of vegan food.

What are the most important lessons you've learned as owner or chef of this restaurant?

It hasn't been about learning something new for me. Instead, it's been about taking the time to practice what I learned before, to do something complete, to strive to create something complete, something where I can say, "Now this is truly very good."

What led you to want to open a vegan restaurant, and/or what led you to the vegan diet yourself?

Ethical reasons. But I never strived to open a restaurant. Initially it was a whim, a shot in the dark, but when customers kept returning I realized that there's a real need for healthy vegan food. I felt an obligation to improve, because I understood we were doing something important for them.

In the time since your restaurant first opened, how has the plant-based food movement changed? Do you find more demand now for vegan food?

Yes, definitely, demand is growing in Israel, especially in the last two years. And I think the main difference is that the attitude of nonvegetarians has changed. Seven years ago many people ridiculed us, but now, over the years, there's a growing understanding that vegan food is healthier.

Since your restaurant first opened, has your view of what constitutes healthy or delicious food changed? Have you changed the types of foods you offer?

No, I already knew that raw food was the healthiest choice. The only personal change I made is that I now frequently drink wheatgrass. This definitely helped me with caffeine withdrawal, and gave me more physical energy. I can see it in my running: I got faster and stronger with wheatgrass juice.

Where do you see the plant-based food movement going in coming years?

Change is slow. For me the real question is when will vegan restaurants become the majority. I believe it'll happen, maybe in thirty, forty, or fifty years.

The principle of this burger is simple: include as many healthy and energizing ingredients as possible. Therefore, the base is sprouted lentils and quite a lot of flaxseed. All other ingredients are included for texture and taste.

Buddha Lentil Burger

Serves 8–10

2   tablespoons olive oil (optional)
1½ cups minced white onion
7   cups sliced white mushrooms
¾   cup sliced celery stalks
3   cups sprouted green or black lentils
1½ cups minced toasted walnuts
10 garlic gloves, minced
¼   green jalapeño pepper, minced well*
1   cup tomato paste
1   cup ground flaxseeds
4   tablespoons tahini mixed with 4 tablespoons water
4   tablespoons soy sauce**
30 fresh basil leaves, minced
1½ teaspoons ground sea salt (or regular salt)
1½ teaspoons ground black pepper

*Wear gloves when handling these peppers and never touch your eyes.

**For a gluten-free version of this recipe, use gluten-free soy sauce or Bragg Liquid Aminos.

Preheat the oven to 375 degrees. Warm the olive oil in a pan and add the minced onion together with the mushrooms and the celery. Sauté for 5 minutes. Drain the vegetable mixture in a colander and press out all the juices and oil. Then put the mixture in a food processor together with the lentils and walnuts. Using a large food processor, work in batches. With the food processor half-full, pulse the ingredients for 5 to 8 seconds until it resembles the texture of ground beef.

Transfer the mixture out of the food processor and into a large bowl, and stir in the rest of the ingredients with a large spoon (or a mixer). Set aside and let it rest for 10 minutes so the ground flaxseeds can bind the mixture. The mixture should be soft and moist.

To make each patty, take about 5 heaping tablespoons of burger mixture and press it flat into a disc onto an oiled baking pan. Bake the patties at 375 degrees. After 10 minutes, flip the patties and rotate the pan around in the oven back to front (for even baking). Bake another 10 minutes. Remove and cool. The patties should be crunchy on the outside and softer on the inside.

Serve in a whole spelt bun with toppings, like our Béchamel "Cheese" (see recipe under Tofu Spinach Lasagna), a vegan Thousand Island dressing (vegan mayonnaise, ketchup, pickles, and dried onion), mustard, lettuce, tomato, red onion, or chives.

Tip: *The healthiest way to prepare these burgers is to dehydrate them rather than baking. After shaping the patties, place them in an oven at 115 degrees for 12 hours.*

Tip: *If you want to make the lasagna gluten-free, replace the pasta with eggplant. Preheat the oven to 400 degrees. Cut 1 medium eggplant into thin slices, put them in salt water for 30 minutes, then drain them and pat them dry. Cover with gluten-free flour and bake in the oven for about 40 minutes, until the eggplant slices are crisp on the outside and soft on the inside. Then follow the steps at right to assemble the lasagna.*

This lasagna remains a favorite even after four years. We make the same lasagna day after day, and there are customers at our brunch buffet filling up the entire plate with it. It's quite easy to make, though a little time intensive.

Tofu Spinach Lasagna

Serves 4–6

2 tablespoons olive oil
1 cup minced white onion
3 cloves garlic, minced
3½ cups defrosted frozen spinach, drained
2 cups cubed potatoes, boiled and drained
4 tablespoons soy sauce
1 teaspoon salt
½ teaspoon pepper
2 cups crumbled tofu, either hard or soft (not silken)
3 cups soy milk
20 ounces lasagna pasta
Buddha Tomato Sauce (recipe follows)
Béchamel "Cheese" (recipe follows)

Note: To protect the pasta layers from shifting due to humidity, work quickly and cover each layer with the next.

Put the olive oil in a saucepan and warm it for 15 seconds. Add the white onion and sauté for 3 minutes. Add the garlic and the spinach and sauté for another 2 minutes. Add the cooked potato cubes, soy sauce, salt, and pepper, and smash the mixture with a potato masher (or with an immersion blender, but be careful not to overmix, or the potatoes will turn to glue). Add the crumbled tofu and stir.

To assemble: Preheat the oven to 350 degrees. Sprinkle soy milk on the bottom of the baking pan, just to make a base. Add 1 layer of lasagna pasta. Top that with the tomato sauce. Add another layer of lasagna pasta. Top that with the tofu-spinach mixture. Add another layer of lasagna pasta. Top with the cheese. Bake the lasagna for 30 minutes. The lasagna is ready when the cheese on top turns golden. Remove and serve. The lasagna will only keep well for 3 days in the fridge, so eat leftovers quickly.

Béchamel "Cheese"

Serves 8

This is our most popular sauce and cheese substitute, based on soy milk, with nutritional yeast for taste, *besan* (chickpea flour) for protein and added thickness, and a little salt and canola oil, creating a rich mayonnaise-style spread.

¼ cup Earth Balance butter substitute
6 tablespoons besan (chickpea flour)
1½ teaspoons salt
3 cups soy milk*
¾ cup nutritional yeast powder
1 to 1½ cups canola oil (weaker blenders require more oil)

* For this kind of cheese you will need soy-based milk; the lecithin in the milk is a binder and results in the mayonnaise-like consistency.

Soften the butter substitute on the stovetop in a stainless-steel pot over a low flame, taking care not to boil it. Mix the *besan* and salt into the butter substitute and stir so that the mixture thickens and makes a roux. Slowly add the soy milk, while continuously stirring. Turn up the flame to warm the mixture, and bring it to a boil still while stirring, until thoroughly combined,

recipe continued next page

and then switch off the burner. Move mixture to a blender and add the nutritional yeast and blend until thoroughly combined.

Add the canola oil in batches: Pour out part of the mixture from the blender into another container, so the blender is never more than one-third full. Put the lid back on tightly and increase the blender to maximum speed. If you have a blender with a small middle lid on the top, open the lid on the top while the blender is running and you will see a hole created by the blender plates. (If your lid doesn't have this, you will have to stop the blender.) Slowly pour the canola oil into the soy milk mixture while the blender runs. You will see that the hole slowly closes. When the hole is closed and the motor of your blender sounds higher (the blades of the knife are running in air), the cheese is finished and you can switch off the blender. Repeat this process, adding oil to the other batches.

Tip: *If resulting cheese is too salty for your taste, you can dilute it with more soy milk in the blender.*

Buddha Tomato Sauce (Marinara Sauce)

We base our tomato sauce on the classic Italian marinara sauce, but we add sun-dried tomatoes for more flavor.

5   sun-dried tomatoes (not packed in oil)
2   tablespoons oil
1   cup minced white onion
2   cloves garlic, minced
1   red bell pepper, diced
½   cucumber, diced
½   zucchini, diced
5   tomatoes, boiled and skin removed, diced (or 1 14-ounce can crushed tomatoes)
1   cup tomato paste
10 fresh basil leaves, minced
½   cup white wine
1   teaspoon salt
1   teaspoon pepper

Soak the sun-dried tomatoes for 30 minutes in enough water to cover them. Do not drain. After 30 minutes, move them to a blender and blend them with the soaking water. Set aside. Sauté the white onion in the oil for 3 minutes in a saucepan. Add garlic, pepper, cucumber, and zucchini and sauté for another 2 minutes. Add tomatoes, tomato paste, sun-dried tomato mixture, basil, and wine, and cook for about 20 to 30 minutes until mixture is reduced by about 30 to 50 percent. Mash with a potato masher or blend with an immersion blender. Taste and add salt and pepper to your liking.

Café Blossom

NEW YORK, NY

466 Columbus Ave.
New York, NY 10024
(212) 875-2600

(Other locations in New York City)

www.blossomnyc.com

A fixture on Manhattan's Upper West Side, Café Blossom is a classy, innovative, and passionate vegan café.

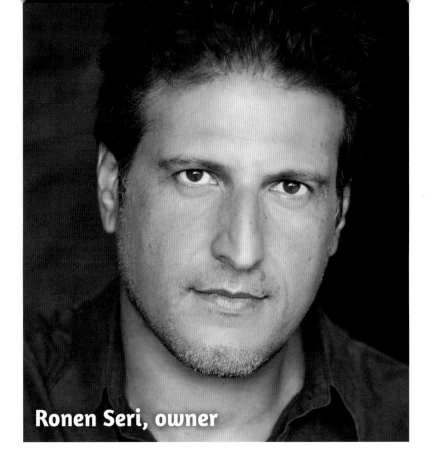

Ronen Seri, owner

Is this your first restaurant?
No. Blossom Restaurant came first. That was in Chelsea.

When did Café Blossom open?
2007.

Do you want to have more than one restaurant?
Yes, we already do. We have Blossom in Chelsea, [a second] Café Blossom on Carmine Street, and V-Note on the Upper East Side.

How many do you hope to have in the future? Will you expand further?
I always think the one I just opened will be my last, but I want as many neighborhoods as possible to benefit from tasty vegan food.

What's your favorite dish on the menu?
Our seitan scallopini is delicious. We currently feature it on the menu at our Chelsea location. At the Upper West Side café I love the pistachio-dusted tofu.

What's your most popular appetizer?
Currently, people are loving the garlic mushroom ravioli.

What's the most popular entrée on the menu?
Our classic Seitan Marsala.

What's your most popular dessert?

Chocolate cake is everyone's favorite. But the key lime cheesecake is a close second.

What do you feel is special about your restaurant?

We have a comfortable atmosphere while still offering upscale food and service. We also have a very passionate staff with regard to animal rights issues.

How often do you change your menu items? Do you have daily or weekly specials?

Seasonally. We offer weekend specials and seasonal specials whenever possible.

Do you have gluten-free, soy-free, and sugar-free options on your menu?

We have several gluten-free and raw dishes and some soy-free options. We use raw agave syrup as a sweetener [in place of sugar] in a few desserts.

What do you do to reduce your environmental impact?

Recycling, LED lighting—and all our takeout containers, plasticware, and bags are made from biodegradable corn oil.

What are the most important lessons you've learned as owner or chef of this restaurant?

I used to be more of a junk-food vegan. Now, while I still favor rich and creamy foods, I also have a greater appreciation for simpler, wholesome vegetable dishes.

What led you to want to open a vegan restaurant, and/or what led you to the vegan diet yourself?

It was all about animals. I was not brought up to think this way, but I had a realization during a meditation retreat. A cow happened upon where I was at the time. I observed this wonderful creature and my perspective changed then and there.

In the time since your restaurant first opened, how has the plant-based food movement changed? Do you find more demand now for vegan food?

There is definitely more demand for vegan food. People are beginning to realize the health benefits as

well as the environmental effects. The word "vegan" itself has become more common, whereas a few years ago, I found myself always having to explain what it meant to people.

Since your restaurant first opened, has your view of what constitutes healthy or delicious food changed? Have you changed the types of foods you offer?

I used to be focused more on trying to convert world cuisine and make vegan versions of international dishes. I still like to do that, but lately I've wanted to play more with grains and vegetables and make them as delicious as possible.

It's a challenge to be a businessperson but also to operate cruelty-free since there are so many restaurants that do not operate this way, so many companies that do not see this as a priority. It is challenging to offer good food without hurting any life.

Where do you see the plant-based food movement going in coming years?

I believe it will expand because of health concerns. 🐢

This is our most popular dish at Café Blossom! It has satisfied many vegans and nonvegans alike for the more than five years.

Seitan Marsala

Serves 4–6

For the mashed potatoes:
6   Yukon Gold potatoes
½   cup Earth Balance butter substitute
3   tablespoons chopped garlic
Salt and pepper, to taste

For the sauce:
1   bottle (750 mL) Marsala wine
1   cup vegetable stock
2   cups port wine
1   tablespoon chopped fresh thyme
1   tablespoon chopped fresh oregano
1   tablespoon chopped fresh chives
½   cup brown sugar
Salt and pepper, to taste

For the fillet and greens:
3   medium bunches kale
2   tablespoons olive oil
1   tablespoon minced garlic
1   teaspoon Earth Balance butter substitute
12 4- to 5-ounce seitan fillets
1   cup flour
4   heads fennel, sliced
4   cups sliced shiitake mushrooms
4   shallots, sliced

Peel and boil potatoes. Place cooked potatoes in bowl, add ½ cup of Earth Balance, chopped garlic, and salt and pepper to taste. Mash together until thick and smooth.

For the sauce: Combine all ingredients into a large pot and simmer for approximately 5 minutes over medium-low heat to dissolve sugar, and then remove from heat.

For the fillet and greens: Sauté kale with olive oil and garlic. In a separate pan, add 1 tablespoon of Earth Balance to pan over high heat. Coat seitan fillets with flour, reduce heat, and place fillets in pan. Once brown, add fennel, mushrooms, and shallots. Sauté for 3 to 5 minutes or until vegetables are cooked, and then ladle Marsala sauce into pan. Reduce heat, cover for 10 minutes, and let the Marsala reduce.

To assemble: Place 2 large scoops of mashed potatoes in a deep dish. Place a handful of kale over the mash. Lastly, place your fillets and veggies on top and add salt and pepper to taste. Each serving should have 2 fillets. Pour remaining Marsala sauce over filets and serve.

Dijon-Glazed Tofu

Serves 4–6

For the eggplant sauce:
2 medium onions, diced
2 large carrots, diced
1 celery stalk, diced
4 cloves garlic, diced
1 tablespoon olive oil
1 eggplant

For the vegetables:
6 small bunches Swiss chard
1 tablespoon olive oil
1 clove garlic, chopped
Juice of 1 lemon wedge
24 baby carrots

For the glaze sauce and tofu:
2 cups Dijon mustard
¾ cup soy sauce
1 cup canola oil
½ cup agave syrup
1 cup water
Salt and pepper, to taste
1 5-ounce piece of tofu, cut into
   3 pieces

To serve:
3 cups black rice (cooked)

For the eggplant sauce: Preheat the oven to 350 degrees. Add the onions, carrots, celery, and garlic to a pan with the olive oil and sauté briefly over medium heat. Peel eggplant and bake in the oven for 15 minutes. Remove eggplant from oven and combine with the sautéed vegetables in the blender. Blend until they have made a smooth puree. (Add water as needed.) The consistency should be thick and creamy.

For the vegetables: Preheat the oven to 350 degrees. Sauté the Swiss chard in a pan with olive oil over medium heat together with the garlic and lemon. Place the baby carrots on a greased pan, and once the oven is at temperature, bake them for 45 minutes.

For the glaze sauce and tofu: In a large bowl, whisk together the mustard, soy sauce, canola oil, agave syrup, water, salt, and pepper. Coat tofu with glaze and grill (or sauté) over medium heat for 5 to 10 minutes. Give the tofu another coat of glaze before plating.

To assemble: Place a liberal amount of eggplant sauce on the center of the plate. Add ½ cup black rice, and place 4 baby carrots on top of the rice. Then place a generous amount of sautéed greens over the rice. Lastly, take the Dijon-glazed tofu and place it on your greens. Repeat with the other servings.

Candle Café

NEW YORK, NY

1307 3rd Ave.
New York, NY 10021
(212) 472-0970

(Other locations in New York City)

www.candlecafe.com

For over twenty years the Candle restaurants have been striving to better the health of the individual and the planet by serving their unique brand of farm-to-table vegan fare. Their organic and seasonal menus and sexy eco-cocktail bars continue to impress a dedicated following of locals, tourists, and celebrities.

Joy Pierson, co-owner and chef

Is this your first restaurant?
Yes. My co-owner, Bart Potenza, purchased a health food store on the Upper East Side of Manhattan in 1984, and renamed it the Healthy Candle in honor of the previous owners' nightly ritual of lighting candles to bless their establishment. I was a customer there and then became the in-house nutritionist and eventually Bart's partner. When we won $53,000 in the Take-5 lottery on a Friday the 13th in 1993, we had the funds to open Candle Café. Then we opened Candle 79 about ten years later and most recently Candle Café West in April 2012.

When did your first restaurant open?
The original Candle Café opened in 1994.

How many restaurants do you hope to have? Will each restaurant have different menus or the same?
We envision a few more Candles in New York City and the greater New York area and then branching out into other markets like Los Angeles, Miami, and other major cities. Because we rely so heavily on local products we imagine that all the menus will not be the same but we will do our best to take our signature items wherever we go.

What's your favorite dish on the menu?
Our Good Food Plate, which allows me to put together whatever grouping of sides that I'm in the mood for with any two dressings or sauces.

What's your most popular appetizer?
Seitan chimichurri has been everyone's favorite for as long I can remember. I try to get everyone to try it, because once they do they are hooked for life.

What's the most popular entrée on the menu?

Seitan piccata with lemon caper sauce. It has been on our menus since we opened and has wowed vegans and meat-eaters alike.

What's your most popular dessert?

Chocolate mousse pie. It is decadent, gluten-free, and you would never know it's vegan. And of course I love it à la mode with our pastry chef Jorge Pineda's handmade coconut–chocolate chip ice cream.

What do you feel is special about your restaurant?

The energy in the room. You just feel like you're in another (and happier) world when you enter one of our restaurants. It comes through our chefs and ends up in the food. It radiates through our staff as they care for people. Our mission is to nourish people, both inside and out, and when we do that our guests feel it and connect with it and it is pure bliss.

How often do you change your menu items? Do you have daily or weekly specials?

We offer four to five daily specials along with three soups per day. We also offer a selection of sides that changes on a daily basis. The choice of specials is left to our talented chefs. The season is the biggest determining factor in what they choose. Our menu selections change about four times a year to go along with the changing of the seasons.

Do you have gluten-free, soy-free, and sugar-free options on your menu?

We have a dedicated gluten-free menu that has about fifteen options on it. [Some] desserts are sweetened with agave and/or maple syrups. And we have a few soy-free options that are not noted on the menu.

What do you do to reduce your environmental impact?

Our to-go flatware and cups are compostable, as are some of our food packing containers. We also invest in alternative energy sources, embrace organic and local produce whenever possible, and use green cleaners. We were the first restaurant in New York City to be certified "green" by the Green Restaurant Association. But the biggest thing we do is turn people on to vegan food, which saves the planet from the damages of factory farming. The tastiest way to decrease your carbon footprint is to be vegan.

What are the most important lessons you've learned as co-owner of this restaurant?

I've learned that the most important thing in business is to inspire people.

What led you to want to open a vegan restaurant, and/or what led you to the vegan diet yourself?

My passion is to heal people with food. I was a practicing nutritionist when I met Bart, who introduced me to the power of plant-based foods. He served me a sandwich and my life was never the same.

In the time since your restaurant first opened, how has the plant-based food movement changed? Do you find more demand now for vegan food?

There is definitely more demand for plant-based foods now than when we first opened. The growth we've seen in the last twenty years has been one of the most exciting parts of this ride.

Since your restaurant first opened, has your view of what constitutes healthy or delicious food changed? Have you changed the types of foods you offer?

Our choices have expanded and we are always interested in accommodating the nutritional needs of our customers. We now have a dedicated gluten-free menu and raw-food options available.

Where do you see the plant-based food movement going in coming years?

Simply put, we see the movement getting bigger and bigger. We expect it to lead to a more compassionate and happier world. 🐷

Porcini-Crusted Tofu

Serves 6–8

2   tablespoons balsamic vinegar
2   tablespoons agave
3   tablespoons soy sauce
3   tablespoons olive oil
¼   teaspoon black pepper
2   tablespoons chopped onions
¼   teaspoon chopped garlic
2   14-ounce packages extra-firm
    tofu, drained and cut into thirds
½   cup dried porcini mushrooms,
    ground into a powder
1   cup unbleached all-purpose
    flour
Pinch salt
Pinch black pepper
2   tablespoons safflower oil
Fried capers (optional)

In a large mixing bowl combine balsamic vinegar, agave, soy sauce, olive oil, black pepper, onions, and garlic. Whisk together the ingredients and pour the mix over the tofu and let it marinate covered in the fridge for at least 2 hours.

To make the crust, in a large bowl, mix the porcini mushroom powder, unbleached flour, salt, and pepper and set aside. Drain the tofu from the marinade and squeeze the excess liquid out of the tofu. Dredge each piece of tofu in the crust, pressing the crust into the tofu with your hands to ensure that the tofu remains completely covered. In a large sauté pan over medium heat, add 2 tablespoons of safflower oil, and let the oil become hot without simmering. Add the tofu to the hot oil, and let it cook for about a minute on each side or until golden brown. Once cooked, take the tofu out of the pan and place on paper towels to absorb the excess oil. You may need to add more oil if the pan starts to become too dry.

Tip: *To assemble the dish pictured opposite, put a 3" ring mold in the center of a plate, arrange a spoonful of sautéed greens of your choice in the mold, and press down with the back of a spoon. Add a scoop of the mashed potatoes (recipe follows) on top of the greens, and press down again. Remove the mold and top with a few pieces of the seitan and fried capers, if using. Drizzle the seitan and the plate with the mushroom gravy (recipe follows). Repeat for the remaining servings.*

Garlic Mashed Potatoes

Serves 4

3 medium Yukon Gold potatoes
1 tablespoon olive oil
2 cloves fresh garlic, minced
1½ tablespoons Earth Balance butter substitute, melted
¼ cup plain soy milk
1 tablespoon chopped fresh parsley

Place the potatoes in a large saucepan and add enough water to cover. Bring to a boil over high heat. Reduce the heat to medium, cover, and cook until the potatoes are tender, approximately 20 to 25 minutes. While potatoes are cooking, heat olive oil in a small sauté pan over medium heat. Add garlic and lightly sauté for 1 to 2 minutes. Mix the sautéed garlic, Earth Balance, and soy milk together, then add to the potatoes. Mash the potatoes with a potato masher to make a fairly smooth puree. If a creamier texture is desired, add more soy milk. Stir in parsley and serve immediately.

Candle Mushroom Gravy

Serves 4

2 tablespoons brown rice flour
2 tablespoons olive oil
½ cup diced white onion
½ cup diced celery
1 cup sliced oyster mushrooms
1 cup sliced cremini mushrooms
1 cup sliced white mushrooms
1 teaspoon fresh thyme
1 bay leaf
2 cups water
1 teaspoon sea salt
½ teaspoon black pepper

In a sauté pan over medium heat, toast brown rice flour. Add 1 tablespoon olive oil and whisk until well mixed. Turn off heat. In another sauté pan over medium heat, sauté onion and celery in 1 tablespoon olive oil for 3 minutes. Add mushrooms and thyme and bay leaf and sauté for another 3 minutes. Pour in water and add salt and pepper and bring to a boil. Once it reaches boil, remove from heat. Remove the bay leaf, transfer the mixture to other pan with flour mixture, and whisk together until smooth. Simmer on medium-low heat for 20 to 25 minutes. Serve warm.

Chaco Canyon

SEATTLE, WA

4757 12th Ave. NE
Seattle, WA 98105
(206) 522-6966

(Second location in Seattle)

www.chacocanyoncafe.com

Chris Maykut, owner and chef
(pictured on right)

Chaco Canyon Organic Café exists to serve the diverse needs of its community and to empower its employees to create a better tomorrow for themselves and the world. Plus, the food is terrific.

Is this your first restaurant?
Yes, but I've worked in several along the way, including San Francisco's Millennium Restaurant with vegan virtuoso Eric Tucker heading the kitchen.

When did Chaco Canyon open?
We opened in September 2003 in our original location. In April 2007, we moved to our current location, and in April 2011 we added our second location in West Seattle.

Do you want to have more locations?
Oh, yes. We're planning for our third location and commissary kitchen to open in fall of 2014. We would love to have six Chaco Canyons in the Seattle area, with the possibility of doing single franchises in Portland and in Vancouver, BC.

What's your favorite dish on the menu?
It really changes every couple months. I love our raw enchiladas and am constantly impressed with how vibrant, tasty, and satisfying they are.

What's your most popular appetizer?
Hands down, our Egyptian Red Lentil Soup. Delicious and nourishing, with a nice hint of lemon and black pepper.

What's the most popular entrée on the menu?
That would be our lentil burger. Voted the best vegetarian burger in Seattle by *Seattle Weekly*, it's ridiculously good. It's not the healthiest thing on our menu for sure, but something that will put a smile on your face.

What's your most popular dessert?
Everything our amazing bakery department puts out is gobbled up. The short answer would be our raw brownies—delightfully simple with only five ingredients.

What do you feel is special about your restaurant?
Our "triple bottom line": valuing people, profit, and planet in all decisions. It's the absolute pillar of our café. We favor people and planet in nearly all of our decisions,

and it's rare that we ever pick profit over the other two. We value our employees as our most important quality, and are committed to everyone having a joyful experience at Chaco Canyon, and that ethic spreads to our community in a very tangible way.

How often do you change your menu items? Do you have daily or weekly specials?

We have a static menu for the most part that has occasional changes, but we add about fifteen items per month as "local and seasonal specials," often teaming up with a local farm and featuring their produce.

Do you have gluten-free, soy-free, and sugar-free options on your menu?

Yes, we have numerous selections for all of those categories and many more that deal with other common allergies: nut-free, allium-free, wheat-free, and so on. We've become a beacon in the Seattle community for not only specialized diets but restrictive diets due to allergies.

What do you do to reduce your environmental impact?

What *don't* we do? Here's a sampling: We're the first certified organic vegetarian café in Washington. We hand-sort, compost, and recycle over eighty percent of our waste. We used low-VOC paint and recycled insulation for our walls. We used all recycled wood for the trim and tabletops. We have *never* provided a disposable spoon or fork in our existence. And much, much more.

What are the most important lessons you've learned as owner or chef of this restaurant?

The best ideas for my business come from my employees and our community, not from me.

What led you to want to open a vegan restaurant, and/or what led you to the vegan diet yourself?

When we opened, Seattle had a dearth of vegan options, few organic options, no raw options, and very few fresh juice sources. Yet there was a huge community in each of these categories that was being underserved. We've been able to create a vegan menu that is beloved by more carnivores than vegetarians—and that's a point of pride.

In the time since your restaurant first opened, how has the plant-based food movement changed? Do you find more demand now for vegan food?

I think we really caught the wave as it was forming; veganism was popular and growing ten years ago, and it's popular and growing now. The difference in my opinion is the rhetoric around it.

Since your restaurant first opened, has your view of what constitutes healthy or delicious food changed? Have you changed the types of foods you offer?

The short answer is yes. What hasn't changed is that I believe there is no one diet that is best for all, and that there are as many perfect diets as there are people in the world. What works for me won't work best for you, and vice versa. Chaco Canyon exists to fill in some gaps for people who need options for their particular diet that they can't get elsewhere.

Where do you see the plant-based food movement going in coming years?

(1) People will move to more urban farming and supporting local farms, which will help plant-based dietary consciousness; (2) Factory farms and GMO-based crap will start to lessen their strangleholds on American food systems; and (3) Vegetarianism and veganism will become part of everyone's weekly, if not daily, regimens. 🐾

Gluten-Free Coconut Strawberry Shortcake Cupcakes

Makes 20 cupcakes

2   cups tapioca flour
1⅓ cups white rice flour
1   cup millet flour
2   teaspoons xanthan gum
2   teaspoons baking soda
1¼ teaspoons salt
1⅓ cups shredded coconut
2⅓ cups sugar
1   cup safflower oil
2⅓ cups coconut milk
1   cup water
4   teaspoons apple cider vinegar
1   tablespoon vanilla extract

For the strawberry filling:
10 ounces frozen strawberries
3   tablespoon plus 1 teaspoon
     cornstarch
½   cup sugar
2   teaspoons margarine
4   teaspoons fresh lemon juice

For the coconut whipped topping:
1½ tablespoons agar powder
2   teaspoons cornstarch
⅓   cup sugar
¼   teaspoon salt
2½ cups coconut milk
1   teaspoon vanilla extract
2   tablespoons coconut oil

Preheat the oven to 325 degrees. Using the whisk attachment, whisk together flours and xanthan gum in mixer for about 3 minutes. Add baking soda, salt, shredded coconut, and sugar, and mix briefly. Remove and set aside. In another mixing bowl, mix together wet ingredients: oil, coconut milk, water, apple cider vinegar, and vanilla extract. Slowly add flour mixture and mix thoroughly, at least 5 minutes at medium-high speed. (This is needed to get the xanthan gum to work its magic.) Grease muffin pans liberally. If using muffin liners, spray the inside of the paper cups liberally as well! Fill muffin wells only two-thirds full. Bake in the oven 30 to 40 minutes, or until a tester comes out clean. Cool completely.

For the strawberry filling: In a small pot, cook the frozen berries over medium-low heat. In separate bowl, combine cornstarch and sugar. When the berries are warm but not hot, add in the cornstarch mixture to the pot. Cook, stirring frequently, until the mixture is thick, bubbly, and translucent. Remove from heat and mix in margarine and lemon juice. Chill in refrigerator.

For the coconut whipped topping: In small saucepan, whisk together the agar, cornstarch, sugar, and salt. Whisk in the coconut milk. Over medium heat, bring to a boil, stirring constantly. Lower heat, continue stirring constantly, and simmer for 5 minutes. Remove from heat, and stir in vanilla extract and coconut oil. Immediately pour through a fine

Tip: *Use a piping bag with the big round tip for the strawberry filling for an easier assembly.*

mesh strainer to remove any agar bits and place in the refrigerator to chill overnight. Remove from the refrigerator and transfer to a mixer. Whip the mixture until smooth and fluffy.

To assemble: Cut a cone-shaped plug out of the top of each cupcake. Pipe coconut whipped topping around the hole. Pipe strawberry filling into the well of the hole until it's level with the whipped topping.

Quinoa is a grainlike crop originally grown in the mountainous regions of Ecuador, Columbia, Peru, and Bolivia. It's considered a complete protein for humans, as it contains a balanced set of essential amino acids. It's gluten-free and easily digestible, making it an excellent grain alternative. This is a great way to use extra quinoa.

Quinoa Tabbouleh

Serves 4–6 (as a side dish)

2½ cups quinoa
3¼ cups water
1   cup minced fresh parsley
    (about ½ bunch)
2   cups peeled, seeded, and diced
    cucumber (½" dices)
Leaves from 3 stalks of mint,
    minced
¼   cup diced red onion (¼" dices)
1   teaspoon salt
2   tablespoons apple cider vinegar
⅓   cup olive oil

Combine the quinoa with 3¼ cups water in a pot. Bring to a simmer and then reduce heat to low. Cover and cook for 30 to 35 minutes. Remove from heat and let sit covered for an additional 5 minutes. Fluff quinoa with a fork and cover and cool it in the refrigerator at least 4 hours. Once chilled, add quinoa to a large bowl with all the other ingredients. Mix together with a spoon and serve immediately or chill.

Tip: *It's easy to make variations on this recipe. You can mix red and black quinoa together with white (for example, cook 2 cups white quinoa with ½ cup red quinoa or ½ cup black quinoa) or use other grains like barley, farro, red rice, buckwheat, or millet.*

Choices Café

MIAMI, FL

379 SW 15th Rd.
Miami, FL, 33129
(305) 400-8895

(Second location in Miami)

www.mychoicescafe.com

Choices Café's mission is to serve delicious, plant-based meals and to operate as part of a larger organic and plant-based food movement.

Alex Cuevas, owner

Is this your first restaurant?
Yes.

When did it open?
August 2011.

Do you want to have more than one restaurant?
Absolutely, yes.

What's your favorite dish on the menu?
The Mental Lentil Wrap (with black beans, quinoa, lentil "meat," plantain, pico de gallo, vegan cheese, and avocado).

What's your most popular appetizer?
Our quesadilla, which is made fresh and oozes with vegan cheese, organic spinach, and mushrooms.

What's the most popular entrée on the menu?
VA's Insane Mexican Wrap (with black beans, quinoa, soy chorizo, plantain, pico de gallo, and vegan cheese).

What's your most popular dessert?
Our gluten-free brownies, which we bake in-house and offer in both walnut and peanut butter varieties.

What do you feel is special about your restaurant?
I feel that my restaurant is special because of the people who work here, our customers, the quality, organic ingredients we use, the love that we transmit into our food, and most importantly the spirit of the plant-based mission behind which we are operating.

How often do you change your menu items? Do you have daily or weekly specials?

Our menu has been a work in progress, and it is still evolving and growing. We offer daily soup and dessert specials, as well as entrée specials a few days per week, depending on our local produce options.

You mentioned gluten-free brownies. Do you have other gluten-free, soy-free, and sugar-free options on your menu?

Yes, we have all three. About ninety percent of our desserts are gluten-free and soy-free, and all of our wraps can be made gluten-free. We also have a variety of raw, sugar-free desserts and smoothies.

What do you do to reduce your environmental impact?

First and foremost, we use all plant-based ingredients. In the food business, I believe that's the biggest contribution to the eco cause. We also use more than ninety-five percent organic food, we utilize only eco-friendly cleaning products, eco-friendly, compostable wares for take-away, we compost our food waste, and, of course, we recycle.

What are the most important lessons you've learned as owner or chef of this restaurant?

Running a restaurant is hard! We are dedicated to our mission and to having a positive impact at a macro level, but it would definitely be easier to do something less intense and less complicated.

What led you to want to open a vegan restaurant, and/or what led you to the vegan diet yourself?

I've been a vegetarian since I was ten years old. I became vegan at age twenty. It is very important for me to help disseminate the information that I've learned about the atrocities in animal welfare, not only in this country but all over the world. There is an overabundance of reasons to adopt this lifestyle of kindness and love. If more people knew about all of the benefits, I believe more people would become vegan, or vegetarian at least. One of the main goals for me is to offer a platform for people to open their minds toward the possibilities of learning more about a plant-based diet. Having a meal at our restaurant is, in essence, a "teaching through taste buds" experience.

In the time since your restaurant first opened, how has the plant-based food movement changed? Do you find more demand now for vegan food?

I believe we've already had a significant amount of impact, even in our short time here in Miami. The number of customers continues to grow on a daily basis, which makes us extremely excited about the progress. We believe that the movement will only continue to expand. We are motivated and cannot wait to grow our organization to meet the demand.

Since your restaurant first opened, has your view of what constitutes healthy or delicious food changed? Have you changed the types of foods you offer?

Since starting the restaurant, we've envisioned offering a gradual introduction to healthy, plant-based foods. We have some classic American dishes, which include sweet potato fries, vegan burgers, and desserts, to entice people who are new to this lifestyle. We also offer many raw items, as well as a full menu of juices and smoothies, to encourage the adoption of a healthier plant-based diet once these types of folks start patronizing our café regularly.

Where do you see the plant-based food movement going in coming years?

I believe the plant-based food movement is growing, which is fantastic. But I also see what I would call eco-posing. It's very trendy to say "eco-friendly," "organic," and "green." But in reality it's very difficult for a food-based organization to be truly eco-friendly unless it is plant-based entirely. What I believe will happen is that specialized vegan restaurants will become more and more popular, as this sort of awareness grows. This would be momentous, since the implications are that there would be less suffering in the realms of human health, karma, the environment, and, of course, animal well-being. I look forward to this day. 🐾

This hearty burger was originally developed by an employee to honor his grandfather, a man who spent more than fifty years practicing vegetarianism in Colombia, despite the difficulties of breaking from prevalent meat-eating traditions. This dish was a way to celebrate his family heritage of animal advocacy and *ahisma*, the philosophy of harmlessness. The Simran was a homegrown veggie burger perfected by adding a few modern touches and some Choices flair to original ingredients that were available in the 1940s. The Simran burger became a customer favorite as soon as it was launched, and it has been a staple on our menu ever since.

Simran Burger

Makes 18 patties

1½ cups dry chickpeas soaked in water overnight (preferably 2 nights)
1½ cups lentils soaked in water overnight (preferably 2 nights)
7 cloves garlic
1 onion, cut into quarters
1 to 2 yellow bell peppers, seeded, stemmed, and cut into quarters
4 cups frozen peas
½ cup tamari or soy sauce
1½ teaspoons pepper
Cooking oil (optional)

Drain the soaked chickpeas and lentils, ensuring they are dried and drained fully. Chop garlic, onion, and yellow bell pepper together in food processor. Add peas, chickpeas, and lentils; blend in food processor into a fine paste. (This can be done in batches if the food processor is small.) In small batches, place mixture into cheesecloth bag and squeeze to wring out moisture. (The mixture should be very dry, almost claylike.) Add tamari and pepper, mixing lightly by hand or by pulsing in the food processor. Shape mixture into burger-size patties. With little to no oil, heat patties through by grilling in a pan at medium-high heat for approximately 2 minutes on each side, or until browned. Serve immediately, either on a bun, or atop a bed of greens.

Tip: *Uncooked Simran patties can be wrapped and stored in a refrigerator for up to 2 days.*

These fudgelike brownies are so rich and delicious; they have become a staple on our menu. If you try them out at home, we predict they will become a staple in your kitchen, too. They're packed with vitamin E, omega-3s, and antioxidants. Your taste buds *and* your body will thank you.

Raw Brownie Bliss Bites

Makes 16 brownie bites

For the brownies:
1   cup walnuts or pecans (or a mixture of both)
1   cup pitted dates
5   tablespoons raw cacao powder
1   tablespoon raw agave syrup
¼   teaspoon sea salt

For the frosting:
1   cup pitted dates
¼   cup raw cacao powder
¼   cup coconut oil
¾   cup filtered water

For the toppings (optional):
Goji berries
Cacao nibs
Shredded coconut

Chop nuts in a blender or food processor. Add dates and blend until combined. Add remaining brownie ingredients and blend until you achieve a fudgelike consistency. Line a 9 x 9 pan with parchment paper. Pour brownie mixture into lined baking pan. Place in the refrigerator for 1 hour to set.

To make the frosting, combine all ingredients in a blender or food processor, and blend to achieve a smooth, spreadable consistency. Pour the frosting into a small container and cool in the fridge for an hour.

After both the frosting and the brownie base are cooled and set, remove both from the fridge and top brownie mix with frosting. Add optional toppings or other toppings of your choice.

Tip: *The chocolate frosting also doubles as a tasty dip for strawberries.*

Coox and Candy

STUTTGART, GERMANY

Sulzbachgasse 14
Stuttgart, Germany 70372
+49-711-50446004

www.coox-candy.de

A combination of historic ambiance, hearty vegan food (based on traditional German cuisine), and decadent desserts, Coox and Candy has become a must-eat stop for vegan travelers in Germany.

Kathrin Friedrich, owner and chef

Is this your first restaurant?
Yes, it is.

When did it open?
February 2011.

Do you want to have more than one restaurant?
We would like to grow and open a small take-away shop in the center of the city and maybe another restaurant in the next two years. In the meantime, we've been putting together our own vegan snack-food truck.

What's your favorite dish on the menu?
I personally love our Golden Crispy Tempeh served with snow peas, carrots, and quinoa.

What's your most popular appetizer?
Green Bruschetta: cucumber and avocado on roasted bread.

What's the most popular entrée on the menu?
Hummus Rosé with Chicory Leaves: delicious hummus paired with beetroot and served with fresh chicory leaves and bread to dip.

What's your most popular dessert?
Our delicious homemade cream cakes, especially the traditional German Schwarzwälder-Kirschtorte (Black Forest cake).

What do you feel is special about your restaurant?
Our great atmosphere in an old house in Bad Cannstatt, our gorgeous and friendly service staff, and a creative menu serving fresh vegetable cuisine as well

as new vegan interpretation of classic meat dishes like *roulladen* (German roulade) and schnitzel, using tofu and seitan products.

How often do you change your menu items? Do you have daily or weekly specials?

We have a seasonal menu for spring, summer, and autumn/winter. Moreover, we change the menu every week and have varying daily specials. This is especially important for our many regular guests who are looking for variety.

Do you have gluten-free, soy-free, and sugar-free options on your menu?

We have some gluten-free options on the menu: mashed sweet potatoes, rice, or millet as side dishes, and our salads and soups. We use many soy products (tofu, tempeh, soy milk, soy cream) but we can arrange some soy-free meals on request. And we offer agave syrup if someone doesn't like sugar in tea/coffee. We don't use stevia yet. Our cakes always use normal sugar.

What do you do to reduce your environmental impact?

We use eco-electricity in our house; our website is also hosted on a server using eco-electricity. We have electric hand dryers in our bathrooms instead of paper towels. We buy only fair-trade coffee, fair-trade tea, and fair-trade soy products.

What are the most important lessons you've learned as owner or chef of this restaurant?

It's so much easier to explain the vegan lifestyle if you offer somebody a delicious meal, a sweet dessert, and good coffee, instead of talking to the person in the street showing him bloody pictures of dead animals.

What led you to want to open a vegan restaurant, and/or what led you to the vegan diet yourself?

We were looking for a job combining our love of vegan cooking and cuisine with our deep need to fight for animal rights. I became a vegetarian when I was thirteen, after seeing how a neighboring farmer killed a little lamb. I became a vegan when I was twenty, after I realized that even organic milk and eggs mean that some baby animals have to be born and killed for my consumption habits.

In the time since your restaurant first opened, how has the plant-based food movement changed? Do you find more demand now for vegan food?

Our restaurant was really popular from the first day we opened. Lots of newspapers and TV stations came along to interview us. And now, lots of people know about this one vegan restaurant in Stuttgart and talk about us. As a result, even more people became curious about our place, and now we're completely booked nearly every evening. Thanks to that big media coverage, more and more people came to understand what vegan really means. We don't have to explain the reasons for our food choices as often anymore.

Since your restaurant first opened, has your view of what constitutes healthy or delicious food changed? Have you changed the types of foods you offer?

What's changed is my appreciation for the preferences of our clients. We discovered that they aren't so enthusiastic about whole foods like whole-grain pasta, brown rice, or Ayurvedic dishes. Many of our guests are more into vegan interpretations of classic meat dishes; for example, our veggie "duck" filet with homemade bread dumplings. It's a seitan-based duck alternative, served with dumplings, brown sauce, and braised red cabbage or vegan schnitzel. These are not primarily healthy dishes, but they're delicious. At the same time, for the more health-focused customer, we serve fresh juices, raw food, and classic vegetable dishes. Another trend we've acknowledged on the menu is green smoothies; we began serving these in the summer of 2013 and people love it!

Where do you see the plant-based food movement going in coming years?

It's becoming bigger and bigger! 🐷

Celery-Breaded Cutlet with Wild Rice and Mixed Vegetables

Serves 4

For the celery cutlets:
12 cups water
2   teaspoons salt
2   firm celery roots
    (approximately 2 pounds),
    peeled and cut into ½" slices

For the mixed vegetables in a light sauce:
4   large carrots
12 radishes
2   cups Brussels sprouts
1   large onion, finely chopped
2   cloves garlic, chopped
2⅛ cups soy milk
½   cup cornstarch
1 to 2 teaspoons salt, to taste
½ to 1 teaspoon black pepper,
    to taste
¼ to ½ teaspoon freshly grated
    nutmeg, to taste
1¼ cups canola oil

For the breading:
¾   cup bread crumbs
¾   cup flour
1   teaspoon salt
1   teaspoon turmeric
½   teaspoon pepper
2⅛ cups cold water
Rapeseed oil for frying

To assemble:
2   cups wild rice mixed with
    white rice, cooked according to
    package instructions and kept
    warm
1   lemon, sliced (garnish)

For the celery cutlets and mixed vegetables with sauce:
Start with the celery cutlets, so they have time to cool before they are breaded. Bring approximately 12 cups of water to a boil, then add salt. Add celery root slices to the salted water, bring to a boil again, reduce heat, and cook until al dente (5 to 7 minutes). Meanwhile, peel and slice the carrots into ⅓" slices, trim the radishes and wash thoroughly. Brush Brussels sprouts with oil and, using a knife, cut a ¾"-deep X at the base of each. Take celery root out of the water and let cool. Save the salted water for later.

Now prepare the sauce: Place the onion on a baking sheet, brush with a little bit of oil, and put it under the broiler until golden brown; add the garlic and broil again for 1 minute. Pour soy milk into a saucepan; add the broiled onion and garlic and bring to a boil. When the sauce boils, bind with the cornstarch and once again bring to a boil. Season the mixture with salt, pepper, and nutmeg. Puree the sauce with a hand blender, until the onions are fine and the spices are well distributed. Keep circulating the blender as you add the canola oil in a thin stream.

In the celery water, cook the vegetables, adding separately: Start with the carrots and cook for about 10 minutes; then add the radishes and cook for 5 to 7 minutes; finally, cook the Brussels sprouts until al dente (10 to 12 minutes). Drain the water and immediately add the hot vegetables into the sauce.

For the breading: Put the bread crumbs in a shallow bowl. In a separate bowl, stir flour, spices, and water until smooth. Dip the celery slices in the liquid mixture, coating them

well; shake them off and then roll them in the bread crumbs. Heat oil in a pan and fry both sides of the cutlets until golden brown.

To assemble: Distribute vegetables and warm rice on plates, add the cutlets, garnish with lemon slices, and serve.

Saffron Rice with Barberries with a Pot of Flavorful Vegetables

Serves 5

For the rice:
1   cup rice
2   teaspoons salt
½   teaspoon crushed saffron threads
¼   cup dried barberries*

For the vegetables:
1   large onion, chopped
8   tablespoons oil
3   tablespoons black mustard seeds
2   tablespoons whole coriander seeds
4   cups warm water
2   teaspoons salt
1¼ cups sliced carrots (½" slices)
¾   cup peeled and diced potatoes (1" dices)
1   red bell pepper, seeded and cut into 1" pieces
1   yellow bell pepper, seeded and cut into 1" pieces
¾   cup red lentils, rinsed**
¾   cup yellow lentils, rinsed**
1   tablespoon turmeric
1   teaspoon ground cumin

For the chutney:
½   cup tamarind paste*
½   cup date paste*

For the garnish:
Parsley
Black mustard seeds
Fresh fruit

* Available in Turkish or Persian-Indian grocery stores.

** In contrast to other lentils, must not be soaked.

Bring a large pot of water to a boil and cook the rice according to the package directions with salt and saffron. Meanwhile, rinse the dried barberries under hot running water and set aside. When the rice is cooked, carefully fold in the barberries.

Fry the onion in 8 tablespoons of oil in a large pot with the black mustard seeds and whole coriander seeds. Add 4 cups warm water then salt and bring it to a boil. Gradually add the individual vegetables, according to the cooking time: First, add the carrots in the boiling water and cook them for 15 minutes. Then add the potatoes and cook for another 10 minutes. Then put in the bell pepper pieces. Finally add the red and yellow lentils and let the whole mixture cook for another 15 minutes. The lentils and starchy vegetables will begin to bind the liquid in the pot. Once the boiling vegetables are cooked, add turmeric and cumin, taste, and add salt as needed.

To make the chutney, combine the tamarind paste with the date paste in a large bowl and puree both ingredients together with a hand blender. (You can also use a food processor.)

To assemble: Arrange everything together on plates and garnish with fresh parsley, black mustard seeds, and fruits of your choice (kumquats and physalis are fun additions).

Cornbread Café

EUGENE, OR

1290 W. 7th Ave.
Eugene, OR 97402
(541) 505-9175

www.cornbreadcafe.com

> Cornbread Café is a family-friendly vintage vegan diner, as down-home as Eugene, Oregon, itself.

Sheree Walters, owner and chef

Is this your first restaurant?
Yes.

When did it open?
The restaurant opened July 1, 2011. In 2010, we operated out of a parked food trailer.

Do you want to have more than one restaurant?
Yes. I have a dream of easy access drive-thru restaurants along I-5, although I'll consider my dream realized with just one.

What's your favorite dish on the menu?
Fettuccine Alfredo. I like this dish because of its simplicity and its uncanny similarity to traditional fettuccine Alfredo. It's got all the flavor and creaminess, but a lot less fat, no cholesterol, and most importantly, it's vegan!

What's your most popular appetizer?
The Fries Deluxe combo, with unCheese sauce and cashew gravy.

What's the most popular entrée on the menu?
Chicken Fried Tempeh with cashew gravy.

What's your most popular dessert?
Frozen Peanut Butter Pie.

What do you feel is special about your restaurant?
It has a community feel to it—very diverse clientele and everybody feels welcome. We also have a very large percentage of nonvegetarians who regularly dine with us!

How often do you change your menu items? Do you have daily or weekly specials?
Our core menu stays the same, with new additions about every six months. We offer at least one daily special.

Do you have gluten-free, soy-free, and sugar-free options on your menu?

We have a lot of gluten-free options, quite a few soy-free options, and we have plans to add a sugar-free dessert to the menu.

What do you do to reduce your environmental impact?

Our food scraps are picked up by a local gardener who runs his car on our used cooking oil. We use compostable takeout containers and utensils, one-hundred-percent recycled dinner napkins and toilet paper, and earth-friendly cleaning supplies and hand soap. Most of our staff rides their bikes to work, and our wholesale items are delivered to local markets via bike. We also give a ten-percent discount to folks who walk or ride the bus to the café, as well as a twenty-percent discount to folks who get $20 or more of biofuel from our local SeQuential Biofuel Station. The café was painted with no-VOC paint and all of the décor is reused. As far as our food goes, ninety-five percent of our menu is organic, we buy most of our ingredients locally, and all brews on tap are made by our fellow local businesses.

What are the most important lessons you've learned as owner or chef of this restaurant?

Organization is key, and baby steps are crucial. Pay attention to customer demands and critiques. Clear communication with staff is a must.

What led you to want to open a vegan restaurant, and/or what led you to the vegan diet yourself?

I have planned to open a vegetarian restaurant for the past twenty years (even before I became vegetarian). I had plans to become vegetarian for many years before I finally made the commitment, but I didn't fully make the connection between the

animals I loved and the animals I had been eating/exploiting until years later. Once that clicked, I quickly gave up dairy and eggs, too. It's a no-brainer for a vegan to open a vegan restaurant. It evolved into a vegan restaurant several years before the Cornbread food cart opened. I fully enjoy creating cruelty-free meals that have all the taste and texture of the comfort foods most of us grew up with.

In the time since your restaurant first opened, how has the plant-based food movement changed? Do you find more demand now for vegan food?

I think it's changed quite drastically! I'm noticing more every day that nonvegetarian folks are opening up their minds to either giving up meat or consuming a lot less of it. The mainstream seems to really be making the connection between what they eat and how they feel—both physically and mentally. The vegan food movement has only just begun! If you look at how many "traditional" restaurants are out there, we have a long way to go before the market is even close to being saturated. But it just keeps getting better!

Since your restaurant first opened, has your view of what constitutes healthy or delicious food changed? Have you changed the types of foods you offer?

When the food cart opened, we were mostly catering to the fast-food scene and not necessarily concentrating on the health aspect of veganism. When the restaurant opened, we included some healthier options. There is now a big demand for even more healthy items, including some raw options. We just started offering raw fettuccine Alfredo and will add fresh juices and smoothies to our menu in the near future.

I wouldn't say that my view of what constitutes healthy and delicious has necessarily changed, but my commitment to share more of it with the public has. I know how to do healthy and delicious…watch out! We're just getting started!

Where do you see the plant-based food movement going in coming years?

I see it continuing to grow, but gaining momentum as the years go on. We're in a time of more conscientious thinking, and that's great for all of us—especially our animal friends! 🐷

Chicken Fried Tempeh

Serves 4–8

2   12-ounce packages tempeh
2 to 3 cups canola oil to grease the
    pan and for frying
1½ cups unsweetened soy milk (no
    substitutions)
1½ tablespoons apple cider vinegar
2   teaspoons hot sauce
2   cups unbleached all-purpose
    flour
2   tablespoons baking powder
1½ teaspoons sea salt
1   teaspoon poultry seasoning
⅛   teaspoon celery seed

Preheat the oven to 350 degrees. Slice the tempeh horizontally, then on the diagonal to make 4 triangles per 12-ounce baking tray. Lightly oil the tray and place the triangles on the tray and into the oven. Bake for 12 to 15 minutes, flipping after about 6 minutes.

In a bowl, whisk together soy milk, apple cider vinegar, and hot sauce to make the "buttermilk" ingredients, and set aside.

Combine the flour, baking powder, sea salt, poultry seasoning, and celery seed in a large bowl and whisk together well.

Heat oil in a large, heavy pot. Use shallow oil for a less fatty dish, or a pot full of oil for deep-frying. (If you can, use a thermometer and keep the oil at 325 degrees for best results. You may need to adjust temperature if you are frying a lot of tempeh, as it will cool off.) Always use tongs for safety!

Line up 2 shallow bowls for the dredging process. Fill one with the flour and the other with the "buttermilk." Use one hand for wet and one for dry (unless you like big, globby fingertips!). Take a tempeh triangle in hand and dip it in flour using your dry hand, put it in buttermilk and coat it with your wet hand, then put back in flour and use your dry hand to cover up tempeh before handling. Repeat dipping in the buttermilk and flour once more.

Now you're ready for frying. Using your tongs, gently place the tempeh in the oil. You will need to turn it once so that both sides get all golden brown and crispy. The total frying time is about 4 minutes, depending on how many pieces of tempeh you're frying at once. Fry until a golden-brown color is achieved. Then remove with tongs and place on a paper-towel-lined plate. Repeat the process with the other tempeh triangles.

Serve topped with cashew gravy and enjoy with your favorite sides. It is also very good cold and perfect for a picnic, served with potato salad, baked beans, and biscuits.

Tofu Omelet Sheets

Serves 6

For the omelet:
1½ blocks firm tofu
1½ tablespoons arrowroot
    (or cornstarch) mixed well
    with ¼ cup water
1   tablespoon nutritional yeast
2   teaspoons onion powder
1¼ teaspoons sea salt
1   teaspoon garlic powder
½   teaspoon black pepper
⅛   teaspoon turmeric (for color)
Oil for greasing and frying

For the filling:
Vegan cheese
Chopped vegetables, your choice
    (mushrooms, onions, bell pep-
    pers, asparagus, spinach)
Fresh herbs, your choice (oregano,
    basil, chives)

Preheat oven to 350 degrees. Crumble tofu into food processor bowl and add the rest of the omelet ingredients except the oil. Process until all ingredients are completely blended together and perfectly smooth. It's a good idea to turn off the food processor and give the mixture a good stir with a rubber spatula, then turn it back on to finish.

Lightly oil a jellyroll pan (13 x 18), and line it with parchment paper. Scoop the tofu mixture into pan, and spread tofu evenly to the sides. Take another piece of parchment paper, lightly oil one side of it, and place oiled-side down on top of the tofu. You can also even out the mixture a little easier with this top sheet on—use your hands to gently pat and make sure there are no uneven spots.

Bake for about 12 minutes, checking after 10 minutes. It's a good idea to rotate the pan back to front after about 6 minutes. Remove the pan from the oven when the parchment paper turns yellow.

Once cool, take off top piece of parchment paper. Run a butter knife around the edges to separate the omelet from sides of pan and gently remove the bottom piece of parchment paper. Make 1 vertical cut down the middle and 2 horizontal cuts, making 6 even omelet sheets. Heat a lightly oiled pan over a medium flame. Place the omelet onto the pan, smooth-side down. Sprinkle filling ingredients on half of the sheet and fold. Top with more cheese and cover until hot. Remove and serve.

Skillet Cornbread

Serves 6–10

1 to 2 tablespoons Earth Balance
*   butter substitute*
1   cup cornmeal (medium
*   ground)*
1   cup unbleached all-purpose
*   flour*
½   cup sugar
2   teaspoons baking powder
1   teaspoon sea salt
1   cup soy or rice milk
⅓   cup oil
Egg replacer for 2 eggs (follow
*   directions on box)*

For the topping (optional):
Earth Balance butter substitute
Agave syrup

Preheat the oven to 375 degrees. Put 1 or 2 tablespoons Earth Balance butter substitute (or other vegan margarine) into a 9" cast-iron skillet and put in the heated oven for about 10 minutes.

Add together the dry ingredients (through salt) in a large bowl and whisk together, combining thoroughly. Set aside. In a separate bowl, whisk together all the wet ingredients (soy or rice milk through egg replacer). Add wet ingredients to dry and mix well, just until all of the dry mixture is incorporated with the wet. Some small lumps are okay.

Remove skillet from oven and coat bottom and sides with the melted Earth Balance. Pour (or scrape) batter into skillet, spreading evenly with rubber spatula. Bake for approximately 20 to 25 minutes in the middle of the center rack. Test the center of corn bread with a toothpick after 20 minutes. When the toothpick comes out clean without crumbs sticking to it, the corn bread is done. Let it cool for a few minutes and, if desired, serve with Earth Balance and agave syrup.

Counter Culture

AUSTIN, TX

2337 E. Cesar Chavez St.
Austin, TX 78702
(512) 524-1540

www.counterculturaustin.com

It may look a little like an old-time diner, but don't let that fool you. Counter Culture serves wholesome vegan comfort food made from scratch—and offered at affordable prices—with an emphasis on food that is nutritious and unprocessed.

Sue Davis, owner and chef

Is this your first restaurant?
Yes, but I had a food trailer first for almost three years.

When did Counter Culture open?
April 2012.

Do you want to have more than one restaurant?
Not at this moment in time.

What's your favorite dish on the menu?
Depending on the time of day either the Mac & Cheeze or the Pac Man kale salad.

What's the most popular appetizer on the menu?
Spicy baked artichoke dip.

Most popular entrée?
The Philly seitan sandwich.

Most popular dessert?
Rotating flavors of our cashew-based Cheezecake.

What do you feel is special about your restaurant?
It has a real Austin vibe, laid-back and not pretentious but with some style.

How often do you change your menu items? Do you have daily or weekly specials? How do you choose those specials?

The menu is set but we're constantly offering daily and weekly specials. Sometimes they're based on what's being grown locally; other times it's what we're craving or what someone has requested.

Do you have gluten-free, soy-free, and sugar-free options on your menu?

Yes to all three. We have lots of gluten-free options, including the Mac & Cheeze and bread for some sandwiches. Most desserts are gluten-free. We have half a dozen soy-free dishes. Most of our desserts are sugar-free, sweetened with dates. All of these are clearly marked on our menu.

What do you do to reduce your environmental impact?

We use a local company that sources the most environmentally friendly compostable packaging. And we use another local company that recycles and composts over ninety-five percent of our waste. Our regular trash cans never fill up! We shop locally as much as possible and use organic ingredients whenever possible. We also collect spent water to water our patio plants, and we hope to plant a veggie and herb garden in the fall.

What are the most important lessons you've learned as owner or chef of this restaurant?

Make sure you are experienced in the industry, do your research, don't rush into anything, and be ready to live there.

What led you to want to open a vegan restaurant, and/or what led you to the vegan diet yourself?

After working in many restaurants I decided that I'd like to open my own, as I've worked for myself in the past in other fields. Love for all animals is the number-one reason the restaurant is vegan. Environment and health come after.

In the time since your restaurant first opened, how has the plant-based food movement changed?

I know we've opened omnivores' eyes to delicious food that they didn't know existed.

Do you find more demand now for vegan food?

There is a growing consciousness about animal rights, health, and the environment, and as we evolve as a species I see plant-based eating becoming more common.

Since your restaurant first opened, has your view of what constitutes healthy or delicious food changed? Have you changed the types of foods you offer?

I'm constantly challenged with providing healthy food at a fair price. I've realized that some people don't necessarily want the healthiest food when they eat out. Eating out is a treat, so we offer some luxury items and "splurge" food.

Where do you see the plant-based food movement going in coming years?

Growing bigger and bigger, I hope. 🐷

Pasta with Pumpkin Curry Sauce

Serves 4

For the pasta and veggies:
Pinch salt
14 ounces pasta of your choice
4   cups Chinese broccoli, kale, or
    other green vegetable

For the curry sauce:
3 to 4 cloves garlic, roughly
    chopped
1½ tablespoons roughly chopped
    fresh ginger
1   fresh red or green chili, diced
    (optional)
½   14-ounce can coconut milk
1   14-ounce can pumpkin puree
2   tablespoons lime juice
1   tablespoon tamari
1   tablespoon curry paste
1   teaspoon vegetarian fish sauce
    (optional)

For the garnish (optional):
Fresh cilantro leaves
Shredded red cabbage

Bring a large pot full of water and a pinch of salt to boil, add the pasta, and boil over medium heat. Cook until noodles are al dente (testing the noodles 2 minutes before they're due to be ready). Once the pasta is cooked, drain the water and set the noodles aside.

In the same pot, bring several cups of water to boil. Pour a large bowl of water and add ice cubes. Gather together the 4 cups of green vegetables and, using a slotted spoon, quickly dip them in the boiling water in batches of about 1 cup, cooking them for about 30 seconds. Then quickly dunk the veggies in ice water to shock them and place them on a paper towel to dry.

Next, prepare the curry. Place all of the curry ingredients in a blender and blend until you have a smooth sauce. Remove and toss with cooked pasta and vegetables. Add garnish, if using. Serve at room temperature or heat briefly in a saucepan.

> **Tip:** *Other add-ins to consider include roasted beets, chickpeas, and pumpkin seeds. You can use sweet potato instead of pumpkin. A gluten-free version can easily be made using rice or quinoa instead of pasta as a base.*

Pumpkin-Chocolate Chip Bread Pudding

Serves 4–6

2 cups oat milk, or your favorite kind of nondairy milk

1½ cups pumpkin puree

½ cup date paste

1 banana, very ripe

1 teaspoon vanilla

1 teaspoon ground cinnamon

½ teaspoon ground ginger

¼ teaspoon ground nutmeg

1 tablespoon tapioca flour

½ cup chocolate chips

8 slices whole-grain bread (stale is fine), cut into 1" cubes

Preheat your oven to 350 degrees. While the oven comes to temperature, add all the ingredients in the order listed, minus the bread cubes, into the blender. Blend until thoroughly combined. Place the bread cubes on a baking tray and toast in the oven for 5 minutes.

When the bread is toasted, combine it with the pumpkin mixture in a bowl and let it soak for 5 minutes. Pour this mixture into individual ramekins and bake in the oven for 20 minutes, or until the tops have browned. Let sit for at least 5 minutes before serving. Serve warm as is or with vegan vanilla ice cream.

El Piano

MÁLAGA, SPAIN

c/ San Juan de Letran 13
Malaga, Spain 29012
+34-952-217886

(Other locations in Granada, Spain and York, England)

www.el-piano.com

Serving award-winning, fabulous vegan and gluten-free tapas and entrées, El Piano brings a Spanish twist to plant-based food. The entire enterprise is grounded in sustainability and local community involvement, and all food is made on-premises from locally sourced fresh produce.

Magdalena Chávez, founder

Is this your first restaurant?
El Piano York, in the United Kingdom, was the first to open.

When did it open?
El Piano York opened in 1997. El Piano Granada, in Spain, was our second restaurant to open, in 2007. And El Piano Málaga in Spain became our third restaurant in 2011.

How many restaurants do you hope to have in the future? Will you expand further?
At the moment we hope to expand in Spain.

What's your favorite dish on the menu?
The one dish that has never left the menu in fifteen years and the one longtime staff members still happily eat is lentil dhal, a simple blend of lentils, curry, coconut milk, and fresh coriander.

What's your most popular appetizer?
The menu gets revised frequently, so this changes, but probably baba ghanoush.

What's the most popular entrée on the menu?
The dhal probably, as described above.

What's your most popular dessert?
In the UK, that would be our sticky toffee pudding. In Spain, our Brownie Andalus.

What do you feel is special about your restaurant?
We maintain a broad commitment to our product, our customers, our community, and push for education and sustainability. All our food is wholly vegan and wholly gluten-free. We offer free classes and workshops on vegan, gluten-free cooking. And our customers and our staff are stakeholders in the businesses.

How often do you change your menu items? Do you have daily or weekly specials?
The UK restaurant has a printed menu that changes every six months. The Spanish operations are different; the food changes daily and there is no printed menu.

Do you have gluten-free, soy-free, and sugar-free options on your menu?
Yes to all.

What do you do to reduce your environmental impact?
The core focus of El Piano is sustainability, and that begins with the food, which is vegan. We also source local ingredients to reduce our carbon footprint. Next is the packaging: It's one-hundred-percent biodegradable, except for cellulose bags, which have a ten-percent plastic content. We do not use air-conditioning. In the wintertime, we make use of our outside spaces for cooling. Deliveries are made by bicycle (happily all three cities are fairly flat). And staff members share rides.

What are the most important lessons you've learned as owner or chef of this restaurant?
Give knowledge away. People return to a restaurant for so much more than just the food.

What led you to want to open a vegan restaurant, and/or what led you to the vegan diet yourself?
The decision to have a vegan and gluten-free menu wasn't driven by a desire to exclude any diners.

We wanted the maximum number of people with dietary restrictions to be able to eat the maximum amount of food on the menu and to be able to eat it with others.

In the time since your restaurant first opened, how has the plant-based food movement changed? Do you find more demand now for vegan food?
No idea. Some of our customers do come because it is vegan, but just as many, or more, come because of our other qualities. In the UK there is more demand and the overall number of vegans within the population is greater.

Since your restaurant first opened, has your view of what constitutes healthy or delicious food changed? Have you changed the types of foods you offer?
Not really. We offer what people want. And we're aware that people can't want things they haven't encountered. There's always a balance to be struck between what's familiar and what's cutting edge. Recently in the UK we offered a number of raw-food options that we later removed from the menu, as no one ordered them. In Spain, however, raw foods are more popular.

Also, any new trends or options have to fit within our environmental policies of being local and organic. For example, we are not much taken with the so-called "superfoods," as they are rarely organic or local to Spain or the UK—and they're almost never fairly traded.

Where do you see the plant-based food movement going in coming years?
Urban plant-based food production is going to grow exponentially in the coming years. We're already planning to use the external walls of our buildings to grow both ornamental and edible crops. Out of necessity, food is going to become a local issue, involving business and the community. Laying down the rails for this type of cross-sector cooperation is essential, and as people in the food industry, we have an important role to play in this, and a responsibility to do our part. 🐾

This is a big favorite with many customers in both Spain and the UK.
The syrup is based on Arabic flavors and will last months in the fridge.

Granada Chai

Makes approximately 2 cups

2⅛ cups water
2 to 3 black tea bags
½ cinnamon stick
½ teaspoon ground nutmeg
10 green cardamom pods
½ red chili, chopped
A few coriander seeds
Sugar, to taste
1 cup soy, coconut, or rice milk

Combine all the syrup ingredients, except the milk, in a saucepan and bring to simmer. Simmer gently for 20 minutes. Taste and adjust the sugar to your desired sweetness.

To make the chai, heat your desired milk in a saucepan. Remove from the heat, pour it into a mug, and add the syrup to taste.

Based on a traditional Peruvian recipe, this dish was developed in Málaga by the Peruvian cook there. It's typical for us to use our international team to introduce new items to the menu. The beauty of this dish is that it is different every time because it is a way to make an original use of leftovers. It reinforces our commitment to sustainability and variety.

Peruvian Leftovers Pie

Serves 8–10

For the outer layers:
10 cooked potatoes
Salt, to taste
Juice of 1 lemon
Pinch turmeric
½ fresh red chili,
    chopped very finely

For the filling:
Anything you like, even leftovers...
    Typical fillings would be salads,
    beans, pasta, veggie burgers, or a
    mix thereof. Avoid frozen foods, as
    they'll add too much moisture to
    the pie as they thaw.

For the topping:
9 ounces tofu
½ cup olive oil
Juice of ½ lemon

For the garnish:
1 red pepper, finely chopped
1 handful fresh parsley, chopped

Mash the cooked potatoes with the salt, lemon juice, turmeric, and chili. Using half of the mashed potatoes, cover the base of a round, silicone, ceramic-based springform pan. Now add a layer of filling, as little or as much as you wish. Cover with the rest of the mashed potatoes. Using an immersion blender, blend the topping ingredients (tofu, olive oil, and lemon juice) and smooth a thin layer of the mixture atop the pie.

Garnish with chopped red pepper and parsley. Serve cold.

Evolution

SAN DIEGO, CA

2965 5th Ave.
San Diego, CA 92103
(619) 550-1818

www.evolutionfastfood.com

A drive-thru vegan restaurant that proves that fast food can be healthy, too.

Zachary Vouga, manager

Is this your first restaurant?
This isn't the owners' (Rich Robinson and Mitch Wallis) first restaurant. Mitch Wallis's first restaurant opened in 1984 inside a fitness club in Tucson. And he has opened seven more since then.

When did it open?
This restaurant opened as Kung Foods in November 2004, a vegetarian restaurant with similar entrées and aesthetic. It reopened in 2008 as Nature's Express. Finally in 2010, we downsized and rebranded as Evolution.

Do the owners want to have more than one restaurant?
The owners plan to open many Evolutions across America.

What's your favorite dish on the menu?
The portobello sandwich, or the "Honey" Mustard Chick'n Wrap.

What's your most popular appetizer?
Chick'n Tenders with five homemade dipping sauces.

What's the most popular entrée on the menu?
The bacon cheeseburger, made with tempeh bacon, a tempeh patty, and tapioca cheese, or the California Burrito.

What's your most popular dessert?
New York cheesecake with fruit topping.

What do you feel is special about your restaurant?
We are one of the only (if not the only) vegan restaurant with a drive-thru window. Also we pride ourselves on our specialty homemade soft-serve and our one-of-a-kind raw milkshakes. And another standout quality of Evolution is our speed; we strive to provide gourmet vegan meals in less than four minutes.

How often do you change your menu items? Do you have daily or weekly specials?
Every morning we conjure a new special entrée. We also create a new soup each day and new soft-serve flavors two to three times per week.

Do you have gluten-free, soy-free, and sugar-free options on your menu?
Yes, many. On top of all of our juices and most of our smoothies, all of our sandwiches can be made both gluten- and soy-free. In addition, we try to cater to soy-free and gluten-free customers with our daily soups and specials.

What do you do to reduce your environmental impact?
We use plant-based containers and utensils that contain no plastic. We recycle all of our used cooking oils, glass bottles, cardboards, etc. And we're a ninety-nine percent GMO-free restaurant, soon to be one-hundred percent.

What are the most important lessons you've learned as owner or chef of this restaurant?
In the words of Mitch Wallis, owner of Evolution, "Everything boils down to love: loving our customers and staff and food and suppliers." I would add that patience, humility, love, and passion can shine through your cooking and take it to the next level.

What led you to want to open a vegan restaurant, and/or what led you to the vegan diet yourself?
I became vegetarian in 2004 and vegan in 2011. My stepmom was a huge source of inspiration and

support in my plant-based endeavors, and now it's snowballed into an exciting and encompassing lifestyle.

In the time since your restaurant first opened, how has the plant-based food movement changed? Do you find more demand now for vegan food?
Definitely. The best change is that a substantial number of consumers now view vegan as another cuisine category like Mexican or Chinese, so it's not seen as super extreme and you don't have to become vegan to enjoy a good vegan meal.

In the time since your restaurant first opened, has your view of what kinds of food choices to offer changed?
There has definitely been a move toward more fusion foods: creative combinations from many cultures and time periods.

Where do you see the plant-based food movement going in coming years?
Evolution embodies a huge part of the future plant-based food movement. We are the only drive-thru vegan restaurant that is poised to grow into an international chain, providing a meaningful alternative to the fast-food giants. 🐾

Lentil Curry Stew

Serves 6

⅓ cup olive oil
4 cups diced onion
¼ cup minced garlic
1¼ quarts water
¼ cup tomato paste
¼ cup curry powder
2 teaspoons ground cinnamon
¼ cup agave syrup
½ cup coconut milk
1 teaspoon cumin
1⅓ cups lentils
2 cups thinly sliced red pepper
2 cups sliced carrots
1½ cups green peas, preferably fresh
1 tablespoon sea salt

Heat a saucepan over a medium flame; add the olive oil, and once that's heated add the onions. Sauté the onions 5 to 7 minutes until translucent. Add garlic and stir for a moment. Add the water, tomato paste, curry powder, cinnamon, agave syrup, coconut milk, cumin, and lentils and bring to a simmer, then cook for 3 to 5 minutes. Throw in the pepper, carrots, and green peas, and simmer until lentils are cooked completely, approximately 20 to 30 minutes. Once the lentils are cooked, add the sea salt, remove from the heat, and serve.

Live Coconut Cacao Cheesecake

Makes one 9" pie

For the filling:
4   young coconuts
1   cup raw agave syrup
¾   cup raw cashews
½   cup coconut oil warmed to liquid
1   tablespoon raw cacao powder
1   teaspoon vanilla
Pinch salt, preferably Himalayan sea salt

For the crust:
2½ cups Brazil nuts or cashews
½   teaspoon ground cinnamon
Pinch ground nutmeg
Pinch salt, preferably Himalayan sea salt
⅛   cup to ¼ cup agave syrup

> **Timing:** *Pie must chill at least 24 hours before serving.*

For the filling: Carefully crack open the coconuts. (You won't need the coconut water, so feel free to pour it into a jar and save it in your fridge to drink later.) With a spoon, carefully remove the meat from the shell. Try to avoid getting pieces of coconut shell fiber in the mix. Place the coconut flesh into a food processor and process until smooth. Add the agave syrup, cashews, coconut oil, raw cacao, vanilla, and salt into the running food processor. Once the mixture is completely smooth, pour it out into a bowl and set aside while preparing the crust.

For the crust: Add the Brazil nuts (or cashews) to the food processor and process the nuts until they resemble a fine crumb. Toss in the cinnamon, nutmeg, and salt. Add agave syrup. The crust mixture should have a crumbly but not soggy texture.

To assemble: Press the crust mixture into the bottom of a lightly oiled 9" round pan. Pour the coconut filling mixture into crust. Allow to set at least 24 hours in the freezer before slicing and serving.

Funky Pies

SYDNEY, AUSTRALIA

2/144-148 Glenayr Ave.
Sydney NSW 2026, Australia
+61-451-944-404

www.funkypies.com.au

See HappyCow reviews at
www.happycow.net/book/funky-pies

Funky Pies is cozy, its couches are comfortable, its food is scrumptious— and what a choice of pies!

Angie Stephenson, owner and chef

Is this your first restaurant?
Yes.

When did it open?
April 2009.

Do you want to have more than one restaurant?
Yes.

What's your favorite dish on the menu?
The Nepalese lamb curry. This pie was made by a gorgeous Nepalese guy, Bachhu, who worked for us. He's since been married and had a beautiful little baby girl. He still pops in for the occasional fly-by pie.

What's your most popular appetizer?
Coffee, if you can call that an appetizer. While you wait for your food, you can sip on a delicious, fair-trade, organic latte. Soy is the only milk currently available. We're looking at sourcing creamy milk from coconuts and almonds soon.

What's the most popular entrée on the menu?
The Rockin' Roll. It's our version of a sausage roll: We use a veggie mince and fry up some onion and garlic together with some fresh rosemary from a friend's garden (anyone's garden really), and it comes together perfectly.

What's your most popular dessert?
The Funky Fudge Brownie. This is the winner amongst our treats, with our Caramel Slice (a biscuit base with hard caramel in the middle and chocolate on top) coming a very close second!

What do you feel is special about your restaurant?
We're humble; we're not making a big production out of our veganism, which means we appeal to all sorts of passers-by. It's the reason we don't advertise our veganism; we want everyone to try a Funky Pie without the judgment. It seems to work; we have people coming back for the "beef pie that I had last time."

How often do you change your menu items? Do you have daily or weekly specials?
We have specials when we create a new pie, or when we have a fundraising night/event. Generally our menu stays the same, with the introduction of a new pie now and then.

Do you have gluten-free, soy-free, and sugar-free options on your menu?
Yes! Gluten-free, soy-free, low-sugar pie options and no-sugar dessert items are all available.

What do you do to reduce your environmental impact?
It's a long list! We used lead-free paint to paint the place, environmentally friendly varnish over the tiles, water-saving tap, energy-saving lightbulbs, biodegradable take-away materials, biodegradable wholesale pie packaging, one-hundred-percent recycled napkins and boxes for package pies, and cleaning detergents that are all environmentally friendly and non-animal tested. Even the toilet paper in our bathroom is one-hundred-percent recycled. Our Funky shirts are sweatshop-free. No plastic bags available for take-away.

What are the most important lessons you've learned as owner or chef of this restaurant?
Tough one. I think that you need to be good to your staff. A happy staff makes for comfortable customers. All our beautiful staff have pretty much been here since day one.

What led you to want to open a vegan restaurant, and/or what led you to the vegan diet yourself?
So I can eat what I want every day! Kidding! I wanted to have my own business for a long time, a series of events led me to be able to finance it, and it

went from there. As for being led to the vegan diet, I would say a feeling that I didn't want to contribute to the animal cruelty that I seemed to be drawn to watch on TV. The final straw was seeing a live export ship abandoned in the ocean; the captain and crew jumped ship, leaving all the sheep to burn and drown. You can't help but want to educate yourself, and when you do, it's impossible to turn a blind eye.

In the time since your restaurant first opened, how has the plant-based food movement changed? Do you find more demand now for vegan food?
I think society is more accepting of veganism these days; it doesn't seem to be as extreme as it once was. There are so many more options out there. All the contributors to this book have helped that to no end.

Since your restaurant first opened, has your view of what constitutes healthy or delicious food changed? Have you changed the types of foods you offer?
There are always fads of different foods; however, it's great to open your mind to new foods and flavors. I enjoy suppliers providing us with new food opportunities that we can then share with our customers.

Where do you see the plant-based food movement going in coming years?
I like to think it'll continue to grow. I'd love to see someone come up with a decent vegan Camembert cheese, or a vegan halloumi cheese—then I'd be set. And I think raw foods will take off a bit more, particularly in terms of health. I'd like to see that, rather than people thinking that they can cure illnesses with more pills and potions.

G'day Satay Pie

Serves 6

1   cup diced potato
1   cup diced pumpkin
¾   cup diced sweet potato
2   tablespoons vegetable oil, separated
1   teaspoon chili pepper flakes, plus more to sprinkle
¼   cup finely chopped fresh cilantro (roots, stalk, and all)
2   teaspoons curry spices (use a premixed dried spice mix)
3   tablespoons crunchy peanut butter
1   tablespoon crushed peanuts
1   teaspoon soy sauce
¼   teaspoon salt
2   cups coconut cream
1   package vegan puff pastry
Soy milk for glazing

Preheat the oven to 350 degrees. Spread diced potato, pumpkin, and sweet potato out onto a greased baking tray. Drizzle a small amount of vegetable oil over the top, reserving the rest for the filling. Roast the cubed veggies in the oven for approximately 20 minutes, or until they appear slightly golden brown.

Gently heat the remaining vegetable oil in deep frying pan, and add chili flakes and cilantro. When oil is bubbling, add curry spices. Stir well. Cook for another 2 minutes.

After the spices have been mixed through, giving off an intense aroma, add the peanut butter, crushed nuts, soy sauce, and salt, and cook for another 2 minutes, constantly stirring. Next, turn up the heat and add the coconut cream. Bring to a boil and then turn off the heat. Finally, once veggies are perfectly roasted, add them to the frying pan and gently stir through the coconut sauce.

Preheat the oven to 400 degrees. To assemble the pie, grease 6 round 5" diameter pie tins, about 1.5" deep. Using your favorite vegan puff pastry, cut out 6 large circles and 6 smaller circles (equivalent to the base and top of your pie tin). Press the pastry base into the tin, ensuring that pastry touches the sides and bottom all the

recipe continued

way up to the rim of the tin and smoothing out any air pockets so the pastry cooks evenly and takes on the shape of the tin.

Evenly distribute the mixture into the 6 formed pie bases. Make sure you don't overfill the pies—it will cause a mini explosion in your oven and leave you with a sticky mess to clean up. Keep the filling to about 1 cup. Place the 6 precut lid discs over the pie fillings; pinch the bottom and top pastry edges together to make a floral edge. Using a pastry brush, glaze the top of the pastry with soy milk and then sprinkle some chili flakes over the top. Stab a couple of fork holes into the pasty to let steam out while they bake.

Load the pies into the oven and bake them for about 25 minutes, or until golden brown.

For the full Funky effect, serve with mashed potato, mushy peas, and gravy.

G-Zen

BRANFORD, CT

2 E. Main St.
Branford, CT 06405
(203) 208-0443

www.g-zen.com

G-Zen is an organic, sustainable, gourmet vegan restaurant. The ingredients are grown locally, and many are homegrown on the Shadle farm, a 270-year-old solar-powered farm and farmhouse in nearby Durham, Connecticut.

Ami Beach Shadle and Mark Shadle, co-owners and chefs

Is this your first restaurant?
G-Zen is my first restaurant. Mark [Shadle, also a co-owner] ran another award-winning vegetarian restaurant for twenty-two years.

When did G-Zen open?
In the fall of 2011.

Do you want to have more than one restaurant?
Yes, we're looking to expand and grow our eco-conscious and vegan business model, probably to a completely different part of the country.

What's your favorite dish on the menu?
Raw pasta. The pasta is made from tricolor vegetables—carrots, daikon, and beets—and the sauce is a sun-dried organic marinara with fresh herbs, topped with a cashew Parmesan cheese. The dish is garnished with G-Zen kale chips.

What's the most popular entrée on the menu?
New Orleans Creole Tempeh. It's a seasoned, blackened house-made tempeh with roasted red pepper Creole sauce, paired with organic garlic greens, mashed red potatoes, and gluten-free corn bread.

What's your most popular appetizer?
Sublime vegan nachos: a huge plate of homemade corn tortilla chips (non-GMO), gluten-free chili, fresh-made guacamole, olives, scallions, our house-made vegan tapioca cheese, and tofu sour cream, topped with cashew Parmesan.

What's your most popular dessert?
Traditional spiced carrot cake with ginger cream frosting and chopped walnuts. When Mark competed in the Culinary Olympics, this was part of his menu.

What do you feel is special about your restaurant?
We live the life that we promote. Our life's passion and our work are so intertwined; it's impossible not to sense that when you enter the restaurant and eat the food we serve. "Food is love" is our motto. We eat, drink, and sleep our vegan mission! We believe that serving pure and organic cuisine, cooked with love and intention, is what transforms our food into something spectacular.

How often do you change your menu items? Do you have daily or weekly specials?
We have a huge chef's-special chalkboard—four feet by six feet—in the restaurant. And we offer farm-to-table specials made from ingredients grown on our own organic farm and local farms. We find most of our inspiration in season and locally.

Do you have gluten-free, soy-free, and sugar-free options on your menu?
Seventy percent of the menu is naturally gluten-free. We specify soy-free dishes. If our desserts have a sweetener, it's rice syrup, coconut nectar, or maple syrup. We don't use straight white sugar or brown sugar.

What do you do to reduce your environmental impact?
First of all, our food is ninety-five percent certified organic. We use compostable packages, no bottled water (only glass), and we give discounts to customers who bring their own takeout containers with them. We compost one-hundred percent of food waste from the restaurant on our farm, fertilizing the food we grow for the restaurant in a virtuous cycle! The food we serve in the restaurant is food we've either grown ourselves or bought from local organic farms or farmers' markets, so transportation costs for our food are absolutely minimal. Currently we grow on our farm about thirty percent of our ingredients—sweet potatoes, kale, butternut squash, heirloom tomatoes, healing herbs (echinacea, mint, rosemary, thyme, basil, oregano), wild blueberries, peaches, apples, Concord grapes, and more. We hope to build a greenhouse so that we can grow year-round.

What are the most important lessons you've learned as owner or chef of this restaurant?
That it's not just about the food—we're part of a movement that's about educating people. G-Zen wants to help create a brighter future together with our community. We have a community table that seats more than twenty people. And we use the restaurant and vegan mobile truck as platforms for learning and growing.

What led you to want to open a vegan restaurant, and/or what led you to the vegan diet yourself?
I was led to the diet for reasons of health. Mark had already run a vegetarian restaurant, and when we saw the success of Gmonkey—our food truck that brought vegan food into the inner city—we decided to try to change the face of vegan eating. And we wanted our restaurant to be a place to take business colleagues and nonvegans and introduce them to vegan cuisine in an elegant, candlelit restaurant. Chef Mark and I have been vegan for more than twenty years and counting. We knew when we opened our own restaurant it would reflect the kind of food we like to eat ourselves. G-Zen is raw and cooked organic vegan cuisine, which represents both the chef/owners' and our passions.

In the time since your restaurant first opened, how has the plant-based food movement changed? Do you find more demand now for vegan food?
The demand keeps growing. Even meat-eaters know that moving toward a vegetarian diet just makes sense. More and more people are getting turned off by the pink slime scare, meat recalls, and mad cow disease, while getting motivated by great books and documentaries advocating the plant-based diet.

Since your restaurant first opened, has your view of what constitutes healthy or delicious food changed? Have you changed the types of foods you offer?
We're moving more in the direction of raw food, and it's taking off like you wouldn't believe.

Where do you see the plant-based food movement going in coming years?
The movement is growing stronger and stronger all the time. Soon quitting meat is going to be like quitting smoking. 🐾

Raw Cacao and Coconut Truffles

Makes 12 truffles

3 cups shredded coconut
1½ cups raw cacao powder
1 teaspoon lucuma powder
   (optional, but gives a rich
   caramel flavoring to truffle)
Pinch Celtic sea salt
⅓ cup raw cold-pressed coconut oil
¾ cup agave syrup or maple
   syrup
1 teaspoon Ceylon cinnamon
   powder
Fresh mint leaves (garnish)

Add 2¾ cups shredded coconut, cacao, lucuma, and sea salt to a large mixing bowl and whisk together by hand. In a small saucepan, slightly warm the coconut oil just enough to liquefy. Add the warm coconut oil and agave syrup or maple syrup to the dry mix and mix well with a wooden spatula.

Use a teaspoon or melon baller and scoop out raw chocolate mixture into small balls. Slightly dampen hands and roll into round teaspoon-size pieces. Finish by rolling each truffle in extra ¼ cup shredded coconut. Dust each with a little Ceylon cinnamon for a final touch.

Place truffles in the fridge for 20 minutes or until slightly hardened.

When ready to serve, leave out at room temperature to thaw for 5 to 10 minutes and garnish with a sprig of fresh mint and a dusting of cacao powder on the plate.

Tricolored Vegetable Pasta with Sun-Dried Marinara and Cashew Cheese

Serves 4

For the noodles:
3   medium beets
3   large carrots
3   medium zucchini

For the marinara:
2   cups sun-dried tomatoes in oil
2   cups diced tomatoes
1   cup pitted medjool dates
1   teaspoon fresh oregano
1   teaspoon fresh rosemary
1   cup fresh basil
2   cloves garlic
Pinch black pepper, to taste
Pinch Celtic sea salt, to taste
Chili pepper flakes (optional)

For the cashew Parmesan cheese:
2   cups raw dried cashews (soaked
     1 hour in water and drained)
1   teaspoon Celtic sea salt
1   tablespoon nutritional yeast
     powder

For the garnish (optional):
Fresh or dried chopped basil
Dried oregano

Equipment needed: spiralizer

For the noodles: Using a spiralizer, cut long noodlelike pieces from the beets, carrots, and zucchini. You can also use a vegetable peeler or the shredder attachment to a food processor to make shorter vegetable noodles. Set vegetable noodles aside.

For the marinara: Combine the ingredients in a food processor with the S blade. Pulse until you get a creamy marinara. Remove and set aside.

For the cashew Parmesan cheese: Place the raw cashews, sea salt, and nutritional yeast into the food processor with an S blade and pulse until it makes a Parmesan cheese texture.

To assemble: In a large mixing bowl, combine all vegetable noodles and sun-dried marinara and toss well until the vegetable pasta is well covered with sauce. Serve on a plate topped with plenty of cashew Parmesan to add a rich and cheesy flavor. Garnish your plate with basil and dried oregano.

Chocolate Raspberry Hazelnut Cake

Serves 10–12

1   cup canola oil
2½ cups maple syrup
1   teaspoon lemon juice
2   tablespoons vanilla extract
1   cup apple juice
3   cups whole-wheat pastry flour
1   cup cocoa powder
3   tablespoons baking powder
½   teaspoon salt

For the chocolate frosting:
1   quart vegan chocolate chips
3   12⅓-ounce packages firm
     silken tofu
3   tablespoons canola oil
1   cup sugar
¾   cup cocoa powder
2   tablespoons vanilla extract

For the filling:
Raspberry preserves
Chocolate frosting (see above)
1   cup crushed toasted hazelnuts

Preheat oven to 350 degrees. Oil and flour three 8" cake pans. Combine wet ingredients (through apple juice) in a bowl and whisk together. Combine dry ingredients in a bowl and whisk together. Add the dry ingredients to the wet and stir until just combined. Pour equal amounts of batter into the 3 cake pans. Place the 3 cake pans in the oven on top of a sheet pan and bake for 20 minutes. Rotate the sheet pan in the oven back-to-front and bake 5 to 10 minutes longer. The cakes are done when the center is springy and cake has pulled away from sides of the pan. Remove and cool the cakes in pans. Once cool to the touch, turn the cakes out onto a cooling rack and finish cooling.

To make the frosting, place the vegan chocolate chips in a double broiler and melt over low heat, stirring as needed. Using a food processor, process tofu until smooth. Add canola oil, sugar, cocoa powder, and vanilla. Process until smooth. Add melted chocolate chips and process until smooth and creamy.

To assemble: Cut cake layers in half horizontally with serrated knife. Alternate raspberry preserves, then chocolate frosting with chopped hazelnuts between all 6 layers. Garnish with remaining hazelnuts.

Green Cuisine

VICTORIA, BC, CANADA

560 Johnson St. #5
Victoria, BC V8W 3C6 Canada
(250) 385-1809

www.greencuisine.com

Homemade, healthy, sometimes exotic, Green Cuisine's flavorful food is served buffet-style.

Andy Cunningham, owner and chef

Is this your first restaurant?
This is the first restaurant I've owned. Other vegetarian restaurants/kitchens where I have worked include Divine Light Mission, London, 1973; Supernatural Restaurant, Newcastle, 1975; East West Restaurant, London, 1980; and The Last Resort, Toronto, 1983.

When did Green Cuisine open?
November 1990.

Do you want to have more than one restaurant?
I want to have only one.

What's your favorite dish on the menu?
Tofu noodle soup with focaccia bread.

What's your most popular appetizer?
Falafel with tahini sauce.

What's the most popular entrée on the menu?
Veggie gratin.

What's your most popular dessert?
White and dark chocolate mousse cake.

What do you feel is special about your restaurant?
Everything! Our main feature is our pay-by-weight buffet that allows people to create their own meals by choosing as much or as little of exactly what they want from our wide selection of hot and cold dishes.

How often do you change your menu items? Do you have daily or weekly specials?
We change our menu daily, though we repeat the most popular dishes approximately once every two weeks. Our menu is posted online every day so that people can see when their favorites are being served.

Do you have gluten-free, soy-free, and sugar-free options on your menu?

We're ninety-five percent gluten-free, and we have many soy-free dishes. Sugar-free is not a big issue with our customers, and we use a variety of sweeteners including dried whole cane juice, rice syrup, maple syrup, and organic cane sugar. All our dishes are clearly labeled with signs listing all the ingredients so people can easily select items to their liking.

What do you do to reduce your environmental impact?

First and foremost, we only offer vegan food! We also recycle everything we can. We compost our own scraps. We run our vehicles on used vegetable oil. We buy local and organic ingredients. We use earth-friendly cleaning products. And we use biodegradable takeout containers for those wanting food to go.

What are the most important lessons you have learned as owner or chef of this restaurant?

The most important lesson I have learned is to stick with your own vision but at the same time draw on the suggestions and feedback of others to keep that vision fresh.

What led you to want to open a vegan restaurant, and/or what led you to the vegan diet yourself?

At the age of eighteen, I looked into where my food came from, having never questioned it or given it a second thought before. Becoming conscious of the fact that meat is dead animals made me become a vegetarian. From the get-go, I loved vegetarian food and cooking: lentils, brown rice, carrots, soba noodles, oatmeal, sunflower seeds, kasha—the list goes on. I discovered a whole world of wonderful ingredients that continue to inspire me to this day. I went on to study macrobiotic cooking at the Kushi Institute and this further helped me refine my cooking style and commitment to a vegan diet and introduced me to yet more fascinating ingredients.

I opened Green Cuisine because I love cooking and I wanted to nourish and bring joy to others with my food. Discovering this way of eating was a revelation for me, and I hope that it can be a revelation for others, too.

In the time since your restaurant first opened, how has the plant-based food movement changed? Do you find more demand now for vegan food?

There is much more demand for vegan food these days. The vegan diet is more accepted and mainstream. I see the vegan movement as a branch of the larger natural-foods movement, which has evolved and will continue to evolve at a rapid rate; people are drawn to it because they want to feel good about their food choices and it tastes so good.

In the time since your restaurant first opened, has your view of what kind of food choices to offer changed? Has your view of what constitutes healthy and delicious food changed?

We offer a way of eating based on whole grains, beans, legumes, and vegetables cooked in a variety of styles, and that hasn't changed. But over the years, we've drawn influence from many different culinary cultures around the world, and we'll continue to develop and offer a wide range of new vegan recipes for our customers. Sometimes what's old is new again. Good honest whole foods prepared with love and care will always have a timeless appeal; not only do they taste delicious, but our bodies instinctively recognize them as wholesome and beneficial.

Where do you see the plant-based food movement going in coming years?

Nowhere but up. Though there may be a few blips on the way! The younger generations are more educated regarding what they eat, and are more knowledgeable and concerned about the environmental impacts of their food choices. Barely a day goes by without the media linking meat-based diets to serious health concerns. At some point, the true cost of meat will be reflected in the cost at the cash register.

The way I see it, animal foods have an image problem similar to tobacco. The Marlboro Man used to look pretty cool, but now, not so much.

With the challenges to feed a growing population on a shrinking planet, people are realizing that veganism is not only a moral option but also a realistic necessity. 🐾

A top seller at Green Cuisine, these whole-grain patties
develop a delicious crispy outer layer when fried.

Quinoa Patties (pictured opposite)

Makes 12 patties

3½ cups water
1¼ cups quinoa
¾ cup millet
½ teaspoon salt
1 cup diced onions
1 cup diced carrots
¼ cup oat flakes
¼ cup potato starch
⅛ cup Bragg Liquid Aminos
⅛ teaspoon cayenne
½ cup chopped walnuts
Oil for frying

In a saucepot, bring the water to a boil. Add the quinoa, millet, salt, onions, and carrots. Return to a boil and simmer for 20 minutes. Add the remaining ingredients, except oil; mix and mash a little with a potato masher. Shape the mixture into patties and put them on a tray in the refrigerator to cool. Just before serving, remove them from the fridge, heat a little oil in a pan, and fry them on both sides until crisp and golden.

A moist, tender cake with a deliciously gooey icing.

Peanut Butter Blondies

Serves 16

For the blondie base:
2¾ cups brown rice flour
1½ cups dried cane juice
½ cup shredded coconut
1 teaspoon baking powder
1 teaspoon baking soda
1 teaspoon salt

1 teaspoon guar gum
1 cup sunflower oil
1 cup vegan butter
2½ cups soy or rice milk
1 tablespoon vanilla
1 tablespoon lemon juice
1 cup chocolate chips, melted

For the icing:
½ cup soy milk or rice milk
½ teaspoon agar powder
¼ cup sugar
½ cup rice syrup
½ cup vegan butter
½ cup peanut butter

Preheat the oven to 400 degrees. In a bowl, combine the dry ingredients (through guar gum). Add the sunflower oil, vegan butter, soy milk, vanilla, and lemon juice one by one to the dry mixture, then mix well.

Separate the blondie mix into 2 batches. Pour half of the batter in to an oiled 12 x 9 rectangular cake pan. Add the melted chocolate chips to the remaining half, mixing well, and then pour that over the first half in the cake pan. Bake for 40 minutes. Test with a toothpick when done. Leave the cake in the pan to cool.

To make the icing, place all the icing ingredients, minus the peanut butter, in a pot and bring to a boil over low heat. Once boiled, whisk in the peanut butter until fully incorporated. Take the mixture off the heat and allow to cool a bit.

To assemble: Spread the slightly cooled icing over the cake (still in the pan). Drizzle a little more of the melted chocolate chips over the icing. Refrigerate until fully cooled, then cut into 16 servings.

These moist brownies are as chocolatey and as nutty as it gets without being overly sweet.

Praline Brownies

Serves 16

*For the peanut butter filling/
frosting:*
½   cup soy milk or rice milk
½   teaspoon agar powder
¼   cup sugar
½   cup rice syrup
½   cup vegan butter
½   cup peanut butter

For the brownie base:
1¼ cups brown rice flour
½   cup dried cane juice
½   teaspoon baking powder
¼   teaspoon baking soda
½   teaspoon salt
½   teaspoon guar gum
4   cups chocolate chips
½   cup vegan butter, melted
¼   cup sunflower oil
1½ cups soy or rice milk
1   teaspoon vanilla
*Peanut butter filling/frosting
   (recipe above)*

For the topping:
1½ cups roasted pecan pieces
¼   cup rice syrup
¼   teaspoon sea salt

Place all peanut butter filling/frosting ingredients, minus the peanut butter, in a pot and bring to a boil over low heat. Once the mixture has boiled, remove from the heat and whisk in the peanut butter. Separate into 2 batches and set aside in a warm place until the brownie base is ready.

To prepare the brownie base, preheat the oven to 400 degrees. Mix the brown rice flour, dried cane juice, baking powder, baking soda, salt, and guar gum together. In a double boiler, melt the chocolate chips and vegan butter and stir into the dry mix along with the sunflower oil, soy or rice milk, and vanilla. Mix well and separate into 2 batches.

Spread the first batch of the brownie base into an oiled 12 x 9 rectangular cake pan. Carefully cover the brownie base with 1 batch of the peanut butter filling, then top that with the remaining half of the brownie mix. Bake for 25 minutes. Remove and cool.

To make the topping, on a sheet tray, roast the pecan pieces in the oven for 9 minutes. Carefully boil the rice syrup and sea salt, add the pecans, and keep heating and stirring to coat the nuts. Remove from the heat.

To assemble: Frost the baked brownies with the remaining half of the peanut butter mixture. Sprinkle the pecans on the top of the brownies. Cool before slicing.

Green New American Vegetarian Restaurant

TEMPE, AZ

2240 N. Scottsdale Rd. #8
Tempe, AZ 85281
(480) 941-9003

(Second location in Phoenix, AZ)

www.greenvegetarian.com

Damon Brasch, owner and chef

Green Restaurant is an award-winning, chef-driven, comfort-food destination, serving one-hundred-percent plant-based foods for the masses.

Is this your first restaurant?
No.

When did it open?
The first location of Green Restaurant opened in Tempe, Arizona, in 2006.

How many restaurants do you hope to have in the future? Will you expand further?
The idea of expanding further is always enticing, but we'll only entertain growth if our ethics and our integrity can support it.

What's your favorite dish on the menu?
Depending on how healthy I'm trying to eat, it's either the Singapore Orange Bowl with our house tofu with orange-soy glaze and organic brown rice or our infamous Big Wac with a side of thyme fries.

What's your most popular appetizer?
Our vegan Buffalo "wings" with dill ranch.

What's the most popular entrée on the menu?
The Original "G" Spicy Chicken Sandwich.

What's your most popular dessert?
The tSoynami: organic vegan soft-serve ice cream folded together with your choice of fruits, cookies, cakes, doughnuts, candy bars, or just about anything decadent you can think of. If you haven't had one, you really should.

What do you feel is special about your restaurant?
The most special thing about the restaurant is the number of omnivores that eat here, and then they come back with more of their friends to prove that vegan food can really taste great. That plus our amazing sweet shop, Nami tSoft tServe and

Coffee, which serves one-hundred-percent vegan pastries, ice cream, and coffee—Yum!

How often do you change your menu items? Do you have daily or weekly specials?

We have specials all the time; people love them. Our menu pretty much stays the same throughout the year, but we always incorporate local and organic vegetables into our specials and menu whenever we can.

Do you have gluten-free, soy-free, and sugar-free options on your menu?

We have a whole separate menu that is entirely gluten-free. And we have some soy-free and sugar-free options, too.

What do you do to reduce your environmental impact?

Of course we recycle; we were one of the first restaurants to start recycling in our area. We use loads of green products such as corn-based cups, postconsumer recycled paper products, renewable birchwood flatware, etc. Our beer menu is all local and regional beers, served only in cans; we also have an extensive wine list that includes many Arizona wines on tap. But the most important environmentally conscious choice we make is, of course, to be one-hundred-percent vegan.

What are the most important lessons you've learned as owner or chef of this restaurant?

The most important thing I've learned about owning and operating Green Restaurant is that the people and community around you are what's most important. When you surround yourself with the best, you will be the best.

What led you to want to open a vegan restaurant, and/or what led you to the vegan diet yourself?

I was in the restaurant game for many years, and although I was a vegetarian myself for over seventeen years, the food I was preparing was not aligned with my personal ethics. In 2008, my entire family went vegan after watching the phenomenal documentary *Earthlings*. I made the choice to never cook with animal products again.

In the time since your restaurant first opened, how has the plant-based food movement changed? Do you find more demand now for vegan food?

The demand for good vegan food is certainly on the rise. With the popularity of movies like *Earthlings* and *Forks Over Knives*, and the scientific evidence of the benefits of plant-based foods, more and more people are gravitating toward a vegan diet.

Since your restaurant first opened, has your view of what constitutes healthy or delicious food changed? Have you changed the types of foods you offer?

I don't think my philosophy has changed in this manner. I have always sought to celebrate food, and to celebrate the preparation of food. It's one of the greatest gifts one can offer. The food I prepare will stay with that person who consumes it for the rest of their life, on some level. I want the food to resonate with them in every way, and contribute to their healthfulness.

Where do you see the plant-based food movement going in coming years?

I think if people continue to make plant-based foods exciting and enticing, we can change people's minds. The more people eating plant-based foods, the better they will feel, and the more they will advocate it to others. This philosophy will bloom and grow more and more. 🐾

Coconut Tofu and Blackened Tempeh with Grapefruit Yuzu

Serves 3–6

For the grapefruit yuzu sauce:
¼ cup agave syrup
¼ cup unrefined cane sugar
½ cup yuzu vinegar*
Juice of 1 large grapefruit
Juice of 1 large lemon
1 tablespoon sambal**

For the tofu:
½ cup shredded coconut
1 30-ounce block extra-firm tofu (preferably sprouted)
¼ cup extra-virgin olive oil

For the tempeh:
1 1-pound block tempeh
1 teaspoon granulated garlic
2 teaspoons ancho chili powder
1 teaspoon kosher salt
1 teaspoon dried thyme
¼ cup extra-virgin olive oil

For the garnish (optional):
12 to 15 segmented grapefruit pieces
Handful microgreens
Alfalfa sprouts

* Yuzu vinegar is commonly found at any Whole Foods, Sprouts, or Asian markets, or online from Amazon.

** Sambal is a chili-based condiment used frequently in Malaysian, Indonesian, and South Indian cooking. Find it in the international section of grocery stores or an Asian food market.

Put all of the grapefruit yuzu sauce ingredients in a sauté pan and cook over medium heat. Stir and cook for about 10 minutes until the sauce is reduced by half. Set aside to cool.

To toast the coconut, preheat the oven to 350 degrees. Place the shredded coconut on a sheet tray and put it in the heated oven. Lightly toast the coconut until golden brown (about 10 to 15 minutes). Put the toasted coconut in a bowl and set aside.

Cut the tofu into 1 x 1 squares. Place the oil in a nonstick pan and heat. Put the tofu in the pan and lightly sauté the tofu cubes in until golden brown. Transfer the sautéed tofu to a bowl with the toasted coconut and lightly toss. The toasted coconut should gently stick to the tofu.

Cut the tempeh into 1 x 1 squares. In a bowl, combine the garlic, chili powder, salt, and dried thyme; mix well, then place the cut tempeh cubes into the bowl. Gently roll the tempeh cubes in the seasoning to coat thoroughly on all sides.

Next, heat the oil in a nonstick pan. Once the oil is hot, place the tempeh into the pan and lightly sauté the seasoned cubes until you achieve a rich blackened look on the outside. This should take 5 to 7 minutes. Continue to move the tempeh around in the pan as you cook it to get an even sear on all sides.

To assemble: With a 6" skewer, spear 1 cube of tofu, then 1 cube of blackened tempeh, then 1 more cube of tofu, then the final cube of tempeh. Repeat this pattern 4 times,

recipe continued

alternating the tempeh and the tofu, to get a "checkerboard" effect. Repeat for 3 additional skewers (4 in total). Top with some microgreens or fresh alfalfa sprouts.

Finally, drizzle 4 to 5 tablespoons of the citrus yuzu glaze over the skewers. Add segmented pieces of grapefruit to garnish, if using.

HappyCow Member Reviews for Green New American Vegetarian Restaurant

Best veg food in the Phoenix area

"Green is my favorite place to eat in the Phoenix area . . . . There are many yummy selections. I have tried nearly everything on the menu and it is all fantastic."

—suecag

Always a success

"The best part of this place is that even my meat-eating friends love it. I am a rather picky eater, but I have never had something that I didn't love."

—kcroe

Making other vegan restaurants Green with Envy!

"I am irrevocably in love with this place! Green was THE most anticipated vegan stop on our summer road trip and it did NOT disappoint!"

—Tigra220

Hangawi
Restaurant

NEW YORK, NY

12 E. 32nd St.
New York, NY 10016
(212) 213-0077

www.hangawirestaurant.com

Escape the stress of New York City to this soothing shrine of vegan Korean cuisine.

Terri (pictured) **and William Choi, owners**

Is this your first restaurant?

No, we owned a Korean restaurant—not a vegetarian restaurant—in Queens prior to opening Hangawi. When we became vegetarians, we decided to sell that restaurant and open a vegan restaurant.

When did it open?

Hangawi opened in December 1994. We also own Franchia Vegan Café at 12 Park Avenue in New York City, which opened in April 2003.

What's your favorite dish on the menu?

The Organic Zen Bibimbap, which is wild mountain greens with vegetables and mushrooms served with organic brown rice. The way to eat this dish is to mix these mountain greens, vegetables, and mushrooms with the rice and chili sauce. This is my favorite dish because it is a very typical Korean dish but our version features mountain greens from the Jeong Bong Mountains of Korea that are handpicked and dried and sent by air to our restaurant.

What's the most popular appetizer?

It's the Combination Pancakes, three types of Korean pancakes: the kimchi (Korean preserved pickle)-mushroom pancake, the leek pancake, and the mung bean–kabocha pumpkin pancake.

What's the most popular entrée on the menu?

The crispy mushrooms in sweet-and-sour sauce made with shiitake and button mushrooms. People love the light crispiness of the mushrooms coated with batter and the tangy taste of the tomato sauce.

What's your most popular dessert?

It is our dairy-free soy cheesecake. People say that our cheesecake tastes better than the cheesecake made with actual cheese.

What do you feel is special about your restaurant?

Dining at Hangawi is a unique Zen experience, from the vegan menu to the total ambience of the space. Diners first need to take their shoes off when entering the dining area, just as they would if entering a Korean house. Then they sit on cushions at low tables (with a well underneath so that they can extend their legs). Zen candles are softly lit on the tables and the diners are transported to a templelike setting far away in the mountains of Korea. As Ruth Reichl wrote in the review of Hangawi in the *New York Times*, "A meal at Hangawi is an experience of all the senses, a chance to escape if only for a little while the stress and bustle of New York City…. The oversize door is an entrance to another world, an invitation to a place where nothing is familiar."

How often do you change the menu items? Do you have daily or weekly specials?

The dishes presented in our prix-fixe Emperor's Tasting Meal are changed every month.

We also have seasonal menus featuring produce available during a particular season, like the matsutake mushrooms in the fall and *todok* (mountain root from Korea) in the winter, as well as spring and summer special menus.

Do you have gluten-free, soy-free, or sugar-free options on the menu?

We have a separate gluten-free menu. For those dishes, we also use tamari soy sauce to substitute regular soy sauce that contains wheat.

What do you do to reduce your environmental impact?

We try to minimize the use of nonbiodegradable materials that are harmful to the environment such as takeout plastic utensils and straws. As much as possible, we also try to use recycled paper products such as recycled paper napkins. In our bathrooms, we have hand dryers that replace paper towels. The used cooking oil is also recycled.

What are the most important lessons you've learned as owner or chef of this restaurant?

We've learned that it's important to believe in our philosophy of a healthy and ethical diet and educate our customers on this belief. When we started Hangawi in 1994, vegetarianism was not as popular as it is today and a Korean vegetarian restaurant was something really alien to the American public. It was important for us to constantly educate the public in our belief that vegetarianism is the safest diet and the most beneficial to our environment. We needed to teach our customers about eating a balanced vegetarian meal. This took a lot of patience and creativity. We're constantly working with our menu to add variety and creativity to our dishes.

What led you to want to open a vegan restaurant, and/or what led you to a vegan diet yourself?

We opened a vegan restaurant because we became vegans and strongly believe that a vegan diet is the safest and the most healthy and ethical way of eating.

We attended a lecture about vegetarianism, and it convinced us to follow a vegan diet.

The professor who gave the lecture talked about the negative environmental effects of a meat-based diet and the horrendous cruelty afflicted on animals in factory farms. He also talked about the karma of the animal spirit that remains in our body after we consume animals. We were convinced that for health, ethical, environmental, and philosophical reasons, we had to adopt a vegan diet.

In the time since your restaurant first opened, how has the plant-based food movement changed? Do you find more demand now for vegan food?

There has definitely been a positive direction in the plant-based food movement in the last ten years. More and more people, especially young people in urban areas such as New York City, are becoming vegans with the awakening of the green movement.

In the time since your restaurant opened, has your view of what kinds of food choices to offer changed? Has your view of what constitutes healthy or delicious food changed?

It has always been our belief that a healthy vegan diet must be a balanced diet comprised of the *um* (yin) foods such as green vegetables and fruits and yang foods such as the root foods like carrots, potato, radish. A balance of the *um* and yang foods is our basic principle of a healthy vegan diet. Recently, we started offering more gluten-free and organic options in the menu as we believe that foods that are free of pesticides and artificial fertilizers are definitely healthier and taste better. 🐮

Tofu with Broccoli in Spicy Garlic Sauce

Serves 4

For the sauce:
¼ cup peeled and minced apple*
¼ cup peeled and minced pear*
¼ cup small pieces orange
3 teaspoons minced onion*
2 teaspoons minced garlic*
1 tablespoon sugar
2 tablespoons sesame oil
2 tablespoons sake (fermented rice wine)
10 tablespoons water
10 tablespoons gluten-free tamari**

For the tofu and broccoli:
10½ ounces tofu (medium firm)
½ medium-size eggplant
Soybean oil for frying
3½ cups broccoli pieces (cut into 2"-long segments, including crown)
2 teaspoons minced garlic*
2 tablespoons soybean oil to sauté
2 teaspoons minced fresh ginger*

* You can use a food processor to mince these ingredients.

** Available at Whole Foods and all major health food stores.

In a mixer, blend all of the sauce ingredients together until well combined. Transfer this mixture from the blender into a saucepot. Simmer for 2 to 3 minutes over a low flame. Set aside.

Cut the tofu into triangles of approximately 2 x 1 x 1 and ½" thick. Slice the eggplant into thin slices, approximately 2" in length. Steam the sliced eggplant in a steaming pot for about 5 minutes. Set eggplant aside.

Heat 1" of soybean oil in a deep wok until the oil is very hot. Deep-fry the tofu pieces in the wok with oil for 30 seconds. Remove them from the oil using a slotted spoon or a spider and place them on a plate with a paper towel to soak any excess oil. Deep-fry the broccoli in the same oil for 5 seconds. Remove them from the oil and place on a plate with a paper towel. In a separate frying pan, heat 2 tablespoons of soybean oil until the oil is hot. Sauté the minced garlic and ginger pieces until they are golden brown. Add the cooked tofu, broccoli, and steamed eggplant and sauté for 20 seconds.

To assemble: Add the sauce and sauté the broccoli, tofu, and eggplant together with the sauce for 30 seconds.
Serve on a large plate.

Stuffed Shiitake Mushrooms with Almond-Cinnamon Sauce

Serves 4 (as an appetizer)

For the shiitake mushrooms and stuffing:
- 2 tablespoons finely minced carrot
- 10 ounces minced medium-hard tofu
- ½ cup finely minced oyster mushrooms
- 3 tablespoons minced fresh parsley
- ¼ cup finely minced onions
- Pinch black pepper
- 1 teaspoon sesame seeds
- 1 teaspoon mushroom powder*
- ½ teaspoon salt
- 2 tablespoons sesame oil
- 1 teaspoon ginger paste (blend ginger with a little water)
- 1 teaspoon potato powder*
- 8 medium-size shiitake mushrooms
- Grapeseed oil for frying

For the almond sauce:
- 3 tablespoons finely chopped almonds
- 2 tablespoons water
- 1 tablespoon mirin (sweet Japanese rice wine)
- 1½ teaspoons agave syrup
- 1 tablespoon corn syrup
- Pinch salt

For the cinnamon sauce:
- 3¾ cups water
- 4 cinnamon sticks
- 2 tablespoons soy sauce
- 1 tablespoon sugar
- 1½ tablespoons potato powder

* Available at Asian markets.

For the shiitake mushrooms and stuffing: Mix the carrot, tofu, oyster mushrooms, parsley, and onions together in a large bowl. Add black pepper, sesame seeds, mushroom powder, salt, sesame oil, ginger paste, and potato powder and mix well again.

Wash the shiitake mushrooms well and cut the stems away. Make little patties with the minced ingredients and stuff the patties into the shiitake mushrooms where the stem has been cut away. Add a little oil to a saucepan, heat the oil, and pan-fry the stuffed shiitake mushrooms on both sides until the stuffing turns golden brown.

For the almond sauce: Blend the almonds with water, mirin, agave syrup, corn syrup, and salt until the mixture becomes milky and consistent.

For the cinnamon sauce: Boil 3¾ cups of water with the cinnamon sticks in a pot for 10 minutes, until the cinnamon flavor melts into the water. Remove the cinnamon sticks from the pot and add the soy sauce and sugar to pot. In a separate bowl mix a little water with the potato powder until the potato powder becomes a paste. Add the potato powder paste to the pot, stirring the mixture well over a low flame until it becomes consistent.

To assemble: First pour the almond sauce onto a plate followed by the cinnamon sauce. Place the stuffed shiitake mushrooms on top of the sauce and serve.

Karyn's On Green

CHICAGO, IL

130 S. Green St.
Chicago, IL 60607
(312) 226-6155

(Other locations in Chicago)

www.karynsongreen.com

Elegant, stylish, contemporary, and nestled in the midst of Chicago's Greektown neighborhood, Karyn's on Green makes vegan sexy.

Karyn Calabrese, owner and chef

Is this your first restaurant?
No, it's my third.

When did it open?
January 2010.

How many restaurants do you hope to have in the future? Will you expand further?
I'd like to have a food truck and open restaurants in LA, Vegas, and three more in Chicago.

What's your favorite dish on the menu?
"Crab" sliders.

What's your most popular appetizer?
Our arugula flatbread.

What's the most popular entrée on the menu?
Roasted portobello with root vegetable hash, sautéed greens, and crispy leeks.

What's your most popular dessert?

The peanut butter chocolate chip brownie.

What do you feel is special about your restaurant?

It's contrary to what people think of when they picture a vegan restaurant. It's unique and very sexy. We have a bar with alcoholic and nonalcoholic beverages.

How often do you change your menu items? Do you have daily or weekly specials?

The menu is fixed, but we do have daily and weekly specials that we announce on Twitter and Facebook.

Do you have gluten-free, soy-free, and sugar-free options on your menu?

Yes, we have soy-free and sugar-free menu options. In addition, we have a separate gluten-free menu. Also, some raw options are available.

What do you do to reduce your environmental impact?

All of our takeout containers are environmentally friendly. We buy as much local farm produce and goods as possible.

What are the most important lessons you've learned as owner or chef of this restaurant?

Finding and inspiring the right team to work with is essential to run a successful business.

What led you to want to open a vegan restaurant, and/or what led you to the vegan diet yourself?

A vegan diet was a revolutionary and educational experience for me. All the women in my family died young, and I didn't want to follow in their footsteps. I was a vegan for a couple years, then a raw foodist. It has now been forty-five years [that] I have lived this way. There wasn't enough of a variety of vegan restaurants when I was going through my transition.

In the time since your restaurant first opened, how has the plant-based food movement changed? Do you find more demand now for vegan food?

I definitely think the market is expanding. Sixty-five to seventy-five percent of our customers aren't vegan; they simply like the food and ambience.

In the time since your restaurant first opened, has your view of what kinds of food choices to offer changed? Has your view of what constitutes healthy or delicious food changed?

No, I generally choose my menu by what appeals to me.

Where do you see the plant-based food movement going in coming years?

I see more growing acceptance, more understanding of why we should eat this way. I spend a lot of time educating people at free information seminars twice a month at one of my restaurants. 🐢

Coconut-Squash Soup with Garbanzo Bean Garnish

Serves 8

2   butternut squash
1   tablespoon olive oil
1   cup cooked garbanzo beans, drained and dried
½   teaspoon paprika
½   teaspoon sea salt, plus more to taste
½   teaspoon raw sugar
56 ounces canned coconut milk
Water as needed
Chili oil (garnish; optional)

Preheat the oven to 350 degrees. Line a large baking sheet with parchment paper. Set aside.

Slice off the stems of the squash. Cut the squash in half lengthwise. Remove and discard the seeds. Place the squash halves cut-side down on the prepared baking sheet. Roast in the preheated oven for 1½ hours, or until the squash is very soft. Let cool to room temperature.

Meanwhile, heat the oil in a medium skillet on medium heat (the skillet is ready when a drop of water sizzles in the pan). Add the garbanzo beans. Cook and stir for about 5 minutes, or until they are browned. Drain the garbanzo beans. Transfer them to a medium bowl with the paprika, salt, and sugar. Mix well. Set aside.

Peel the roasted squash halves and put them in a large saucepan. Add the coconut milk. Simmer on medium heat for about 20 minutes, stirring frequently. Transfer the squash mixture to a blender. Process on high speed for about 2 minutes, or until smooth, stopping occasionally to scrape down the blender's sides. Add 1 to 2 tablespoons of water as needed to thin the soup to the desired consistency. Season with more salt, to taste.

Ladle the squash into serving bowls and top each serving with some of the garbanzo beans.

Top with a drizzle of chili oil if you like. Feel free to prepare the soup in advance; time only makes it more flavorful.

Lettuce Love Café

BURLINGTON, ON, CANADA

399 John St.
Burlington, ON L7R 2K3 Canada
(905) 637-2700

www.lettucelovecafe.com

Canada's first one-hundred-percent gluten-free vegan restaurant, Lettuce Love Café features local and organic plant-based cuisine created with deliciously vibrant flavors.

Kelly Childs, owner and chef

Is this your first restaurant?
Not really. My husband Ken has been in the restaurant business all his life, and he has been very influential in our journey.

When did this restaurant open?
May 2010.

You have two restaurants. Do you want to have more?
Definitely we are moving toward more locations. We feel there is such a demand for what we do. Right now, we have people who drive from Toronto, Guelph, or London, Ontario (a one- to two-hour trip), and they aren't even fazed by the drive. They just want to be a part of our culture and eat here as often as they can. And we want to be able to provide food to them wherever they live!

What's your favorite dish on the menu?
Oooh, that's a hard one. For breakfast, it's either one of our organic green smoothies or green juices, along with a pumpkin seed muffin or our amazing World Peace Cookie (a gluten-free cookie made with oats and cranberries). If it's lunch or dinner, wow, our vegan Caesar salad is to absolutely die for.

What's your most popular appetizer?
Our soups seem to be the most in demand. These are made organic and fresh daily and are hearty and very popular.

What's the most popular entrée on the menu?
We have an incredible sandwich called the B.L.A.T.: Bac'Uns, lettuce, avocado, tomato, and a little sea salt with our house-made mayo on toasted gluten-free bread.

What's your most popular dessert?
Our Mile High Brownie is the best! It came in first place in Toronto's Totally Fabulous Vegan Bake-Off in February 2012, against forty-eight other competitors, and crazily enough, we were the only gluten-free bakery, too! People drive for hundreds of miles for our goodies.

What do you feel is special about your restaurant?
The vibe. It's very special. We have amazing, vibrant colors throughout and groovy music and lighting. We engage with all people who walk in our front door.

How often do you change your menu items? Do you have daily or weekly specials?
We don't change our menu too often because people would be very upset if their favorites disappeared. But we have daily features and daily bakery features.

Do you have gluten-free, soy-free, and sugar-free options on your menu?
We are a one-hundred-percent gluten-free restaurant and bakery. This is a huge feat and we managed to get all gluten-free ingredients for our restaurant and bakery departments.

Also, all our baked goods are soy-free. We have a few items on our café menu that have soy ingredients, but if people ask, we will gladly omit anything with soy in it.

As for sugar-free, we never use refined sugar in anything. As sweeteners, we will use dates, banana, applesauce, maple syrup, coconut nectar, and raw evaporated cane juice.

What do you do to reduce your environmental impact?
Being kind to the environment is one of our three pillars—and as a one-hundred-percent plant-based whole-food café and bakery, we use ingredients that automatically bring us very close to being green and sustainable. You have to follow through, though, with recycled or plant-based packaging and postconsumer recyclable items and print materials. We make purchasing decisions based on how far our products have to travel and how they are packaged. And we share our passion with our staff and customers.

What are the most important lessons you've learned as owner or chef of this restaurant?
The restaurant business is *hard* work. It's twenty-four/seven. Even if you're not physically there, you're still there in your mind. As my husband (and restaurant coach) says, "you paint a picture one brushstroke at a time, and if you don't have that picture in your head, you'll paint a mess."

What led you to want to open a vegan restaurant, and/or what led you to the vegan diet yourself?
Reading *The China Study* was the tipping point for me to change my diet to vegan. I was already vegetarian for a long time and then when I read about the ill effects of dairy and the corrupt dairy and food industry, my blinders came off. I took it one step further and studied plant-based nutrition at Cornell. At the same time, I watched *Earthlings* and I found out more about factory-farmed animals and the cruelty inflicted upon them.

In the time since your restaurant first opened, how has the plant-based food movement changed? Do you find more demand now for vegan food?
Way more demand now! I think the attention given to Bill Clinton and Ellen DeGeneres has helped us all to have a bigger voice. It has become trendy to eat vegan with all these celebrities going vegan and more and more people are realizing the health benefits that come from it.

Since your restaurant first opened, has your view of what constitutes healthy or delicious food changed? Have you changed the types of foods you offer?
We decided to eliminate gluten in the restaurant. That has really been the only change in direction for us. None of us, in our family, have celiac disease or are gluten-intolerant per se; it was a voluntary thing, and now, strangely enough, we have never felt better in our lives.

Where do you see the plant-based food movement going in coming years?
I see it going *huge*. I mean really big. The health-care system in the US is bankrupt. And people are realizing they need *prevention*—that is, nutrition from food, rather than drugs, to fix their ailments. Going plant-based is a natural cure-all, and one I promote wholeheartedly. I love that I have people coming to me from all over the world needing to know the first steps to going plant-based. Later they're thanking us a million times over for helping them get off their medications or reversing their diabetes or losing weight. It's just so rewarding!

My daughter Erinn and I have always had a sweet spot for carrot cake. This one we created without any wheat or gluten in it. We wanted to make sure it was still just as moist and full of flavor as the one we used to bake. Pineapple and coconut help to boost the natural sweetness of carrots, and they also enhance the grated carrot in the cake and give you a really nice texture and mouthfeel. We love this one!

Kelly and Erinn's Carrot Cake

Serves 10–16

3½ cups gluten-free all-purpose flour (we use Bob's Red Mill)
1 tablespoon baking powder
2 teaspoons baking soda
1½ teaspoons xanthan gum
1 teaspoon salt
1½ teaspoons ground cinnamon
1 teaspoon ground ginger
¼ teaspoon allspice
1¼ cups unsweetened coconut milk
1 teaspoon apple cider vinegar
2 cups evaporated cane juice
¼ cup maple syrup
2 teaspoons pure vanilla extract
1¼ cups canola oil or melted coconut oil
¼ cup hot water
3½ cups grated carrots
¼ cup shredded unsweetened coconut
¼ cup drained pineapple pieces
½ cup raisins

For the cream cheeze frosting:
1 cup palm shortening or Earth Balance shortening*
1½ cups vegan cream cheese
2 tablespoons coconut nectar or maple syrup
Pinch sea salt
2 tablespoons vanilla extract
6½ cups powdered sugar, sifted
½ cup shredded coconut (garnish; optional)

These are organic and nonhydrogenated.

Preheat oven to 350 degrees. Prepare three 9" cake pans with nonstick spray or parchment paper cut to line the bottom of pans.

To a medium-size mixing bowl, add the flour, baking powder, baking soda, xanthan gum, salt, cinnamon, ginger, and allspice, and dry whisk to combine. Set aside. In small bowl, combine coconut milk and apple cider vinegar and let sit for about 5 minutes.

In a large bowl combine evaporated cane juice, maple syrup, vanilla, and oil and mix with a hand or standing mixer. Add the coconut milk and vinegar mixture and mix again with an electric hand mixer. Add the dry mixture to the wet mixture in the large bowl and process with a mixer until combined and the batter begins to thicken (due to the xanthan gum). Gently add in the hot water and stir until combined. Fold in the carrots, coconut, pineapple, and raisins.

Pour the batter equally into 3 cake pans. Place the cake pans into the heated oven and bake for about 25 minutes, or until a toothpick inserted in center comes out clean.

For the frosting: With an electric hand mixer or a tabletop mixer with the paddle attachment, blend the shortening and the cream cheese until combined. Add the coconut nectar (or maple syrup), salt, and vanilla, and continue to mix until combined. Add the sifted powdered sugar in small batches until combined, then mix on high speed for about 2 to 3 minutes until you have desired consistency. Keep covered in sealed container in refrigerator until ready to use.

Cool the cake. Then gently remove the layers and place the first layer on the serving plate that the final cake will rest

on. Place three-fourths of the frosting onto the layer and smooth out to edges; add the second layer and repeat with the remaining frosting, gently smoothing out to edges and on the sides with a wide knife or spatula. If you're using coconut to garnish: Over top of a cookie sheet (or a sheet of parchment or foil), place a handful of coconut in your hand and with the palm of your hand, push the coconut in place on all sides of the cake until fully covered. (The cookie sheet will catch all the coconut that falls and you can clean up quickly and neatly.)

My husband loved and missed Reubens once we went to a one-hundred-percent plant-based diet. It became my mission to reproduce a vegan version as best as I possibly could.

Tempeh Reuben

Serves 4

For the tempeh marinade:
⅛ cup beet juice
¼ cup pickling or sauerkraut juice
2 tablespoons olive oil
⅛ teaspoon minced garlic
Juice of ½ lemon

For the Russian dressing:
½ cup vegan mayo
¼ cup ketchup
2 tablespoons finely diced dill pickles
1 teaspoon finely diced red onion
¼ teaspoon garlic powder
⅛ teaspoon brown mustard (optional)

For the tempeh:
1 9-ounce package of tempeh
½ cup Daiya Cheddar-Style Shreds

To assemble:
8 slices of gluten-free bread (we use Organic Works Chia Buckwheat Bread)
1 cup sauerkraut, drained (we use nonpasteurized for a healthier fermented option)

For the tempeh marinade: Place marinade ingredients into a small mixing bowl and whisk together very well or put into a small food processor and process until combined, about 5 seconds. Pour the marinade into a 13 x 9 roasting pan or cake pan.

For the Russian dressing: In a small mixing bowl, use a spoon to gently combine dressing ingredients until fully incorporated.

For the tempeh: Heat a steamer pot. Once hot, place the tempeh in the steamer for about 5 minutes, until you see it slightly swell and plump up.

Take the tempeh out of the steamer, place on a chopping block, and let it cool to the touch. Cut it in half so you have 2 rectangular blocks. Then take each rectangular block and slice it carefully through the middle so that you have 4 thin rectangles.

Place the tempeh in the prepared 13 x 9 pan and marinate the pieces on both sides for about 30 minutes minimum in the fridge. (You can marinate overnight and store the tempeh slices in a sealed container for up to 3 days.)

Heat an iron skillet over medium heat. Once hot, put the 4 tempeh slices in the skillet. You should hear them sizzle. Sear on the first side for about 4 minutes and then flip over each piece of tempeh. Sprinkle 2 tablespoons of Daiya shreds on each tempeh piece and then place a lid on the skillet to melt the cheese for about 3 to 4 minutes.

To assemble: Toast the bread. Top 4 slices with 2 tablespoons of Russian dressing and 2 to 3 tablespoons of sauerkraut, then place the tempeh with melted Daiya on top. Top with 1 more tablespoon of sauerkraut and final slice of toast.

Loving Hut

HOUSTON, TX

2825 S. Kirkwood Rd. #100
Houston, TX 77082
(281) 531-8882

(Other locations worldwide)

www.lovinghut.us

Harry Mai, owner and chef

At Loving Hut Houston, all items are one-hundred-percent vegan, prepared with the secret ingredients of love and care, and served with warm customer service at affordable prices.

Is this your first restaurant?
Yes.

When did it open?
Loving Hut Houston was opened by the original owner on October 25, 2009.

How many restaurants do you want to have?
Loving Hut itself is an international vegan chain restaurant with over 200 locations around the world. In the United States alone, there are 42 locations, and the restaurant franchise is still growing here in the US and around the globe.

What's your favorite dish on the menu?
Mongolian Wonder, a soy protein with onion, bell pepper, and ginger sautéed in a homemade sauce.

What's your most popular appetizer?
Golden Rolls with carrots, cabbage, celery, jicama, mushroom, and soy protein served with a sweet and sour sauce.

What's the most popular entrée on the menu?
Golden BBQ Vermicelli: BBQ soy protein with lettuce, cucumber, carrot-radish pickle, and roasted peanuts.

What's your most popular dessert?
Silky flan.

What do you feel is special about your restaurant?
We believe that many restaurants are able to prepare good vegan food. However, we feel our commitment is unmatched in providing one-hundred-percent pure vegan food with the passion of sharing our love and care for people. At Loving Hut

Houston, customers feel safe to know that all menu items are one-hundred-percent vegan. Our goal is to provide the best and healthiest ingredients possible in all the food we prepare, such as non-GMO rice oil, organic sugar, organic flour, organic ketchup, and sea salt, among others. Above all, love and care truly are our secret ingredients.

How often do you change your menu items? Do you have daily or weekly specials?

Our customers are very attached to our current menu. Therefore, we try not to change it too often. Approximately every six months to a year, we review and update our menu items according to economic considerations, and we add new items as requested and supported by our customers.

Do you have gluten-free, soy-free, and sugar-free options on your menu?

Yes, we do. We have a few menu items that are gluten-free and soy-free. Also, customers can ask our service staff about accommodating for other special diet needs.

What do you do to reduce your environmental impact?

We pay very close attention to the environmental impact that our restaurant may have on our planet. We use biodegradable containers for to-go orders. We recycle all recyclable materials, and we use energy-saving lightbulbs. In fact, a vegan diet has the lowest carbon footprint on our environment. We encourage people, especially our customers, to have more plant-based meals by informing them of the benefits of a vegan diet using pamphlets, and posters, and showing selected programs on the TV monitor in our restaurant.

What are the most important lessons you've learned as owner or chef of this restaurant?

Creating a menu with fresh and healthy ingredients that are organic or non-GMO, without using MSG, all the while keeping prices low is perhaps the highest priority we have as the owners of Loving Hut Houston. We've had to learn how to balance health concerns with taste and price factors to support our business model.

What led you to want to open a vegan restaurant, and/or what led you to the vegan diet yourself?

Love and compassion for all beings have led us to become vegans ourselves. We wanted to open a vegan restaurant to save more lives and reduce the suffering of our animal coinhabitants on Earth. In addition, we wanted to reduce the effects of climate change, and the vegan diet can stop the majority of the causes of global warming. By serving delicious, plant-based meals, we encourage people to adopt the compassionate, healthy, and planet-saving vegan lifestyle. We are so happy to know that Loving Hut Houston has made a difference. Many customers have shared stories with us about how their lives have changed to become more peaceful, more positive, healthier, and happier since they have started to dine at our Loving Hut.

In the time since your restaurant first opened, how has the plant-based food movement changed? Do you find more demand now for vegan food?

The plant-based food movement has made obvious progress. Now, a lot more people have started eating vegan food. The general public is more in tune with the need to eat healthier. At Loving Hut Houston, every day we see more and more new customers coming to dine and becoming vegans.

Since your restaurant first opened, has your view of what constitutes healthy or delicious food changed? Have you changed the types of foods you offer?

We have many customers starting to suggest additional healthy items. We also have many new customers who just became vegan still wanting to eat foods that taste rich.

Where do you see the plant-based food movement going in coming years?

Our beautiful planet and our animal friends still need a lot of help from us. However, we really believe the plant-based food movement is going to spread much faster in the coming years as the foundation has been built up with efforts from all directions. Vegan food definitely has received attention in our society and around the world. 🍲

Fabulous Phở: Aulacese (Vietnamese) Traditional Soup

Serves 6–8

For the phở soup base:
- 3 pounds jicama
- 3 pounds daikon
- 2 Fuji apples (optional)
- 2 gallons filtered water
- ½ pound shallots
- 3 yellow onions
- ¼ cup sliced fresh ginger (see instructions on the next page for removing skin before slicing)
- ¼ cup rock sugar (optional)
- 2 bags phở seasoning (preferably Phở Hoa brand; each package includes 4 small bags)*
- 2 tablespoons vegan mushroom seasoning**
- 3 tablespoons sea salt
- 2 tablespoons sugar

To assemble:
- 4 ounces white wood-ear mushrooms (optional)
- ½ pound dried vegan soy protein***
- 3 slices fresh ginger
- 2 pounds fresh phở noodles*
- 4 to 8 slices vegan protein balls***
- 4 to 8 thin slices vegan ham***
- 1 6-ounce piece tofu, lightly fried and sliced (optional)
- 4 stalks green onions, finely chopped
- ½ yellow onion, thinly sliced
- 2 tablespoons extra-virgin olive oil or vegan butter
- ½ bunch fresh cilantro, chopped
- 1 pound bean sprouts
- Small bunch fresh Thai basil
- Hoisin sauce*
- Sriracha hot chili sauce*
- 1 lemon, cut into wedges

* Can be found at Asian grocery store.

** Chef's Wonder seasoning can be purchased at any Loving Hut.

*** Can be purchased online.

Wash the jicama, peel off the skin, and dice it into 1" cubes. Wash the daikon and dice it into 1" cubes. Wash the apples, if using, and dice them into 1" cubes. Place the jicama, daikon, and apples into a large stockpot. Make sure the pot is large enough to hold 3 gallons of water. Add 2 gallons of filtered water, turn the heat to high, and boil for at least 1 hour. Lower the heat and use a slotted spoon to take the cubes out.

While waiting for the soup base to boil again, use the open flame on the burner to burn the shallots, yellow onions, and ginger until the skin slightly blackens. (Use metal tongs, not your hands, to hold the vegetables.) Take out the vegetables and wash off the burned skin. You may use a knife to scrape the burned skin off more easily. Cut each yellow onion into 4 pieces. Slice ginger into thin slices. After the soup base has boiled for about 1 hour, set the heat to low and use a slotted spoon to take the vegetables out.

Add burned shallots, burned yellow onions, and burned ginger into the soup base. Add rock sugar to the soup base, if using. Add the phở spice bags into the soup base. Increase the heat to high and continue to boil the soup base for an additional 30 minutes. Add vegan mushroom seasoning, sea salt, and sugar into the soup base. Mix well. Adjust vegan seasoning, salt, and sugar to your taste. Keep warm on the stovetop over low heat while serving, or store the soup base in the refrigerator for later use.

To assemble: If using the white wood-ear mushroom, soak the mushroom in tap water for 1 hour or until soft then cut in small blocks about 1 x 1. To prepare the dried vegan soy protein, boil water in a small pot, add a few slices fresh ginger, then add dried vegan soy protein and boil for about 3 to 5 minutes or until it becomes soft. Take it out and wash it with tap water twice and then hand-squeeze the soy "beef" to remove the excess water.

Use a small pot to boil about 8 cups of water. Take about 3 ounces of phở noodle, enough for 1 bowl, and place in a wire basket. Dip the noodles into the boiling water for about 20 seconds or until the phở noodle becomes soft. Place the phở noodles into a serving bowl. Add several pieces each of vegan soy protein, vegan protein ball, vegan ham, tofu, white wood-ear mushroom (if using), chopped green onions, and sliced yellow onions. Heat the soup base to boil and add several ladles of the base to the serving bowl. Add 1 teaspoon of olive oil or vegan butter. Add some chopped fresh cilantro, bean sprouts, fresh basil leaves, hoisin sauce, Sriracha sauce, and a wedge of lemon.

Spicy Cha Cha

Serves 4–8

3   cups all-purpose flour
2   teaspoons sugar
1   cup cornstarch
2   teaspoons and 3 cups rice oil
1   teaspoon baking soda
2   teaspoons sea salt
3   cups water
2   pounds vegan sea crescents
    (aka "vegan shrimp") each
    sliced in half*
3   cups bread crumbs
1   red bell pepper, diced
1   green bell pepper, diced
4   stalks celery, diced
½   yellow onion, diced
4   stalks green onion, finely
    chopped
2   tablespoons vegan mushroom
    seasoning
2   teaspoons dried hot chili
    powder

Can be purchased online.

Put the all-purpose flour, sugar, cornstarch, 1 teaspoon rice oil, baking soda, and a pinch of sea salt in a large bowl. Add water slowly and mix well until it becomes a thick batter.

Dip the vegan sea crescents into the flour mixture then roll the vegan sea crescents in the bread crumbs. Make sure each vegan sea crescent is fully covered with the bread crumbs.

Add 3 cups of rice oil in a deep frying pan or a medium-size pan, then turn the burner to medium heat. Place the vegan sea crescents into the pan and fry them until they become golden in color. Take the vegan sea crescents out and set aside on a plate with a paper towel to blot any excess oil.

Add 1 teaspoon of rice oil into a hot pan. Add all diced vegetables (bell peppers, celery, onions) and stir-fry for 30 seconds. Add the fried vegan sea crescents. Sprinkle with vegan seasoning, sea salt, and dried hot chili powder. Stir well for an additional 10 seconds. Remove from the heat and serve alone or ideally on a bed of chopped lettuce with steamed rice.

Lovin' Spoonfuls

TUCSON, AZ

2990 N. Campbell Ave., Suite 120
Tucson, AZ 85719
(520) 325-7766

www.lovinspoonfuls.com

Casual, cozy, and comfortable, Lovin' Spoonfuls is all about food prepared with love. There's good chemistry all around in this restaurant, which is owned and operated by a woman with a PhD in, naturally, chemistry.

Dr. Margaret "Peggy" Raisglid, owner and chef

Is this your first restaurant?
Yes, it is. I worked at restaurants when I was in college and I've been able to apply some of the lessons learned back then to what I'm doing now.

When did it open?
In September of 2005.

Do you want to have more than one restaurant?
I'm currently working on a franchise package.

What's your favorite dish on the menu?
Tied for my personal favorites are our signature dish, the Piccadilly Nut Loaf with steam-grilled veggies, mashed potatoes, and mushroom-Burgundy gravy, and the linguini with "meat"-balls and our own chunky marinara, garlic bread, and an organic spring-mix side salad with sesame-Dijon dressing.

What's your most popular appetizer?
Hands down, the Golden Nuggets with "honey"-mustard dipping sauce. Although…the cashew mushroom pâte with toast points won an award from *Vegetarian Times* magazine.

What's the most popular entrée on the menu?
The Route 66 "bacon" "cheese"-burger for lunch and the country-fried "chicken" dinner in the evening.

What's your most popular dessert?
Chocolate fudge brownie pie on top of a chocolate-chip cookie crust. A very close second is the chocolate fudge cake.

What do you feel is special about your restaurant?
So many vegetarian restaurants look like granola-crunching, hippie places. When I developed the concept for Lovin' Spoonfuls, I really wanted to create a place with a warm, inviting, slightly upscale atmosphere and offer dishes that were familiar to people. I wanted people to feel comfortable about coming with their growing family, nonveggie friends, or perhaps their business associates. My hope was to appeal to veggies and nonveggies alike.

How often do you change your menu items? Do you have daily or weekly specials?
The menu has certainly evolved over the six years that we've been open, expanding our selections for various types of diets. We also have a different lunch and dinner special every day, and we always have holiday specials, with Thanksgiving being the biggest day of the year [for us].

Do you have gluten-free, soy-free, and sugar-free options on your menu?
Yes to all three. Our number of gluten-free customers is growing the most rapidly. For breakfast we have gluten-free waffles, pancakes, and scrambles. We bake our own gluten-free bread for toast and sandwiches. We've also taken the fats and oils out of all of our sauces and most of our soups so, now we've also expanded our fat-free options.

What do you do to reduce your environmental impact?
We offer sturdy, nondisposable takeout containers, which cost $5 for a one-time purchase. After that, customers just bring it back in, it gets sent back to our commercial dishwasher, and then the next one is free. When customers call in their order, they simply say, "Make it green." This way no disposables are consumed at all. In addition, we are participating in a compost program with the University of Arizona. All of our food waste is collected and picked up by the university for composting.

What are the most important lessons you've learned as owner or chef of this restaurant?
When I first opened, with limited restaurant experience, what helped me the most was hiring people with a lot of experience who could show me the ropes. Another thing I learned was that it's very helpful to have a book with all the ingredients for each dish by the register so that you (or any employee facing the customers) can answer all questions with complete accuracy.

What led you to want to open a vegan restaurant, and/or what led you to the vegan diet yourself?
I became a vegan in August of 1989, after hearing two women at my friend's church talk about all the issues associated with eating meat. They addressed the health and ethical issues, the cruelty in the meat, dairy, and poultry industries, and the huge negative environmental impact. As a result, I have been developing vegan recipes that resemble nonvegan counterparts for over twenty years. I am ethically committed to a vegan lifestyle and decided that the best way to promote veganism was to show people how tasty vegan meals can be. That's when my career as a chemist and engineer took a new turn, and I opened up a restaurant.

In the time since your restaurant first opened, how has the plant-based food movement changed? Do you find more demand now for vegan food?
Absolutely. So many more people are becoming aware of the benefits of a whole-food plant-based diet.

In the time since your restaurant first opened, has your view of what kinds of food choices to offer changed? Have you changed the types of foods you offer?
I used to think in order to be healthful, food only had to be vegan. It now seems clear that a more optimum diet includes more whole foods; minimum processing; and less fats, oils, sugar, and salt.

Where do you see the plant-based food movement going in coming years?
There is no question that this movement is gaining momentum, increasing as more and more people are recognizing the benefits. And we're living on a planet that simply can't sustain such a large human population of meat-eaters, so sooner or later, we're all going to arrive at a largely plant-based diet. 🍂

Green Chili Polenta

Serves 12

6   cups water
2   cups polenta-grade cornmeal
¼   cup vegan Parmesan
1   teaspoon garlic salt
1½   teaspoons Louisiana-style
       hot sauce
1   cup (8-ounce can) diced, fire-
       roasted green chilies
2   cups corn (frozen or fresh)
1   cup shredded vegan cheddar
       (like Daiya) , distributed
       evenly over top
2   cups diced tomatoes
¼   cup chopped fresh basil

Preheat the oven to 350 degrees. In a large pot, bring the water to boil. Rapidly stir in the polenta. Simmer, covered, for 15 minutes.

Remove pot from heat and add the Parmesan "cheese," garlic salt, hot sauce, green chilies, and corn. Spread in an 8 x 8 baking pan. Sprinkle with vegan cheddar. Top with fresh, diced tomatoes and fresh, coarsely chopped basil. Cover with foil (or an inverted cookie sheet), place the pan in the oven, and bake until hot throughout (approximately 20 minutes).

Lucky Leek

BERLIN, GERMANY

Kollwitzstrasse 54
Mitte, Berlin, Germany 10405
+49-030-66408710

www.lucky-leek.de

Sebastian Happe-Sinémus, co-owner, and Josita Hartanto, co-owner and chef

Serving creative gourmet cuisine in a cozy environment, Lucky Leek operates in a city that is fast becoming the epicenter of the European vegan movement.

Is this your first restaurant?
Yes.

When did it open?
We started on April 1, 2011.

Do you want to have more than one restaurant?
No, we are focusing on one project only. It's important to be able to have full control over what you serve your guests.

What's your favorite dish on the menu?
We change our regular menu every week, and have a new daily menu every day, so my favorite dish changes all the time!

What's your most popular appetizer?
All our appetizers are popular. We're always careful to create and arrange them in ways to make them look and taste unique, fresh, and exciting.

What's the most popular entrée on the menu?
Our homemade seitan has always been very popular. We steadily improve our recipes to surprise our guests with new flavor combinations and a diversity of texture. Many of our guests are new to veganism, and they want to eat something familiar, not experimental. For those guests, we offer new interpretations of "classic" dishes.

What's your most popular dessert?
All of our desserts are something you shouldn't miss. We really put a lot of work, creativity, and love into them, and we're addicted to our own sweets.

What do you feel is special about your restaurant?
Everything we serve is done in house. That way we can assure the quality, and we'll have direct contact with our guests to constantly improve and vary our creations.

How often do you change your menu items? Do you have daily or weekly specials?

We change our menu every week, and we have daily specials.

Do you have gluten-free, soy-free, and sugar-free options on your menu?

We always have gluten-free meals on the regular menu. Some of our meals can be done without soy and most can be done without sugar. If you have any dietary restrictions, just let us know, and we'll create something to suit your needs.

What do you do to reduce your environmental impact?

We mostly use regional and seasonal ingredients. We also use renewable energy, commute by bike as much as possible, and inspire everyone around us to go vegan.

What are the most important lessons you've learned as owner or chef of this restaurant?

Every day is a challenge that you should enjoy. Never give up, even when everything seems to go wrong.

What led you to want to open a vegan restaurant, and/or what led you to the vegan diet yourself?

I've been a vegan for many years before I opened my own place, and I worked in many different restaurants. After I spent some time working as head chef in a vegan restaurant, I felt like I needed more freedom to experiment and express myself.

In the time since your restaurant first opened, how has the plant-based food movement changed? Do you find more demand now for vegan food?

More vegan places have opened in our city since we first opened. Even "old-fashioned" pizza parlors and traditional delis offer vegan alternatives now. In Berlin, you can see how fast vegan acceptance has grown, and with it the demand for vegan products.

Since your restaurant first opened, has your view of what constitutes healthy or delicious food changed? Have you changed the types of foods you offer?

Yes, it's always in flux, and we always find new ways to realize new ideas.

Where do you see the plant-based food movement going in coming years?

I think the acceptance is growing very fast. Information on how healthy plant-based food is and how sustainable it is spreads incredibly fast and makes many people rethink their choices. It gets easier to go vegan, as more and more products are available. In general, I would say that the number of vegans/vegetarians is steadily growing and still is far from reaching a zenith! 🍂

Peach Polenta and Vanilla Tomatoes

Serves 4

For the vanilla tomatoes:
24 cherry tomatoes
4 tablespoons olive oil
2 tablespoons agave syrup
1 tablespoon white balsamic vinegar
1 vanilla bean, scraped and split
Pinch salt

For the polenta:
4 peaches
2⅛ cups soy milk
2⅛ cups water
1 tablespoon olive oil
1 teaspoon salt
1 rosemary branch
1¾ cups polenta
Vanilla tomatoes (see recipe above)
Fresh basil

For the vanilla tomatoes: Preheat the oven to 325 degrees. Score an X on the top of the cherry tomatoes with a sharp knife and put in boiling water for 20 seconds. After that, shock them in cold water. Peel the skin off the tomatoes with a small knife. In a bowl, stir together the rest of the ingredients. Add the tomatoes. Pour the tomatoes and sauce into a tray, and put them in the oven for 10 minutes. Set aside.

For the polenta: Wash the peaches, slice in half, remove the pits, and cut into slices. In a saucepan, boil the soy milk, water, olive oil, salt, and rosemary. Once the mixture has come to a boil, remove the rosemary branch and stir in the polenta and let it boil into a thick puree while constantly stirring for 5 to 8 minutes. Add the peach slices. Remove from the heat and immediately add the vanilla tomatoes and the basil. Sprinkle the polenta with some olive oil and serve.

Avocado Apple Tatare with Walnut Bonbons

Serves 4

For the tatare:
2   Granny Smith apples
2   ripe avocados
1   shallot
10 mint leaves
Salt, to taste
Freshly ground pepper, to taste
Juice and zest of ½ lime
1   tablespoon walnut oil

For the chive cream:
½   bunch fresh chives
1   cup soy yogurt
1   tablespoon lime juice
1   tablespoon vegetable oil
2   tablespoons vegan cream
Salt, to taste
Freshly ground pepper, to taste

For the bonbons:
1   handful walnuts
2   tablespoons chopped fresh
    parsley
4   dried tomatoes
1   grape tomato
1   tablespoon agave syrup
12 wonton leaves

To assemble:
Fresh dill (optional)
Fresh sprouts (optional)

For the tatare: Peel skin off the apples. Cut the avocados in half lengthwise. Remove the pits and scoop out the avocado flesh, running a spoon along the inside of the skin. Cut the avocado halves and the apples into fine cubes and cut the shallot and the mint leaves into fine strips. Then carefully stir the avocado, apples, shallot, and mint leaves together and season with salt, pepper, lime juice, lime zest, and walnut oil.

For the chive cream: Cut the chives into short strips. Put all the ingredients into a blender and mix the ingredients together. Add salt and pepper, to taste.

For the bonbons: Place all the ingredients, except for the wonton leaves, into the blender and blend together. Put a tablespoon of the blended filling onto a wonton leaf, roll up the leaf by moistening the ends of the leaves, and twist them to enclose the filling (like a bonbon candy). Deep-fry the wontons in a deep pan.

To assemble: Serve the wonton bonbons together with the tatare and the chive cream. Garnish with fresh dill or sprouts (optional).

Luna's Living Kitchen

CHARLOTTE, NC

2102 South Blvd.
Charlotte, NC 28203
(704) 333-0008

www.lunaslivingkitchen.com

Luna's Living Kitchen is a plant-based, raw foods restaurant demonstrating the core beliefs that living food is a labor of love and that health, beauty, and art can be served on a plate.

Juliana Luna, owner and chef

Is this your first restaurant?
Yes.

When did it open?
July 2010.

Do you want to have more than one restaurant?
Yes! It's our hope to see raw and organic vegan food in every city in the United States, and we would love to participate in this movement as much as we're able.

What's your favorite dish on the menu?
The Living Bagel, a raw, savory bagel made with almonds, flax, zucchini, and rosemary, topped with cashew sour cream and fresh, organic tomato, onion, avocado, basil, sprouts, and jalapeños.

What's your most popular appetizer?
Tricolored hummus, a raw hummus made from sunflower seeds.

What's the most popular entrée on the menu?
Lunasagna.

What's your most popular dessert?
Lemon-berry cheesecake.

What do you feel is special about your restaurant?
There are many unique things about Luna's Living Kitchen. Being one of the only restaurants in our area to serve fresh, organic, and local foods is something that we're proud of, but the most special thing about our kitchen is all of the people, from the chefs to the farmers, who make each day a wonderful communal experience.

How often do you change your menu items? Do you have daily or weekly specials?
We like to change our menu items seasonally to reflect the agricultural diversity in our region. We don't have daily or weekly specials, but occasionally we serve special entrées for holidays or events.

Do you have gluten-free, soy-free, and sugar-free options on your menu?
We are one-hundred-percent soy-free and do not use any refined sugars or syrups in our dishes. The majority of our menu items are gluten-free.

What do you do to reduce your environmental impact?
The first thing that we do is to buy organic produce (with an emphasis on locally grown food), which supports sustainable farming and agricultural practices. In addition, we separate all organic waste from our café and distribute it to a variety of composting projects. And we use compostable disposables for all of our carry-out supplies.

What are the most important lessons you've learned as owner or chef of this restaurant?
Patience, hard work, and discipline. It is not an easy thing to be a vegan pioneer in the South, but with dedication and passionate attention to detail, we have seen a tremendous positive response from our local community.

What led you to want to open a vegan restaurant, and/or what led you to the vegan diet yourself?
Many studies on the benefits of the vegan diet (such as the China Study) helped me to understand the life-affirming power of a plant-based approach to food. I saw the changes that happened in my own

life when I tried it, and I simply wanted to share that with others. Seeing others change and benefit from what we do has only fueled this desire more.

In the time since your restaurant first opened, how has the plant-based food movement changed? Do you find more demand now for vegan food?
It has, in fact, changed a great deal, and we see a much bigger audience that is steadily growing, largely due to the many wonderful films that have emerged on the subject of diet and the food industry in the last several years.

Since your restaurant first opened, has your view of what constitutes healthy or delicious food changed? Have you changed the types of foods you offer?
We started with the perspective of using the simplest and most natural ingredients in our dishes, and this has largely remained unchanged. However, we've grown increasingly fond of incorporating superfoods into our food and beverages, such as spirulina, chia seeds, and maca, to name a few.

Where do you see the plant-based food movement going in coming years?
We see it going as far as we and others like us can take it. It is simply a matter of education so that consumers make the right choices in supporting local, organic, and sustainable agriculture. Thanks to the Internet, this message is spreading like wildfire, and we have nothing but high hopes for the future of food and healthy eating! 🍃

Gaia was the goddess of earth in Greek mythology, so it's fitting that this raw "stir fry" dish features an abundance of fresh vegetables. This dish is light and great for summer.

Gaia's Treasure

Serves 8

For the Gaia's Sauce:
1   cup rice vinegar
1   cup coconut aminos
¾   cup agave syrup
⅔   cup lemon juice
½   cup and 2 tablespoons olive oil
¼   cup tahini
12 cloves garlic
¼   cup sesame oil
3   tablespoons ginger juice
    concentrate
1   teaspoon black pepper
½   teaspoon salt

For the cauliflower rice:
3   cloves garlic
1   teaspoon salt
1½ teaspoons black pepper
1½ pounds cauliflower, chopped
    roughly

For the zucchini noodles:
4   medium-size zucchini, cut into
    thin strips

To assemble:
½   cup carrots
½   cup shiitake mushrooms
½   cup cauliflower
1   cup broccoli
Fresh parsley (garnish)
Fresh chives (garnish)
Microgreens (garnish)

Equipment needed: *spiralizer*

Add all sauce ingredients to a blender and blend for 60 seconds. Set aside.

To make the cauliflower rice, place the garlic, salt, and pepper in a food processor and pulse until the garlic is in minced pieces. Remove. Place the cauliflower into the food processor and pulse until diced to rice-size pieces. Then add the garlic mixture and incorporate thoroughly.

Using a spiralizer, make "noodles" out of the zucchini. (If you don't have a spiralizer, you can use a mandoline slicer or potato peeler to make thin strips of zucchini, cut into ¼" noodles.)

To assemble: Marinate your vegetables in the Gaia's Sauce for about 15 minutes.

Place the zucchini noodles in a serving bowl, add some cauliflower rice, and top with marinated vegetables. Garnish with fresh parsley, chives, or your favorite microgreens.

Muesli is a staple breakfast in the Swiss Alps, packed with heart healthy oats, fruit, and protein. This quick and easy recipe can be whipped up the night before and served in minutes for breakfast.

Swiss Bircher Muesli

Serves 6

9 cups oats
2½ cups grated apple
1 cup raisins
Zest of 4 oranges
1 tablespoon ground cinnamon
¼ teaspoon salt
1 cup orange juice (juice of the
   above 4 oranges)
3 cups dairy-free milk (almond,
   coconut, or hemp milk)
2 tablespoons agave syrup
Banana slices (garnish)

Combine the oats, grated apple, raisins, orange zest, cinnamon, and salt in a container with a lid. Juice the oranges and combine juice with the milk and agave syrup in a separate bowl. Add wet ingredients to the dry container and incorporate thoroughly. Seal the container and refrigerate overnight. Serve the following day with fresh banana slices.

At our restaurant, we serve this dish for breakfast or dessert. Chia are stealthy seeds packed with omega-3s and fiber, but combined with homemade cashew milk, they plump to create a decadent pudding that tastes like vanilla tapioca.

Chia Pudding

Serves 7

25 dates, pitted and soaked overnight

4 cups water

½ cup cashews (soaked for at least 1 hour)

⅛ teaspoon salt

¼ teaspoon ground cinnamon

4 teaspoons vanilla extract

½ cup chia seeds

6 tablespoons maple syrup

To make the cashew milk, combine dates, water, cashews, salt, cinnamon, and vanilla extract in the blender. Pulse 3 times. In a mixing bowl, measure out the chia seeds. While whisking constantly, pour the blended cashew milk mixture over the chia seeds. Whisk for 2 additional minutes once all the milk is poured over seeds. Transfer to a clean container and refrigerate overnight. Serve the next day with a drizzle of maple syrup to sweeten.

Millennium

SAN FRANCISCO, CA

580 Geary St.
San Francisco, CA 94102
(415) 345-3900

www.millenniumrestaurant.com

Millennium turns globally influenced, California fine dining vegan, bringing a world-class chef to a world-class city.

Chef Eric Tucker, co-owner and chef

Is this your first restaurant?
No.

When did Millennium open?
Fall of 1994.

Do you want to have more than one restaurant?
Of course.

What's your favorite dish on the menu?
They're all very good or else they wouldn't be on the menu. At the moment the favorite is possibly our pastry roulade, filled with smoked chard and potato Florentine over a rich mushroom cream with roasted maitake and lobster mushrooms.

What's your most popular appetizer?
Arborio rice and sesame-crusted king trumpet mushrooms with yuzu ponzu and *togarashi* (Japanese chili pepper).

What's the most popular entrée on the menu?
They're all equally popular.

What's your most popular dessert?
Well, I particularly love Ryan and Ariana's blackberry pie with "buttermilk" ice cream, but the most popular is actually the Chocolate Almond Midnight (a white chocolate mousse with a cashew crust and mocha-chocolate filling).

What do you feel is special about your restaurant?
All of it! It has its own vibe and culture.

How often do you change your menu items? Do you have daily or weekly specials?

Throughout a season, you'll see three-fourths of the menu change, whether it's a complete new dish or variant on an existing dish with coming-into-market seasonal produce. We run a tasting menu Thursday through Saturday, which showcases new product ideas, or whatever is our current muse. We do winemaker dinners, farmers' market dinners, dinners on farms, all tomato and chili dinners where we get into the fields and pick our produce, wild mushroom and foraged foods dinners where I'm up in the hills foraging mushrooms twigs and weeds, etc.

Do you have gluten-free, soy-free, and sugar-free options on your menu?

Yes.

What do you do to reduce your environmental impact?

We compost, recycle, buy local, and keep our refrigeration equipment in good working order.

What are the most important lessons you've learned as owner or chef of this restaurant?

To be humble, to be grateful, and to be hands-on. This and any restaurant is only as good as each and every guest's dining experience, not some stars in some newspaper. There are no laurels to rest on. Cookbooks, media coverage, and Twitter feeds mean nothing if a guest has a lousy experience.

What led you to want to open a vegan restaurant, and/or what led you to the vegan diet yourself?

Millennium is a continuation of the former Milly's in San Rafael. It still holds on to the vision of Milly's owners of a fine dining vegan restaurant. Millennium and I are deeply indebted to them.

In the time since your restaurant first opened, how has the plant-based food movement changed? Do you find more demand now for vegan food?

It's more available and mainstream and seems to ebb and flow here in the Bay Area. There's certainly more interest and knowledge in vegetable-based cuisine than there was twenty years ago.

Since your restaurant first opened, has your view of what constitutes healthy or delicious food changed? Have you changed the types of foods you offer?

Well, not really!

Where do you see the plant-based food movement going in coming years?

I see more integration into mainstream restaurants that offer quality vegan and healthier food choices. 🐷

This summer entrée, while influenced by Middle Eastern cuisine, is firmly rooted in seasonal California produce. There may be a lot of components to it, but it typifies how we put together a dish at Millennium. It's worth the trouble to seek out Rosa Bianca or Tuscan Rose eggplants as they are lower in oxalic acid and thus sweeter, without requiring salt like standard eggplant.

It's also well worth the trouble to broil fresh tomatoes until the skin blisters and chars, imbuing the tagine with a smoky/roasted quality. Feel free to embellish the tagine with other summer vegetables such as roasted zucchini and cubes of roasted eggplant.

Pistachio-Crusted Eggplant Napoleon

Serves 6

For the eggplant:
- 2 cups coarsely ground shelled pistachios
- 3 cups white rice flour
- ½ cup tapioca flour
- 2 teaspoons salt
- ½ teaspoon black pepper
- Soy milk, as needed
- 2 to 3 Rosa Bianca or Tuscan Rose eggplants, sliced into ½" thick rounds (12 rounds total)
- Vegetable oil, as needed

For the lemon tofu "cheese":
- 1½ pounds medium-firm tofu, drained and crumbled
- 2 cloves garlic, minced
- 4 tablespoons extra-virgin olive oil
- 2 to 3 sage leaves, thinly sliced
- Zest of ½ lemon
- Pinch chili pepper flakes
- 1 tablespoon nutritional yeast
- Juice of 1 lemon
- Salt and pepper, to taste

For the tomato, leek, and artichoke tagine:
- 2 pounds whole San Marzano or plum tomatoes
- 3 tablespoons extra-virgin olive oil
- 1 tablespoon minced fresh ginger
- 1 teaspoon ground coriander
- 1 teaspoon ground fenugreek
- ⅓ teaspoon turmeric
- ½ teaspoon chili Urfa or Aleppo chili pepper flakes (or substitute crushed red pepper flakes)
- 1 teaspoon dried mint
- 2 teaspoons fresh thyme (or ½ teaspoon dried thyme)
- 1 cinnamon stick
- 4 cups sliced leeks, cleaned and sliced ⅓" thick
- 4 cloves garlic, thinly sliced
- Pinch salt
- 1 tablespoon tomato paste
- 2 cups vegetable stock, or as needed
- 4 cups quartered fresh blanched or frozen artichoke hearts
- 2 cups cooked Corona beans (or substitute any large cooked bean)
- 1 teaspoon arrowroot, dissolved in cold water
- Salt and pepper, to taste

For the cilantro-cardamom coulis:
- 4 tablespoons olive oil
- ¼ yellow onion, sliced in half
- 2 cloves garlic
- 1 serrano chili, seeds removed
- 1 teaspoon cardamom seeds
- 1 cup loosely packed cilantro leaves
- Juice of ½ lemon
- Salt and pepper, to taste

For the Israeli couscous salad:
- 2 cups cooked Israeli couscous
- 2 tablespoons minced yellow onion
- 4 tablespoons minced parsley or cilantro
- Juice of ½ lemon
- 1 teaspoon extra-virgin olive oil
- Salt and pepper, to taste

To assemble:
- 2 cups frisée leaves
- Herb of your choice (optional)

recipe continued next page

For the eggplant: Preheat the oven to 400 degrees. Combine the ground pistachio, flours, salt, and pepper in a mixing bowl and combine well. Place the soy milk in another mixing bowl. Place a piece of eggplant in the dry pistachio/flour dredge, coat well, then place in the soy milk, then dredge again in the flour mix. Place the finished eggplant slice on a well-oiled sheet pan. Follow with the remaining eggplant slices.

Place the pan in the oven and bake. Flip the eggplant over after 6 or 7 minutes. After a total of 12 to 14 minutes, remove from the oven and set aside.

For the lemon tofu "cheese": Place the crumbled tofu in a mixing bowl. In a pan, sauté the garlic in the oil over medium-low heat until just starting to brown. Remove from the heat and add the sage, lemon zest, and chili flakes. Stir together ingredients in the pan, then pour over the tofu. Add the nutritional yeast, lemon juice, salt, pepper, and more yeast to taste. Stir or knead to incorporate the ingredients. Set aside.

For the tomato, leek, and artichoke tagine: Place the tomatoes on a baking pan and broil until the skin on top is blackened. Cool to room temperature. Peel the skin off the tomatoes. (It should slip right off.) Try to keep the tomato in one piece.

In a large saucepan, heat the olive oil over medium-low heat and add the ginger, coriander, fenugreek, turmeric, chili, dried mint, thyme, and cinnamon stick until they sizzle—for 20 seconds or so. Then add the leeks, garlic, and a pinch of salt. Sauté 5 minutes, stirring often. Add the tomato paste and sauté another 30 seconds, followed by the stock. Simmer covered for 10 minutes or until the leeks are soft. Add the artichoke hearts and simmer 5 minutes. Follow with the peeled tomatoes and add the 2 cups cooked beans, and simmer another 5 minutes. Stir in the arrowroot slurry until just thickened. Add the salt and pepper.

For the cilantro-cardamom coulis: In a sauté pan, heat oil and pan-char the onion, garlic, and chili over high heat. Sauté until they are 25 percent blackened. Remove from the heat, stir in the cardamom seeds, then place in a bowl to cool to room temperature. When cool, place in a blender with the remaining ingredients, then blend until smooth. Add salt and pepper.

For the Israeli couscous salad: Combine the couscous with the remaining ingredients. Set aside.

To assemble: Preheat the oven to 400 degrees. On an oiled sheet pan, set down an eggplant slice, top with ¼ cup of tofu "cheese," then top with another eggplant slice. Repeat with the remaining eggplant slices to make 6 Napoleons. Place the sheet pan in the oven and bake 10 to 12 minutes or until heated through. To serve, place a portion of the tagine in shallow pasta bowl. Follow with a portion of the couscous salad in the center of the plate. Top with a Napoleon. Combine the frisée leaves with the herbs and top the Napoleon with the frisée herb salad, if using. Spoon 2 tablespoons of the cilantro-cardamom coulis around the plate. Serve.

Mi Vida

MIAMI, FL

7244 Biscayne Blvd.
Miami, FL 33138
(305) 759-6020

www.mividacafe.net

Mi Vida offers tasty, fresh, vegan cuisine made from local and organic produce. Watch your chef prepare your meal as you enjoy the magical atmosphere of this urban vegan oasis.

Daniela LaGamma, owner and chef

Is this your first restaurant?
Yes.

When did it open?
April 5, 2011.

Do you want to have more than one restaurant?
Yes.

What's your favorite dish on the menu?
Canelones de verdura, a pancake-style dough filled with spinach and cashew cheese and topped with tomato-basil sauce.

What's your most popular appetizer?
Eggplant a la Italiana, eggplant rolls filled with tofu and veggies and served with tomato-basil sauce.

What's the most popular entrée on the menu?
Vegan seitan-and-mushroom sloppy joe.

What's your most popular dessert?
It's a seasonal dessert: the raw vegan passion-fruit pie.

What do you feel is special about your restaurant?
The vibe. We always try to keep the good energies up!

How often do you change your menu items? Do you have daily or weekly specials?
Items on our menu vary depending on the availability of seasonal and organic produce. Our specials change quite often, usually weekly.

Do you have gluten-free, soy-free, and sugar-free options on your menu?
Yes.

What do you do to reduce your environmental impact?
We recycle and we encourage our customers to bring their own containers for their pickup orders, offering a ten-percent discount if they do so. And we have many more ideas that we are planning on incorporating in the near future.

What are the most important lessons you've learned as owner or chef of this restaurant?
There are too many lessons learned by me to pick only a few. With such a varied customer base I find myself constantly doing a lot of research. Almost every day someone comes in with a new tale that makes me curious to learn more.

What led you to want to open a vegan restaurant, and/or what led you to the vegan diet yourself?
There are many things that led me to a vegan diet, but I must say caring for animals is my main reason. I've been vegetarian for more than twenty years, and vegan for about three years. So for me, being vegan is a lifestyle rather than a diet. I wanted to promote this kind of lifestyle by showing people that healthy food can also be delicious.

In the time since your restaurant first opened, how has the plant-based food movement changed?
Even though we haven't been open for that long, I can see a difference. I've noticed people are

now much more aware of the importance of incorporating greens and raw foods into our diets.

Do you find more demand now for vegan food?
Absolutely. I think the rise in cancer and other terminal diseases is really starting to have an effect on our community. People are seeing now that pills and artificial remedies don't solve much, and that preventing disease by maintaining a healthy lifestyle goes much further.

Since your restaurant first opened, has your view of what constitutes healthy or delicious food changed? Have you changed the types of foods you offer?
Yes, and I embrace that. I believe, as a restaurant owner, it is important to have an open mind. Change is always necessary if you want to improve.

Where do you see the plant-based food movement going in coming years?
I believe this is the food of the future. I see it becoming more popular over the years until it takes over and finally becomes the way we all eat. 🐷

Canelones de Seitan or Tempeh

Serves 4 (2 rolls per serving)

For the crepes:
- 1 cup all-purpose flour
- 1 teaspoon olive oil
- 3 cups unsweetened, unflavored almond milk
- Pinch salt
- 1 teaspoon baking powder

For the filling:
- 4 cups ground seitan or tempeh
- 1 tablespoon olive oil
- 1 cup diced red, yellow, and orange peppers
- 1 cup diced onion
- ½ cup diced green pepper
- ½ cup diced tomato
- 1 handful basil, chopped
- 1 cup capers
- Salt and pepper, to taste

For the tomato sauce:
- 4 Roma tomatoes
- 1 handful fresh basil
- 1 tablespoon olive oil
- Salt and pepper, to taste
- Nutritional yeast (garnish)

For the crepes: In a large mixing bowl, whisk together the flour and the oil. Gradually add in the almond milk, stirring to combine. Add the salt and baking powder; beat until smooth.

Heat a lightly oiled frying pan over medium-high heat. Pour or scoop the batter onto the pan. Tilt the pan with a circular motion so that the batter coats the surface evenly. Cook the crepe for about 2 minutes, until the bottom is light brown. Loosen with a spatula, turn, and cook the other side.

For the filling: In a food processor, grind your choice of seitan or tempeh (one or the other; don't use both) until it looks like bread crumbs. Add the olive oil to a pan over medium heat and sauté the seitan or tempeh with all the other ingredients together for about 5 minutes.

For the tomato sauce: Blend all ingredients together in a food processor.

To assemble: Preheat the oven to 350 degrees. Place some of the filling mix in the center of a crepe, then roll it. Do the same for each of the *canelones* and place them on a tray. Put the tray in the oven and bake for 15 minutes or until they're hot. In a saucepan, warm up the tomato sauce before serving.

Place 2 *canelones* per plate, pour some warm tomato sauce over them, and sprinkle with nutritional yeast right before serving.

Mudra Café

MILAN, ITALY

Piazza XXIV Maggio, 8
Milan, Italy 20123
+39-345-451-2459

www.mudramilano.com

Launched by an Italian couple fascinated with Indian culture and the principles of nature, Mudra Café is an organic vegan restaurant and cultural space uniting the disciplines of holistic wellness, natural food, and the arts.

Monica Maya Devi and Marco Fracchiolla, owners and chefs

Is this your first restaurant?
Yes.

When did it open?
2010.

Do you want to have more than one restaurant?
Maybe.

What's your favorite dish on the menu?
Tagliata ai Carciofi e Chardonnay: sliced seitan with artichokes, olives, and Chardonnay.

What's your most popular appetizer?
Tagliere Mudra: wheat salami with organic bread and homemade vegan mayonnaise.

What's the most popular entrée on the menu?
Lasagna di kamut: kamut Italian organic lasagna.

What's your most popular dessert?
Vegan organic tiramisu.

What do you feel is special about your restaurant?

The ambience, the natural food, an elegant but cozy atmosphere, where everybody feels at home and people can relax and feel good.

How often do you change your menu items? Do you have daily or weekly specials?

Yes, we have daily specials and different menus for each season. We serve only seasonal food.

Do you have gluten-free, soy-free, and sugar-free options on your menu?

Of course—lactose-free, gluten-free. All our dishes are also free from refined sugar or additives.

What do you do to reduce your environmental impact?

We divide the trash into paper, plastic, and glass, and we have a low carbon footprint in terms of electrical usage.

What are the most important lessons you've learned as owner or chef of this restaurant?

That people who come to us are gods and goddesses and everyone is divine. When you serve God, you are doing something for the Universe.

What led you to want to open a vegan restaurant, and/or what led you to the vegan diet yourself?

We've been vegan for the past fifteen years. It was a natural choice for us.

In the time since your restaurant first opened, how has the plant-based food movement changed? Do you find more demand now for vegan food?

Now in Italy there is more consumer demand, and it's an expanding field.

Since your restaurant first opened, has your view of what constitutes healthy or delicious foods changed? Have you changed the types of foods you offer?

The vision is the same, but we always add new things and new dishes for our clients to give them the best.

Where do you see the plant-based food movement going in coming years?

It will grow in Italy but we also see lots of potential in India. 🍃

Tagliata ai Carciofi e Chardonnay

Serves 4

4   artichokes
½   cup lemon juice
2   tablespoons extra-virgin olive oil
2   tablespoons soy sauce
1½ cups seitan
1   cup black olives
1   cup Chardonnay
Black pepper
Gomasio*

* Available in health food stores.

Preheat the oven to 360 degrees. Clean the artichokes by removing the stems and the hard outer petals and cutting off their thorny tops. Then cut the artichokes in half, dividing them down the length of the buds, and cut those halves into slices, around ⅛". Rinse the artichoke pieces immediately and place them in a bowl filled with water and lemon juice to prevent them from becoming oxidized. Let them rest for a few minutes in the water and lemon juice, then drain them and place them in a baking dish. Reserve the marinating water for use later.

Add the extra-virgin olive oil and soy sauce to the dish, coating the artichoke evenly, and let it marinate for about 10 minutes. After marinating, place the pan in the oven and bake for 20 minutes.

In the meantime, take the seitan and slice diagonally into small pieces. Place in a pan and sprinkle with soy sauce, olive oil, and a drop of water, and slightly warm the seitan so that it softens further.

Once the artichoke has baked a full 20 minutes, remove the pan and reheat the oven to 350 degrees. Add the seitan and olives to the baking pan, dousing the whole mixture with the Chardonnay and a little marinating water. Mix the contents of the pan and reinsert it in the oven. Bake again for 10 minutes. Once cooked, portion out the artichoke-seitan into dishes and finish with a light dusting of black pepper and gomasio.

Raw Pumpkin Lasagna with Italian Pesto

Serves 4

For the lasagna:
10 porcini mushrooms
4 tablespoons olive oil
2 tablespoons tamari
1 small pumpkin
½ cup lemon juice
1 teaspoon Himalayan sea salt

For the pesto:
1 cup fresh spinach
½ cup fresh sage leaves
½ cup pistachios
¼ cup extra-virgin olive oil
½ teaspoon salt
1 tablespoon lemon juice
1 teaspoon nutritional yeast
   flakes

For the vegan cheese:
½ cup macadamia nuts
½ cup cashews
⅓ cup water
½ teaspoon salt
1 teaspoon natural yeast flakes
½ tablespoon fresh lemon juice

For the garnish:
1 grated macadamia nut

Start with the lasagna. Preheat the oven to 110 degrees. Cut the mushrooms into slices, season with 2 tablespoons olive oil and tamari, and place them in the oven to dry for 2 hours.

Remove the pumpkin skin and seeds and cut the flesh into ⅛" slices and marinate with remaining olive oil, lemon juice, and salt.

Gather together all the ingredients for the pesto and load them into the food processor. Pulse the food processor until the ingredients form a paste.

Move the pesto into another container, clear out the food processor, and load in all of the ingredients for the vegan cheese. Pulse the food processor until the vegan cheese binds together.

To assemble the lasagna, on a plate add the first "sheet" of lasagna with pumpkin and top that with a layer with mushrooms followed by pesto and finally cheese. Repeat with a second layer of pumpkin, mushrooms, pesto, and cheese. Finish with a final layer of pumpkin and decorate with grated macadamia.

Native Foods Café

MULTIPLE LOCATIONS

1775 E. Palm Canyon Dr.
Palm Springs, CA 92264
(760) 416-0070

www.nativefoods.com

(Other locations throughout the US)

Native Foods Café is delicious, fun, plant-based food that is chef-crafted and made in-house every day, including homemade tempeh and seitan. Everything is under $10 and designed to appeal to everyone—from vegans to carnivores!

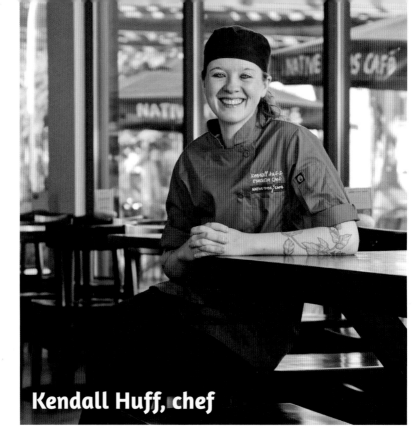

Kendall Huff, chef

Is this your first restaurant?
Our first restaurant opened in 1994 in Palm Springs, California, and we now have twenty locations…and plan to add more!

What's your favorite dish on the menu?
I love the Scorpion Burger. It's homemade blackened tempeh, chipotle sauce, romaine, carrots, avocado, and onions. It's my go-to sandwich!

What's your most popular appetizer?
It's a tie: our Native Nachos with Native Chipotle Crema and Native Cheese or the Native Chicken Wings. It's all in the batter!

What's the most popular entrée on the menu?
Again, head to head are the Rockin' Moroccan Bowl (tofu or Native Chicken marinated in our homemade Moroccan sauce with grilled veggies and quinoa, topped with currants and toasted almonds) and the Twister Wrap (salad greens, fresh avocado and cucumber salsa, creamy chipotle sauce, and your choice of crispy, blackened, or grilled Native Chicken in an organic whole wheat wrap).

What's your most popular dessert?
Peanut butter parfait! It's creamy whipped peanut butter filling layered between Boogie Bar crumbles and chocolate chips, sweetened with agave syrup. And it's gluten-free!

What do you feel is special about your restaurant?

We have such passionate team members and guests. It's a special place to work and the guests always tell us the vibe is awesome, warm, and welcoming. We are also very community-oriented: We celebrate Native Community Days each month by giving back a portion of sales to a local group, such as animal rescues, children's education organizations, environmental groups, and community or school garden programs.

How often do you change your menu items? Do you have daily or weekly specials?

We change our menu two to three times per year with the seasons. We have daily specials and once a month we do Special Meals, where we introduce a new menu offering for three days.

Do you have gluten-free, soy-free, and sugar-free options on your menu?

We sure do! We have an additional menu in-house that is very detailed. We want everyone to be able to eat at Native.

What do you do to reduce your environmental impact?

No meat! We only serve plant-based food, and we use one-hundred-percent recycled napkins and to-go boxes.

What are the most important lessons you've learned as owner or chef of this restaurant?

You've got one opportunity to gain a guest for life on their first visit. We are very welcoming and, as a fast casual restaurant, we've found out guests love the little extra table touches: checking in on how they like their food, offering free drink refills. You have to have great food and great service. If you have only one of those, you've lost them!

What led you to the vegan diet yourself?

Growing up on a farm in the Midwest, you get pretty attached to animals. One day, when I was seven and my sister was nine, our favorite cows went missing. A year or two later, our parents explained where they ended up. Enough said! Became vegan!

In the time since your restaurant first opened, how has the plant-based food movement changed? Do you find more demand now for vegan food?

Oh yes. Chicago has really been our proving grounds where we've found ninety-five percent of our guests are *not* vegan or vegetarian. Yay! We feel like the stigma of veganism is being eradicated.

Where do you see the plant-based food movement going in coming years?

It's going mainstream. You see so many mainstream restaurants now offering several vegan options. Plus the number of people who claim to be vegan have doubled in the past five years! 🐷

Bistro Steak Sandwich

Serves 4–6

1 teaspoon olive oil
4 French rolls or bread of choice
4 ounces Seitan Steak* (recipe follows)
6 tablespoons Native Blue Cheese (recipe follows)
3 Oven-Roasted Tomatoes, very cold (recipe follows)
½ cup Crispy Shallots (recipe follows)
½ cup baby arugula
1 teaspoon chopped fresh parsley

* This requires 8 to 12 hours of marinating time.

Brush the olive oil on the French rolls and place them in a warm pan. Toast and repeat briefly on other side of the bread. Remove and set aside. In a pan, sear the steak seitan for two minutes on each side.

On the bread, spread 2 tablespoons of Native Blue Cheese. Place the hot steak seitan on top of the cheese. Then spoon 4 tablespoons Native Blue Cheese on top of the seitan. Arrange 3 pieces of roasted tomatoes on top of the blue cheese, skin side down. Place ½ cup of Crispy Shallots on top of the tomatoes. Place the arugula on top of the shallots. Sprinkle with parsley.

Crispy Shallots

3 cups thinly sliced shallots
⅛ teaspoon and ½ teaspoon sea salt
⅛ teaspoon black pepper
⅛ teaspoon garlic powder
2 cups soy milk
1 cup all-purpose flour (for tossing)
Vegetable oil for frying

Place shallots in a bowl and add the salt, pepper, garlic powder, and soy milk. Soak the shallots for 2 hours and strain from the liquid.

In batches, toss a handful of soaked shallots in a large bowl with flour. Make sure to coat the shallots well. (They should feel dry.) Repeat until all shallots are breaded. Drop 2 cups of flour-dusted shallots in a stockpot with oil and fry for 1 to 1½ minutes or until golden brown. Remove using tongs or slotted spoon. Place on a baking sheet lined with paper towels to remove extra oil. Repeat until all shallots are done. Sprinkle the Crispy Shallots with salt and store in a shallow container.

Native Blue Cheese

1 cup vegan mayonnaise
2 teaspoons tahini
2 teaspoons garlic powder
4 tablespoons lemon juice
2 tablespoons apple cider vinegar
½ teaspoon black pepper
½ teaspoon sea salt
1 12-ounce box silken tofu

In a mixing bowl, whisk together the mayonnaise, tahini, garlic powder, lemon juice, vinegar, black pepper, and salt. Crumble the tofu into the bowl, keeping the pieces small (no larger than ¼ x ¼) and fold into the mix.

Oven-Roasted Tomatoes

1 cup sectioned Roma tomatoes (see sectioning instructions at right)
3 or 4 cloves garlic
⅛ teaspoon sea salt
⅛ teaspoon black pepper
½ tablespoon olive oil
1 tablespoon plus 1 teaspoon thyme, whole sprigs
½ tablespoon chopped fresh parsley

Preheat the oven to 350 degrees. Cut ¼" off the top of each tomato (the vine end). Then cut in half. Cut each half into 3 equal pieces for 6 pieces total, per tomato. Place the tomatoes in a bowl. Add the other ingredients and toss well. Lay the tomatoes out on a small sheet pan. Place in the oven and bake for 30 minutes. After removing them from the oven, remove the whole thyme sprigs and garlic. Cool completely and serve cold.

Seitan Steak

½ cup soy sauce
¼ cup lemon juice
½ cup olive oil
½ cup water
2 teaspoons garlic powder
1 teaspoon black pepper
6 cloves garlic
1 pound peppered seitan

To make the marinade, place all ingredients, except the seitan, into the blender and blend until smooth. Split the marinade into 2 batches and save 1 batch in the fridge for another time. Using a thin blade, slice all the peppered seitan. Place the seitan in a pan. Pour the marinade over the seitan and allow to marinate for at least 8 hours, no more than 12 hours. Strain the seitan from the marinade. There will not be a lot of liquid left over. Allow the seitan to strain for 10 minutes. Serve warm or in the Bistro Steak Sandwich.

Peacefood Café

NEW YORK, NY

460 Amsterdam Ave.
New York, NY 10024
(212) 362-2266

(Second location in New York City)

www.peacefoodcafe.com

See HappyCow reviews at
www.happycow.net/book/peacefood-cafe

Named after the simple idea that peace begins on your plate, Peacefood Café is a vegan restaurant focusing on providing delicious, innovative food to vegans and nonvegans alike.

Peter Lu and Eric Yu (pictured), owners

Is this your first restaurant?
Yes, and our second location opened in March 2011 in Manhattan near Union Square.

When did Peacefood open?
June 22, 2009.

Is the new restaurant designed differently?
Yes, we designed the new restaurant ourselves from scratch [based on] the way that we see it: as a new generation of vegan restaurant.

What's your favorite dish on the menu?
The Shanghai dumplings—the vegan ones are better than the originals.

What's your most popular appetizer?
It's a three-way tie among the daily soups, Shanghai dumplings, and chickpea fries.

What's the most popular entrée on the menu?
Another tie: the Japanese pumpkin sandwich, French horn (king oyster) mushroom panini, and Peacebowl (three vegetables served with brown rice and ginger oil).

What's your most popular dessert?

So many popular ones: chocolate ganache cake, grasshopper cookie sandwich, key lime pie, etc.

What do you feel is special about your restaurant?

We provide affordable, delicious, conscious food to the public. As owners, we are both very hands-on, participating in all aspects of the business. It's like inviting friends over for dinner at our home; we want to make sure they will have a positive and memorable experience.

How often do you change your menu items? Do you have daily or weekly specials?

The main menu doesn't change because we do provide a great variety of vegan food, but we do have daily specials for lunch and dinner.

Do you have gluten-free, soy-free, and sugar-free options on your menu?

We have gluten-, soy-, and nut-free items. We also have raw options.

What do you do to reduce your environmental impact?

As a vegan restaurant, we have helped reduce the carbon footprint. We also do not sell bottled water and encourage customers to drink the filtered water we provide.

What are the most important lessons you've learned as owner or chef of this restaurant?

We have to be conscientious in what we are doing and generous to everyone—customers and employees. We also need to keep a positive attitude, and our meditation/yoga practices help us keep ourselves centered.

What led you to want to open a vegan restaurant, and/or what led you to the vegan diet yourself?

We were vegetarians for about eight years; at the time, Eric was a stricter vegetarian and I was an ovo-lacto vegetarian. Then I stumbled into Colleen Patrick-Goudreau's *Compassionate Cooks* podcast and we turned vegan on New Year's Day 2007. We,

as owners, are both vegan, and this is the best way to spread the message to be compassionate to animals.

In the time since your restaurant first opened, how has the plant-based food movement changed? Do you find more demand now for vegan food?

I think there are more and more vegan restaurants opening. Yes, the demand is much greater now than even a few years ago. That's why we've opened a second location.

Since your restaurant first opened, has your view of what constitutes healthy or delicious foods changed? Have you changed the types of foods you offer?

Things change all the time; we have to keep improving ourselves based on what we learn from our operations, and we try not to follow all the trends and fad diets even though some are plant-based. We want to provide delicious vegan comfort food for people. Our goal is to make vegan food accessible to people.

Where do you see the plant-based food movement going in coming years?

The plant-based food movement will grow tremendously in the coming years. It is good for personal health, the environment, and the animals. It can solve so many problems in the world; most importantly it shows that we care for our animal companions and don't consume them like a commodity. 🍲

Roasted Spaghetti Squash, Cauliflower, Garlic, and Mashed Potatoes with Porcini Mushroom Gravy

Serves 4

1 cup whole cloves garlic
5 tablespoons olive oil
4 pounds spaghetti squash, cut lengthwise into quarters
Salt and pepper, to taste
1 head cauliflower, florets cut from stem

For the mashed potatoes:
1½ pounds peeled potatoes, cut into large cubes
4 tablespoons vegan butter
1 cup unsweetened rice milk
Salt and pepper, to taste

For the porcini mushroom gravy:
3 tablespoons olive oil
½ cup diced white onion
Pinch salt
3 cloves garlic, minced
2 ounces dried porcini mushrooms, rinsed and soaked in 2 cups warm water until soft; reserve liquid
2 cups sliced mixed mushrooms* (small pieces)
1 tablespoon Dijon mustard
3 cups vegetable broth
2 tablespoons cornstarch mixed with ¾ cup cold water
2 tablespoons vegan butter

*White, oyster, white beech, or any of your choice will do.

For the vegetables: Preheat the oven to 350 degrees. Place the peeled garlic cloves and 4 tablespoons olive oil in a pan over medium heat and cook until light brown. Reserve oil.

Brush the spaghetti squash with 1 tablespoon olive oil and sprinkle with salt and pepper, to taste. Spread out on a cookie sheet lined with parchment paper, then cover with foil paper. In a bowl, toss cauliflower florets and fried garlic with reserved oil. Add salt and pepper to taste; spread cauliflower and garlic on a cookie sheet, uncovered. Place both squash and cauliflower florets in the preheated oven. Remove the cauliflower after 15 minutes, or until they are soft. Remove the squash after approximately 1 hour, when a fork can easily pierce the squash.

For the mashed potatoes: Put potatoes in a large pot and add water to just above the top of potatoes. Bring water to boil, then uncover. Continue the boiling until water evaporates and potatoes are soft, about 10 minutes. Remove pot from heat. Strain any remaining water and mash the potatoes with fork. Add vegan butter, rice milk, and salt and pepper. Mix very well and set aside, covered.

For the porcini mushroom gravy: Heat 3 tablespoons olive oil in a large sauté pan. Add onions and a pinch of salt, and stir-fry for 2 minutes. Add minced garlic, all the mushrooms, and mustard; keep stirring the pan for another 3 to 5 minutes, then add more salt and pepper to taste. Add the liquid from the soaked porcini and the vege-

table broth, bring the sauce to boil, then lower it down to simmer. Continue cooking for another 10 minutes. Pour in the cornstarch mixture and butter, stir for another minute, then remove the pan from heat.

To assemble: Arrange each plate with a piece of squash, top with cauliflowers and garlic, and set mashed potatoes next to them. Ladle gravy on top of the potatoes and vegetables. Serve immediately.

Award-Winning Chickpea Fries

Serves 4–6

5   cups water
2   tablespoons nutritional yeast
    powder
1   tablespoon dried fenugreek
    leaves
¼   cup shredded unsweetened
    coconut
4   tablespoons olive oil
1   tablespoon minced garlic
1   tablespoon minced fresh ginger
4   tablespoons blended spices*
1½ cups chickpea flour
Salt and pepper, to taste

*To make the spice blend, mix
together a pinch of each: ground
coriander, turmeric, cumin, chili,
fenugreek seeds, nutmeg, cinnamon, cardamom seeds, bay leaf,
fennel, and onion flakes, or use a
commercial Indian spice pack.

Combine water, nutritional yeast, dried fenugreek leaves, and shredded unsweetened coconut. Stir and mix well, and set aside in a bowl. In a heavy pot, pour in olive oil and add minced garlic and ginger; sauté over medium heat for 3 minutes. Add blended spices and sauté for another minute, and add mixture in the bowl. Then add flour. Stir constantly to keep mixture from sticking on the bottom of the pot. Stir about 20 minutes until the thickness of the mixture resembles cookie dough. Remove from heat and add salt and pepper to taste.

Transfer mixture to an oiled cookie sheet, spread evenly, and let it cool in refrigerator overnight. To serve, cut mixture into 3 x ¼ rectangles, then deep-fry them in preheated oil or bake them in an oven at 350 degrees for 20 to 35 minutes until they are golden brown. Serve immediately with our Caesar Dipping Sauce (see recipe below).

Caesar Dipping Sauce

Serves 4–6

2   tablespoons tofu sour cream
4   tablespoons Vegenaise
½   piece fermented bean curd*
½   tablespoon nutritional yeast
    powder
1   teaspoon lemon juice
Salt and pepper, to taste

*Available at Asian markets.

Mix all the ingredients in a bowl. Refrigerate 2 hours before serving.

Plant

ASHEVILLE, NC

165 Merrimon Ave.
Asheville, NC 28801
(828) 258-7500

www.plantisfood.com

Jason Sellers, co-owner and chef

Plant makes meatless meals creative, sexy, and colorful, and serves them in a calm, relaxing space—in one of the hippest towns in America.

Is this your first restaurant?
Yes, first one, sole location.

When did it open?
We opened August 16, 2011.

Do you want to have more than one restaurant?
We'd love to have another location in a bigger, slightly more metropolitan market, where we could also have more space for a bigger kitchen and a full bar.

What's your favorite dish on the menu?
My favorite dish is the one I'm standing over as a customer tells me that he or she is having the best meal they could have imagined. If I'm sitting down to eat, I'd have to go with the Wild Forest: locally foraged maitake and chicken-of-the-wood mushrooms, smoked jalapeño mashed potatoes, seasonal sautéed vegetables, and a grilled garlic crostino.

What's your most popular appetizer?
Our most popular appetizer is either the aged "cheese" plate or the smoked hummus; it changes from week to week.

What's the most popular entrée on the menu?
Right now, the most popular dish is the [above-mentioned] Wild Forest.

What's your most popular dessert?
Our most popular dessert is the Blackout Pie: chocolate–peanut butter mousse, cookie crust, and strawberry-balsamic ice cream.

What do you feel is special about your restaurant?
Plant is the creation of three partners and an amazing staff who all possess an ethic, a passion, and a hands-on dedication to be the best we can be. We are great friends and deeply connected to our daily mission. Plant is the first restaurant we've owned and the best restaurant I've ever worked in—it's pretty special to me. We're also the only full-service vegan restaurant in town.

How often do you change your menu items? Do you have daily or weekly specials?

The menu changes according to season and local and regional availability. I like to think about cooking whatever the weather and season tells me makes sense. I occasionally feature a small-plate special on Friday or Saturday night, maybe baby peppers stuffed with pumpkin seed hummus and chipotle cream, or a carpaccio of heirloom tomato, smoked cheese, and lavender oil.

Do you have gluten-free, soy-free, and sugar-free options on your menu?

A lot of the menu is gluten-free, soy-free, and sugar-free, and since we cook to order, every dish can be redesigned to suit those with sensitivities, even those with celiac disease. I think about my customers while creating the menu; if, say, wheat or soy is not essential to the dish, I don't use it. I like the idea that the dishes can appeal to everyone. The most important thing for me when rethinking a dish according to a dietary need is to offer a meal that does not compromise the flavor, texture, or presentation of its original form.

What do you do to reduce your environmental impact?

The most crucial thing we do to reduce the typical impact of a restaurant on the environment is to serve only plant-based foods. We also retrofit equipment to conserve resources, compost, supply local growers, buy locally, buy environmentally savvy products, recycle, and reuse everything we can during day-to-day operations. We've earned a three-star rating from the Green Restaurant Association, and we're working toward our fourth star.

What are the most important lessons you've learned as owner or chef of this restaurant?

The most important thing I've learned is how important and special my partners are to me, and, together, we've learned the importance of a great staff.

What led you to want to open a vegan restaurant, and/or what led you to the vegan diet yourself?

Leslie Armstrong, Alan Berger, and I—the three partners who own Plant—are all ethically vegan. There's not another type of restaurant that we could own. We strove to open in an intimate space with a small menu and an open kitchen, and that's what we got. We love every day as an opportunity to give diners a vegan culinary experience that will bring them back.

In the time since your restaurant first opened, how has the plant-based food movement changed? Do you find more demand now for vegan food?

Since opening, we've found that in the recent wake of popularized media regarding the benefits of a plant-based diet, more people are seeking vegan food for different reasons. Some are literally sent to our restaurant by their doctor, while some search for us after reading about a study or seeing *Forks Over Knives*. People are realizing that they can have the traditional restaurant experience—they can be entertained; they can be intimate; they can celebrate—and they can do so while taking better care of themselves. There's a sense of assimilation for those folks who are new to eating vegan; they can literally have their cake (well, maybe their pie) and eat it, too.

Since your restaurant first opened, has your view of what constitutes healthy or delicious foods changed? Have you changed the types of foods you offer?

We're lucky because we're successfully offering the exact foods we aimed to offer. When you open a restaurant so close to your heart, you realize the risk of a tepid reception. We've had a great response to our food, which makes everyone involved want to work harder to make it better each day.

Where do you see the plant-based food movement going in coming years?

The importance of plant-based nutrition will continue to effect meaningful changes in the restaurant industry, from nonvegetarian restaurants offering animal-free options to the rising quality and prevalence of vegetarian fine dining. 🍵

When it comes to light desserts, nothing beats the interplay of sweet and tart. A generous amount of lime in this parfait lifts the palate and allows for the seasonal fruit to shine. This simple parfait can be made ahead of time and will keep, covered, for a few days. Your parfaits will taste even better if allowed to warm up just slightly after coming out of the refrigerator. At Plant, we serve them with some dehydrated raspberry for a sharp, tart burst.

Raw Lime Parfait

Serves 4

For the crust:
2   cups almonds
¼   teaspoon salt
¾   teaspoon ground cinnamon
½   cup agave syrup
3   dates, pitted and roughly chopped

For the granola:
2   cups almonds
Large pinch salt
Large pinch ground cinnamon
2   teaspoons lime zest
¼   cup agave syrup

For the lime cream:
2½ cups cashews, soaked overnight and drained
¾   cup agave syrup
Zest and juice of 4 limes
2   tablespoons water

To assemble:
Seasonal fruit (garnish; e.g., 16 thin slices apple, 8 berries, or 4 tablespoons diced pineapple)
4   large pinches orange, lemon, and lime zest (optional)
2   teaspoons agave syrup (optional)
4   sprigs fresh mint or 4 edible flowers (garnish; optional)

For the crust: In a food processor, grind the almonds, salt, and cinnamon into a coarse meal. Add agave syrup and dates, and process until a wet, fairly sticky doughlike mix forms. Chill the crust in an airtight container until ready for use.

For the granola (make 24 hours in advance): Grind the almonds in a food processor until ⅛" pieces remain. Combine almond meal and remaining ingredients in a large bowl and mix by hand or with a rubber spatula until uniform. The mixture should resemble a wet granola. Spread the mixture in a single layer on a rubberized baking mat or on a baking sheet covered with parchment paper. Dehydrate in a dehydrator or in a low oven at about 115 degrees for 24 hours, until crisp and crunchy. The granola will crisp as it cools, so don't worry if it's still slightly moist when it comes out of the dehydrator or the oven. Store granola in an airtight container at room temperature.

For the lime cream: Combine all ingredients in a blender and blend until smooth. Add water slowly if necessary, until the mixture is smooth, airy, and no graininess remains. Adjust the agave syrup and lime juice, to taste, to achieve the perfect balance of sweetness and tartness. Chill the cream in an airtight container.

To assemble: Place a ¼" to ½" layer of the crust mixture into the bottom of 4 parfait dishes, 8-ounce glasses, or

any decorative glass serving container. In each glass, alternate layers of granola, lime cream, and your seasonal fruit until only ¼" remains at the top of the glass container. Try to keep your layers even and distinct, and be careful to keep the sides of the serving container clean from smudges. Fill in the remaining ¼" of the glass with granola and a mix of fruit, and chill.

For a finished look, combine the orange, lemon, and lime zest with the agave syrup in a blender and pulse to make uniform. Drizzle the citrus agave syrup over the fruit in each dish or glass just before serving, and add a sprig of mint or edible flower.

In the mountains of western North Carolina, wild mushroom season is most of the year. From morels in the spring, to lobsters, chickens, and boletes in the summer, to blewits and maitake in the fall, we forage them all. In this recipe, we put a simple crispy crust on them and serve them over smoked jalapeño mashed potatoes and seasonal sautéed vegetables. Braising cultivated mushrooms is not always necessary, but we recommend braising wild ones before frying. Cooking wild mushrooms before frying for 1 minute may improve their digestibility. Consult a mycologist in your area before eating anything foraged from the forest.

Wild Forest

Serves 4

For the jalapeño mashed potatoes:
12 cups peeled and diced large Yukon potatoes
2 teaspoons sea salt, or to taste
Large pinch black pepper
½ cup your favorite oil (e.g., olive oil or safflower oil)
¼ cup almond milk
1 tablespoon nutritional yeast
¼ cup minced jalapeños

For the mushroom marinade and braising:
4 cups cultivated-exotic or wild mushrooms*

1 6-ounce block soft tofu
1 teaspoon salt
1 cup vegetable stock
1½ tablespoons paprika, Creole seasoning, or Old Bay seasoning
1½ teaspoons dried basil
1½ teaspoons dried oregano
Large pinch black pepper
2 tablespoons lemon juice

For the mushroom dredge and frying:
3 to 4 cups good-quality olive, safflower, grapeseed, or coconut oil for frying

2 cups all-purpose flour, whole-wheat flour, or brown-rice flour
2 tablespoons paprika
1 teaspoon black pepper
1 teaspoon salt

For the vegetables:
4 heads baby bok choy
1 large red bell pepper
2 tablespoons olive oil
Pinch cumin seeds
1 tablespoon fresh garlic
½ cup cilantro
4 scallions, thinly sliced

* Maitake, beech, or oyster could all be used.

For the jalapeño mashed potatoes: Cover potatoes with water in a saucepot and bring to a boil. Lower heat, add the handful of sea salt, and simmer until tender, about 20 minutes. Potatoes should begin to crumble but not completely fall apart when split. Drain the water well, return the potatoes to the pot, and put pot over very, very low heat, just enough to keep the potatoes from losing temperature. Add salt, pepper, and oil to the potatoes and mash with a potato masher using only vertical

pressure; do not stir. Once mashed, add almond milk, nutritional yeast, and jalapeños. Use a large spoon to stir just until it's uniform and creamy. Be careful not to overmix the potatoes, as they can become gummy and tough. Potatoes can be stored, covered, in a low temperature oven until ready to serve.

For the mushroom marinade and braising: Preheat the oven to 350 degrees. Prepare the mushrooms by trimming any tough or

recipe continued next page

fibrous parts from the base of the mushrooms, and place the mushrooms in a baking dish. Combine remaining ingredients in a blender and blend on high speed until it forms a uniform and smooth marinade. Pour the marinade over the mushrooms, and flip the pieces so that all mushrooms are uniformly wet; some marinade should pool in the bottom of the baking dish. Cover the dish with a lid or foil, and bake in the preheated oven for 20 minutes. Remove the pan from the oven, remove the cover, and let cool.

For the mushroom dredge and frying: Heat the oil over medium heat in a saucepan, wok, or small deep fryer so that the oil is approximately 2" deep. If you have a thermometer, the temperature of the oil should be between 300 and 330 degrees. Combine the flour, paprika, black pepper, and salt in a large mixing bowl or on a large plate. Toss the braised, cooled mushrooms in the dredge, making sure to coat each piece. Once the oil has reached frying temperature, use a slotted spoon or tongs to slide the mushrooms into the oil until there is no room left on the surface for more. Fry the mushrooms for about 1 minute, turning them to cook evenly, until they are light golden brown and crispy. Remove the mushrooms and let cool on a plate with paper towels. Repeat until all the mushrooms are fried.

For the vegetables: Sauté the bok choy and peppers (or your favorite seasonal vegetables) with some good-quality olive oil and a little cumin seed and garlic. Add cilantro (or other fresh herbs) and scallions just before plating. The cumin stands out in the sauté and matches nicely with the jalapeño.

To assemble: Place equal portions of the mashed potatoes on 4 plates, snug some vegetables up next to the potatoes, and stack the mushrooms on top. We like to serve the dish with microgreens and grilled ciabatta rubbed with fresh garlic.

Portobello

PORTLAND, OR

1125 SE Division St.
Portland, OR 97202
(503) 754-5993

www.portobellopdx.com

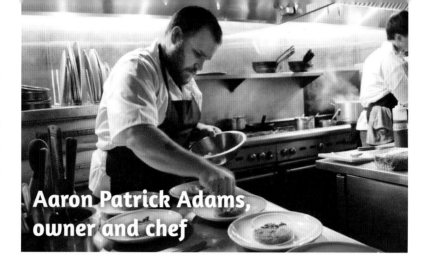

Aaron Patrick Adams, owner and chef

Portobello serves Northwest vegan craft cookery with a Mediterranean bent in an upscale yet casual environment.

Is this your first restaurant?
No. My first restaurant opened in 2002 in Jacksonville, Florida, and was far from being vegan.

When did Portobello open?
Portobello opened in January 2009.

Do you want to have more than one restaurant?
I would love the opportunity to explore some other concepts. I hope to open other restaurants, perhaps in other parts of the country, in the future.

What's your favorite dish on the menu?
That's a hard one. I think I consistently turn to the gnocchi. While we change up the gnocchi with the seasons, those pillowy little dumplings, which I love, stay the same.

What's your most popular appetizer?
I'd say our beet tartare is our most popular. Though our mushroom frites and our cashew cheese–stuffed sweety peps are close seconds.

What's the most popular entrée on the menu?
I think the gnocchi is the most popular, with ravioli coming in a close second.

What's your most popular dessert?
Probably our take on tiramisu. It's been on the menu since day one, and it's the only dish that hasn't changed at all since opening.

What do you feel is special about your restaurant?
We offer a unique take on vegan cuisine. We certainly aren't a health-food restaurant. We're strictly in it to show folks that they don't have to eat animals or animal products to enjoy a decadent meal.

How often do you change your menu items? Do you have daily or weekly specials?
We reprint our menu nightly with at least one or two changes. We're (happily) at the mercy of the local farms that we source from.

Do you have gluten-free, soy-free, and sugar-free options on your menu?

Our menu is virtually soy-free and we offer many gluten-free options. Both are clearly indicated on the menu. We don't offer any sugar-free desserts, per se. We use evaporated cane juice, agave syrup, and maple to sweeten our desserts.

What do you do to reduce your environmental impact?

We compost all food scraps, which is actually very easy to do in Portland, Oregon, as our waste management provider picks up our compost and processes it. We also recycle everything we can. There is a Dumpster for most recycling, one can for glass, one can for garbage, and six cans for compost. Most of our employees arrive to work by bicycle, and we employ a work bike for neighborhood pickups and deliveries.

What are the most important lessons you've learned as owner or chef of this restaurant?

Listen. Listen to your customers and listen to your staff. Make changes where necessary. Never worry about being right, just about being better.

What led you to want to open a vegan restaurant, and/or what led you to the vegan diet yourself?

I had an epiphany while at my old restaurant, where I served foie gras, veal, etc. I realized I needed to make a change. The changes came gradually, and I eventually closed my restaurant down. I felt something inside that told me that I needed to stop and look at what I was doing, how it was affecting the animals caught up in this horrible system, and the impact it had on the health of the environment and my clientele. I moved to Portland, Oregon, sold my car, got on a bike, went vegan, and never looked back.

In the time since your restaurant first opened, how has the plant-based food movement changed? Do you find more demand now for vegan food?

There is an incredible increase not only in demand, but in the wonderful array of products available. I don't know if my palate has adjusted, but it seems

that the products available to us today are a far cry from the vegan products of yesteryear. Cheese is a big one, with the advent of artisanal vegan cheeses. The analogue meats, too, are incredible, though we don't serve them at Portobello.

Since your restaurant first opened, has your view of what constitutes healthy or delicious foods changed? Have you changed the types of foods you offer?

I have removed a ton of soy from the menu. You'll find it on the cheese plate with the Chao Cheese and in the tiramisu. Otherwise, it's gone. A lot of my customers were concerned with overconsuming soy. And we also used to employ more convenience products, like sausages and chik'n when we first opened. We pride ourselves on making all of those types of things in-house now. We have much more of an emphasis on getting vegetables into the mix, rather than relying on mock meats and grains.

Where do you see the plant-based food movement going in coming years?

I think that we'll see more and more omnivorous restaurants offering vegan options. It's sort of bittersweet. I'm happy that folks might eat more vegan food, and that vegans can find things to eat out in the marketplace, but it saddens me that we [as a community will] continue to be complicit in the aiding of business that contribute to the slaughter of animals. I would like to see more exclusively vegan restaurants, but that's a hard sell outside of major metropolitan areas that can support such establishments. 🐄

Butternut Gnocchi with Brussels Leaves, Butternut Velouté, Pepitas, and Pumpkin Seed Oil

Serves 4

4   tablespoons *toasted* pepitas
    (pumpkin seeds)
1   tablespoon olive oil
20 Brussels sprouts
Butternut Velouté *(recipe follows)*
2   tablespoons grapeseed oil
Butternut-Potato Gnocchi *(recipe
    follows)*
1   clove garlic, minced
Salt and pepper, to taste
8   leaves fresh sage, chopped
4   teaspoons pumpkin seed oil

Preheat oven to 375 degrees. Spread *pepitas* on a cookie sheet and drizzle with olive oil. Toss to coat evenly. Sprinkle with salt evenly. Toast in the oven for 7 minutes. Remove and let cool. Store in a sealed container until needed.

Clean the Brussels sprouts, paring off their stems and removing any blemished outer leaves in the process. In a bowl, peel the outer leaves, leaf by leaf, as far down as you can go. You'll end up with several tiny Brussels sprout cores, which you can use in another recipe. Set the Brussels leaves aside for this dish. Heat up the Butternut

Velouté in a saucepot, stirring often and taking care not to burn it. Place a sauté pan on the stove and heat it up on medium-high. Add the grapeseed oil to the sauté pan. Add the gnocchi in the pan carefully. Pan-fry them to a golden brown on both sides. When you flip the gnocchi the first time, add the raw Brussels leaves to the pan. Toss the gnocchi and leaves together. Add the minced garlic and continue to sauté, tossing often to ensure even cooking.

Add a ladle of the butternut sauce to the pan and toss to coat evenly. Season with salt and pepper, to taste.

To plate, place a ladleful of sauce on each plate. Use the back of the bowl of the ladle to swirl the sauce evenly into a large circle on the plates. Carefully spoon the gnocchi and Brussels sprouts leaves into the center of each plate. Sprinkle the plates with *pepitas* and sage. Drizzle with roasted pumpkin seed oil and serve.

Butternut-Potato Gnocchi

Serves 4

- 4 cups large chunks butternut squash, peeled and seeded
- 5 cups large chunks peeled russet potatoes
- 2 cups unbleached fine wheat flour, plus more for dusting
- ⅓ cup Ener-G Egg Replacer
- ¼ clove whole nutmeg, freshly grated
- ½ tablespoon finely ground sea salt
- 4 tablespoons olive oil

Equipment needed: stovetop steamer, potato ricer, and flour sieve

Put a steamer pot on the stove with water and bring up to a boil. Put a large pot of salted water on the stove on high to blanch the gnocchi later. Place the butternut squash and potatoes in the steamer, and steam until fork-tender, approximately 30 minutes.

When fork tender, remove from the steamer and pass the potatoes and butternut through a potato ricer onto a clean, wooden surface, preferably a maple-top table or large cutting board. Sieve the flour and Ener-G Egg Replacer over the top of the potatoes and butternut. Rasp the nutmeg over the top of the flour. Sprinkle the salt all around on top. Create a well in the top of the mound of ingredients and pour the oil inside. Using a dough cutter, pastry cutter, or large cleaver, chop all the ingredients together, trying not to work the dough too much. When the dough is as homogenous as possible using the cutter, start to gather it together with your

recipe continued next page

hands (taking care not to burn yourself if the dough is still hot). Knead lightly.

The dough should be smooth and may be slightly softer than a plain potato gnocchi dough. Dust with flour as needed to keep the dough from getting too sticky. Portion the dough into 4 pieces and scrape your table or board nice and clean. Dust a little flour on your work surface and, using both hands, roll one of the dough portions out in a long snake, about ½" thick. Dust enough so it doesn't stick, but not too much where it slides around on the table. Cut the snake into individual gnocchi.

Put together an ice bath in a bowl of 1 part ice, 2 parts cold water, and keep it near the pot. Check on the pot of salted water, making sure the pot is only simmering and not at a full boil, and drop about a third of the gnocchi into the pot. When the gnocchi are floating on the top, remove them with a slotted spoon and drop in the ice-water bath to stop their cooking. When done, remove the gnocchi from the ice bath and place on a parchment-lined cookie sheet. Continue to cook the gnocchi in batches. These can be made a day in advance if wrapped with plastic wrap.

Butternut Velouté

Serves 4

2 tablespoons grapeseed oil
1 medium yellow onion, peeled and chopped
Pinch salt, plus more to taste
1 large butternut squash, peeled, seeded, and cut into medium-size chunks
1 clove garlic, smashed
6 cups vegetable stock
1 cinnamon stick
1 bay leaf
1 star anise seed
Freshly grated nutmeg, to taste

Place a saucepot on the stove over medium heat, adding the oil. Add the onion to the pot along with a pinch of salt. Slowly cook the onion in the oil, stirring often, until translucent. Add the butternut squash and garlic, stirring well to integrate. Add the vegetable stock to the pot. If the squash is not covered with liquid, add enough to water to cover. Bring to a boil, then reduce to a simmer. Add the cinnamon, bay leaf, and star anise to the pot. Cover and simmer for 30 minutes or until the butternut is totally tender. Remove the pot from the heat. Remove the bay leaf, star anise, and cinnamon stick from the pot and discard. Ladle the mix into a blender, making sure to only fill the blender halfway. Blend until smooth and pour into a container you will store the sauce in. Continue until all of the butternut sauce is blended. Adjust the seasoning with the salt and nutmeg.

Rawlicious

TORONTO, ON, CANADA

2122 Bloor St. W.
Toronto, ON M6S 1M8 Canada
(416) 519-7150

(Other locations in Canada)

www.rawlicious.ca

See HappyCow reviews at
www.happycow.net/book/rawlicious

Rawlicious serves healthy, delicious, raw vegan cuisine in a warm, inviting atmosphere.

Angus Crawford and Chelsea Clark, owners

Is this your first restaurant?
Yes.

When did it open?
April 2008.

Do you want to have more restaurants?
We hope to have many, many more and will definitely expand.

What's your favorite dish on the menu?
The taco wrap—a seasoned nut loaf, salsa, almond cheese, and guacamole, wrapped in a collard leaf.

What's your most popular appetizer?
Spring rolls with our Thai dipping sauce.

What's the most popular entrée on the menu?
Soft corn tacos stuffed with walnut refried beans, guacamole, salsa, shredded romaine, and vegan sour cream.

What's your most popular dessert?
Our blonde macaroons or cheesecake!

What do you feel is special about your restaurant?
Despite our cold climate and the economic temptation to serve cooked food, we have remained one-hundred percent raw from the beginning!

How often do you change your menu items? Do you have daily or weekly specials?
We have seasonal menu items that change twice a year.

Do you have gluten-free, soy-free, and sugar-free options on your menu?

Rawlicious is completely gluten-free and essentially soy-free (except for two items), and we use no white sugar (but do use agave, maple syrup, and dates).

What do you do to reduce your environmental impact?

All of our takeout items are compostable right down to the napkins and cutlery. We use biodegradable cleaning supplies and we compost or recycle ninety-nine percent of our waste.

What are the most important lessons you've learned as owner or chef of this restaurant?

The business is crazy—dead slow one day, ramped the next—so take each day as it comes and focus on the long-term big picture or you'll go crazy!

What led you to want to open a vegan restaurant, and/or what led you to the vegan diet yourself?

We were put on this path when a family member was sick, and we began searching for alternative pathways to healing. Once we started eating healthier, we wanted to share it with our community—and now owning a healthy restaurant has made it easy to eat healthy!

In the time since your restaurant first opened, how has the plant-based food movement changed? Do you find more demand now for vegan food?

The demand for vegan food has definitely been on the rise over the past few years and now it seems more than ever that the general population is aware of the benefits of veganism to the human body and to the environment, which are truly amazing.

Since your restaurant first opened, has your view of what constitutes healthy or delicious foods changed? Have you changed the types of foods you offer?

Our menu is very similar to what it was when we first opened, but we are aware of the growing demand for soy-free options.

Where do you see the plant-based food movement going in coming years?

In a total utopia, plant-based food would be the only food available. In the next ten years or so, the number of vegetarians and vegans is sure to increase along with the demand for truly healthy food. 🍃

This recipe is a great way to satisfy your pasta craving without feeling guilty!
A tool called a spiralizer is used to turn zucchini into noodles—they look so much
like spaghetti it might even fool a few people!

Zuchetti Pesto

Serves 4

6   medium-size zucchini
¼   cup sun-dried tomatoes
1   cup Rawlicious Pesto
     (recipe follows)
10   cherry tomatoes
1   sprig parsley

Equipment needed: spiralizer

Peel the zucchini and create the zucchini noodles by
pushing them through a spiralizer. Slice the sun-dried
tomatoes and cherry tomatoes. Toss the zucchini noodles
with pesto. Garnish with parsley.

Rawlicious Pesto

Makes 1½ cups

1½ cups basil
1   cup spinach
½   cup olive oil
⅓   cup lemon juice
1½ cloves garlic
¼   teaspoon sea salt
¼   teaspoon pepper
¾   cup sunflower seeds (soaked 4
     to 6 hours and drained)

Add all ingredients, except the sunflower seeds, in the
food processor and blend until thoroughly combined. Add
sunflower seeds and combine once more. Remove and
store. The pesto will keep in the fridge for 4 to 5 days.

The bright green color of these tarts alludes to the pop of flavor you get from the first bite! This dessert is creamy and sweet—a perfect picnic treat.

Key Lime Tarts

Makes 4 tarts

For the crust:
¼ cup almonds
½ cup shredded coconut
2½ tablespoons coconut oil
Pinch sea salt

For the filling:
⅓ cup plus 1 tablespoon lime juice
1 avocado
¼ cup agave syrup
¼ teaspoon vanilla extract
Pinch sea salt
½ teaspoon psyllium husks
¼ cup coconut oil
Shredded coconut (garnish)
4 lime slices (garnish)

For the crust: Add the almonds to the food processor and pulse until they become a powder. Add the coconut, coconut oil, and salt and process again until mixture is thoroughly combined. Remove and press this into tart shells or a pie pan.

For the filling: Blend all the ingredients, except the psyllium and coconut oil, in a blender. Once smooth, add the psyllium and the oil and blend.

To assemble: Pour the filling into the crust and set in the fridge for 1 hour or so. Decorate with shredded coconut and a slice of lime.

Real Food Daily

MULTIPLE LOCATIONS

514-516 Santa Monica Blvd.
Santa Monica, CA 90401
(310) 451-7544

(Other locations in West Hollywood, Pasadena,
and LAX Airport)

www.realfood.com

Ann Gentry, owner and chef
(pictured at center)

Real Food Daily is Southern California's premiere organic vegan restaurant, serving an authentic, creative, and nutritionally balanced menu. It's a cherished destination where community values like education, connection, and hospitality are embraced over delicious food that's real.

Is this your first restaurant?
I have three restaurants in the Los Angeles area and one in Los Angeles International Airport.

When did it open?
Santa Monica opened in 1993, West Hollywood in 1998, Pasadena in 2012, and the LAX outpost in 2013.

How many do you hope to have in the future? Will you expand further?
We are the first organic plant-based restaurant to open in an airport. With success, we hope to expand to more airport terminals in the future as well as open more RFDs on the West Coast.

What's your favorite dish on the menu?
Everything has been my favorite at some time or another, but I would have to say my mainstay dish has been The Basics. I like to keep it simple with choosing several macrobiotic staples that give me variety in flavor, texture, and satisfaction.

What's your most popular appetizer?
Our most popular appetizer is, hands down, our Not-Chos. They are perfect for a decadent yet healthy gluten-free option and are especially to die for with our famous cashew cheese recipe. My servers came up with the idea to add our taco mix to this dish, and this brings a whole new dimension to the dish.

What's the most popular entrée on the menu?
The Supreme Burrito is the fan favorite. The basics are rice, beans, tempeh bacon, guacamole, tofu sour cream, lettuce, tomato, and our cashew cheese. People in Southern California have a great appreciation for Tex-Mex style food.

What's your most popular dessert?
Our brownie bowl, chocolate chip cookie, and Faux-Stess Cupcake are a few among many coveted vegan desserts on our menu.

What do you feel is special about your restaurant?
Real Food Daily is a leader in the plant-based green food movement. Since 1993, we have been at the forefront, raising the standards and expectations of

plant-based restaurants. From the genuinely kind employees to the quality fare offered, we're a true center for community gathering and appreciation.

How often do you change your menu items? Do you have daily or weekly specials?

We update our menu four times a year with seasonal changes. Our menu is balanced according to Eastern health philosophies and heart-healthy Western nutrition recommendations.

Do you have gluten-free, soy-free, and sugar-free options on your menu?

We have gluten-free, soy-free, nut-free, and raw options. We also primarily use maple syrup and maple crystals to sweeten our desserts and stray from using refined sugars.

What do you do to reduce your environmental impact?

RFD has always been a champion of the environment by virtue of serving an exclusive plant-based menu using organic produce and ingredients. We participate in the city of Santa Monica's food composting program and even give our unused and leftover cooking oil to a local farmer to use as biofuel in his tractor! In addition to many other environmentally sound business practices, we use green cleaning supplies and energy-efficient appliances in the kitchens and office, and many of our local staff bike, walk, or ride the bus to work.

What are the most important lessons you've learned as owner or chef of this restaurant?

Food is the product, but it's all about the delivery, the experience, the human connection, and the ability to figure out what our guests really want and to serve that to them on so many different levels. We pride ourselves on giving people the full experience.

What led you to want to open a vegan restaurant, and/or what led you to the vegan diet yourself?

When I moved to Los Angeles, I thought I would be moving to the mecca of natural foods. I was astonished to find there was really no organic plant-based restaurant that felt comfortable to me, so I started cooking for myself more. Soon my

friends and coworkers caught on to my vegan dishes and demanded I cook for them, too. I developed a cooking service that expanded to a catered home delivery business and, five years later, opened up my first restaurant.

My style of food is a blend of three influences: my interest in macrobiotics, my roots in Southern food, and the influence of organic produce when I moved to California. My commitment has always been sourcing organic foods, food education, and creating a homey experience for like-minded people—a community.

In the time since your restaurant first opened, how has the plant-based food movement changed? Do you find more demand now for vegan food?

Absolutely. Today there is much more awareness surrounding health and longevity; therefore, a plant-based diet has become much more acceptable and mainstream. All kinds of people are willing to come to a plant-based restaurant these days.

Since your restaurant first opened, has your view of what constitutes healthy or delicious foods changed? Have you changed the types of foods you offer?

Now more and more people are interested in not only vegan cuisine but a wide variety of flavors and textures. Globalization and travel has influenced consumers' tastes. We've addressed the demand in diversity with our seasonal specials as well as by expanding our menu.

As competitors and copycats pop up, we realize our strong suit remains at the core of our mission statement—providing authentic, delicious, certified organic plant-based cuisine that is healthy and nutritious. Surprisingly, it is becoming rare to find genuinely healthy options among the fast-casual plant-based places. At Real Food Daily we provide a premiere culinary experience, which stems from our commitment to providing nutrient-rich dishes.

Where do you see the plant-based food movement going in coming years?

I see the expansion of organic, health-centered restaurants as critical to our society, and anticipate the movement to trend nationally and globally. 🍃

This rice roll has been on the RFD menu since we opened and has always been a favorite because guests are amazed and delighted that sushi can be vegan. We follow the traditional format of rolling rice in nori sea vegetable, but we fill it with an assortment of vegetables, along with some flavorful condiments. Our culinary director, Tara Punzone, created this variation, incorporating her love of pickled vegetables. We like using some of the exotic rice in the marketplace today. If you can't source jade pearl rice, white sushi rice is an easy substitute.

Kimchi Nori Maki Roll

Serves 4

For the sushi rice:
2   cups jade pearl rice
3   cups water
½   teaspoon sea salt
2   tablespoons brown rice vinegar
1   tablespoon mirin

For the sweet miso dipping sauce:
½   cup agave syrup
¼   cup white miso
1   tablespoon tamari
1   tablespoon lemon juice
1   tablespoon minced fresh ginger
2   tablespoons sesame oil

To assemble:
4   sheets toasted nori
4   cups sushi rice
1   handful fresh pea shoots
8   ounces kimchi
8   asparagus spears, grilled
1   firm but ripe avocado, peeled, pitted, and cut into thin wedges
1   red pepper, julienned
2   green onions, cut lengthwise into ¼"-wide strips
6   teaspoons sesame seeds

> *Equipment needed: bamboo mat for rolling sushi, pressure cooker*

For the sushi rice: Combine the rice, water, and sea salt in a 4¼-quart pressure cooker. Lock the lid into place. Bring the pressure to high over high heat. Decrease the heat to medium-low and simmer for 20 minutes. Remove from the heat and let stand for 10 minutes to allow the pressure to reduce. Carefully unlock the lid and remove it from the pot.

Transfer the rice to a large bowl. Drizzle the vinegar and mirin over the rice. Using chopsticks, gently toss the rice to coat it with the vinegar and mirin. Cool the rice completely at room temperature.

For the sweet miso dipping sauce: Place all ingredients except the sesame oil into a high-speed blender and blend. Slowly add the oil and pulse to emulsify. Set aside.

To assemble: Place 1 nori sheet shiny side down on a bamboo mat with 1 long side positioned closest to you. Spread 1 cup of rice in an even layer over the nori sheet, leaving a ½" border on the top long side. Place a few pea shoots facing out on each side. (Allow the leafy tips to stick out of the end of the nori.) Next, place 2 ounces of kimchi in an even line across the rice. Just below the kimchi, arrange 2 asparagus spears facing out, with the tips slightly sticking out of nori. Next arrange a quarter of the avocado slices, red pepper strips, and green onions atop the rice.

Using the bamboo mat as an aid and beginning with the long side closest to you, roll up the nori tightly. Moisten

the opposite long edge with water and seal the roll. Repeat to make 4 rolls total.

Once all rolls have been assembled, cut each roll into 8 pieces, approximately ½"-thick slices, using a large, very sharp knife. Arrange the slices with the cut side up on a platter. Sprinkle with sesame seeds and serve with the sweet miso dipping sauce.

In the early years, when I was at the stove, I created daily specials. As the menu expanded, daily creations became seasonal. Published in my second cookbook, *Vegan Family Meals, Real Food for Everyone*, this main course recipe reflects the style and simplicity of the restaurant's cooking, as it is a one-pot meal comprised of colorful vegetables cooked in a fragrant broth served with whole grains and using whole soy as a plant protein.

One-Pot Vegetables and Tofu with Sesame Rice

Serves 4

1   *medium onion*
1   *large head broccoli, stems removed, florets cut into bite-size pieces (about 2 cups)*
½   *small butternut squash (about 1¼ pounds), peeled and cut into ½" cubes*
2   *medium carrots, peeled and cut*
¼   *head green cabbage*
8   *ounces sugar snap peas, trimmed*
3   *ounces small fresh shiitake mushrooms, stemmed*
1   *cup water*
¼   *teaspoon fine-grain sea salt*
1   *5"-piece fresh ginger, peeled*
⅔   *cup mirin*
6   *tablespoons tamari*
1   *14-ounce block fresh, firm tofu, cut into ¾" cubes*
1½ *cups watercress, stems removed*
Sesame Rice (recipe follows)
2   *scallions, thinly sliced (garnish)*
1   *nori sheet, cut into thin strips (garnish)*

Quarter the onion through the stem end, then place the whole cut onion in the middle of a large cast-iron skillet, doing your best to keep the onion together. Arrange the broccoli, squash, carrots, cabbage, sugar snap peas, and mushrooms in clusters around the onions. Add just enough water to cover the bottom of the skillet (about 1 cup). Sprinkle ¼ teaspoon sea salt evenly over the vegetables. Cover and turn heat to high. Bring to a boil, and then decrease the heat to medium-low and simmer until the squash is crisp-tender, about 12 minutes.

Using a Microplane grater, grate the ginger over a paper towel or sheet of cheesecloth, and then squeeze the pulp to extract 2 teaspoons of ginger juice into a small bowl. Mix in the mirin and tamari with the ginger. Add the tofu and toss to coat. Spoon the tofu mixture over the vegetables and simmer uncovered until the tofu is hot, about 5 minutes. Add the watercress and simmer until it wilts, about 2 minutes.

Serve by dividing the sesame rice equally among the dinner plates or bowls. Using chopsticks, pick small amounts of each vegetable and the tofu and place atop the rice. With a wide spoon, pour some of the broth over the vegetables. Garnish with scallions and strips of nori.

Sesame Rice

1   *tablespoon toasted sesame oil*
4   *cloves garlic, minced*
4   *cups cooked rice (brown, basmati, or jasmine)*
¼   *cup sesame seeds*

Heat the oil in a heavy, large saucepan over medium heat. Add the garlic and sauté until fragrant, about 30 seconds. Stir in the rice and sesame seeds and cook just until heated through, about 3 minutes.

Sage's Café and Vertical Diner

SALT LAKE CITY, UT

234 West 900 South
Salt Lake City, UT 84101
(801) 322-3790

www.sagescafe.com

and

2280 SW Temple
Salt Lake City, UT 84115
(801) 484-8378

www.verticaldiner.com

(Other locations in Salt Lake City)

Sage's Café is a full-service vegan restaurant featuring seasonal, local, and globally inspired cuisine. Vertical Diner, with the same owner, is a hip, circa-1955 vintage diner offering vegan comfort food, local music, and art.

Ian Brandt, owner and chef

Is this your first restaurant?
Yes, Sage is. I opened it on December 21, 1999. I opened Vertical Diner in 2007.

How many do you hope to have in the future? Will you expand further?
I have a third currently, Café SuperNatural. I hope to open a fine dining restaurant in another state some day. I am very interested in Oregon.

What's your favorite dish on the menu?
My favorite dishes on the Sage menu are the shiitake escargot and the tiramisu. At Vertical Diner, the Avalanche is the most popular dish on the menu! The joke is, "You are going to get buried by the Avalanche." It's a large combo plate consisting of two pancakes, house breakfast sausage, hash browns, and tofu scramble.

What's your most popular appetizer?
At Sage, it's the carrot butter pâte with crostini. At Vertical Diner, loyal customers and visitors rave about the Buffalo Tigers at Vertical Diner. This dish is "hot wings" for vegans. They're perfectly spicy and perfectly crisp! And they taste best with one of our local beers!

What's the most popular entrée on the menu?
For Sage, it's the Casseruola, the Magic Wok, and the Mushroom Stroganoff—we have such a perfected menu that all of our entrées are ordered evenly! At Vertical Diner, the most popular entrée on the menu is the American Diner Plate, which is a hefty serving of mashed potatoes topped with our house-made fried seitan and smothered in our savory gravy.

What's your most popular dessert?
Sage's tiramisu. And shoofly cake has been a hit at Vertical Diner!

What do you feel is special about one of your restaurants?
Vertical Diner is a place where we break the myth that "eating vegan is boring." We serve "craveable" foods that feel good to the body, mind, and spirit. We work to make sure both meat-eaters and hardcore vegans are equally comfortable in our space.

How often do you change your menu items? Do you have daily or weekly specials?

At Sage, the seasonal small plates menu and our wine menu change every three months. We have a daily seasonal chef special and a brunch special every Saturday and Sunday. The raw food chef tasting is the last Friday every month. And the pizza night menu is served every Tuesday.

Our menu at Vertical Diner changes as we rotate seasonal and locally sourced produce (we make it a priority to build relationships with local farmers). We serve breakfast all day, every day. And every Sunday night we have Soul Food Sunday: a special American Southern comfort-food menu with favorites like butter beans, collards, barbecued pulled mushroom-stem sandwiches, corn bread, hush puppies, fried pickles, and apple fritters.

Do you have gluten-free, soy-free, and sugar-free options on your menu?

Sage's Café can prepare most of the menu gluten-free. The soup of the day is always prepared gluten-free and soy-free.

At Vertical Diner, people are so happy when they hear that our pancakes, burritos, sandwiches, and almost every item can be ordered gluten-free! We also offer rice milk, almond milk, and other alternatives for those eating soy-free. We work hard to make sure there is an option for everyone at the table!

What are the most important lessons you've learned as owner or chef of this restaurant?

I've learned that people who eat vegan are loyal, compassionate, community focused, and also some of the craziest people I have met, besides myself.

What led you to want to open a vegan restaurant, and/or what led you to the vegan diet yourself?

I felt like being part of the change that I wish to see. I wanted to create my own cosmic bubble here in Salt Lake City that promotes positivity all around!

In the time since Sage first opened, how has the plant-based food movement changed?

Between 1998, when I graduated college and started the Greens Food Cart and then Sage's Café, and now

Sage's Café

I have seen so many more options become available. Thanks to HappyCow for assisting in creating a great veg food scene in the US and beyond!

How has your view of what constitutes healthy or delicious foods changed? Have you changed what you offer?

We have always been aware of the wide range of diets within vegan cuisine and look for ways to serve our guests' needs and preferences. We added donuts to our menu last year based on customer demand and the creativity of our chefs. The donuts are delicious, vegan, made with organic flour—and are not intended to be particularly healthy. We just love serving wonderfully prepared vegan cuisine that is delicious and happens to be healthier than what is served at most restaurants.

Where do you see the plant-based food movement going in coming years?

In 1999, there were twenty or so vegan gourmet restaurants in the US. Now there are hundreds. In 2013, Salt Lake City, with a population of 150,000, become a leading city in vegan plant-based culture, with ten vegan food businesses, cafés, restaurants, and bakeries. It is just the beginning for plant-based foods. 🐾

Sage's Shiitake Escargot

Serves 8–10

For the shiitake marinade:
- ¼ cup balsamic vinegar
- ½ cup Burgundy wine
- ¼ cup minced garlic
- 1¼ cups water
- ¼ cup olive oil
- 2 teaspoons ground rosemary
- 2 teaspoons ground brown mustard
- 1½ tablespoons sea salt
- 1 cup fresh shiitake mushrooms

For the carrot butter pâte:
- 2½ cups peeled and chopped carrots
- ¾ cup macadamia nuts
- ½ cup safflower or canola oil
- 2 tablespoons maple syrup
- ½ tablespoon vanilla
- ½ tablespoon salt

Prepare the marinade the night before: Add all the marinade ingredients together in a bowl and whisk them together, blending until smooth. Soak shiitake mushrooms in the marinade and leave them soaking overnight in the refrigerator, or for 8 hours.

To make the carrot butter pâte, boil the chopped carrots in water for 2 hours. Strain and save stock for future soups or other recipes. Combine boiled carrots and all the other ingredients in the pot. Blend together with an immersion blender until fully combined. Remove to a bowl and chill.

To assemble: Preheat your oven's broiler. Place the marinated mushrooms and a little leftover marinade in a shallow roasting pan. (You can use a soufflé dish or a stainless-steel baking pan.) The layers should not be deeper than 2 mushroom slices. Portion 4–8 tablespoons carrot butter in either the same roasting pan or in a separate roaster. Broil both the mushrooms and carrot butter for approximately 8 minutes. Serve with toasted baguette slices.

Vertical Diner's Tofu Scramble

Serves 2–4

- 1 14-ounce brick firm tofu
- ¼ teaspoon turmeric
- ¼ teaspoon paprika
- ¼ teaspoon white pepper
- 1 teaspoon salt
- 1 tablespoon vegetable oil (sunflower or canola), plus more for frying
- 2 tablespoons nutritional yeast flakes

Drain the brick of tofu and rinse. Press tofu brick between 2 plates with a weight on the top plate to squeeze out excess water. Drain liquid and rinse tofu brick again. In mixing bowl, crumble tofu into large pebble-size pieces and add all of the spices, salt, oil, and nutritional yeast. In an oiled skillet, add tofu and heat slowly over low heat so that the tofu doesn't stick to the pan. Cook until hot and all ingredients are well integrated. Make sure that the tofu is not too mashed. It should be mashed down to dime-to-quarter-size chunks. When making larges batches, mash with a potato masher. Remove and serve.

I modified a vegan version of my grandmother's shoofly cake recipe. It's great for breakfast or as a dessert. Don't forget to drench it in a shot of espresso and a scoop of vegan So Delicious vanilla ice cream!

Vertical Diner's Shoofly Cake

Serves 12

For the streusel:
4   cups all-purpose flour
½   cup shortening, chilled
1   teaspoon salt
1½ cups sugar

For the cake base:
1½ cups water
½   cup sugar
½   cup molasses
1½ tablespoons white vinegar
1   tablespoon baking soda

Start with the streusel. In mixing bowl, mix flour into chilled shortening and add salt and sugar to create a crumble. Preheat the oven to 375 degrees. Grease and flour a 9 x 13 pan well. Set aside.

To assemble the cake base, in a large 1-gallon pot, mix together the water, sugar, molasses, and vinegar. Bring the liquid ingredients to a boil. When the liquid reaches a simmer, turn off heat. Add the baking soda and stir really well to prevent the liquid from foaming over. Pour the liquid into the greased cake pan.

Add the crumble evenly over the liquid in the cake pan, allowing some pieces to sink and some to float. Ideally, half of the crumble will be floating and the other half will be absorbed into the liquid.

Place the cake pan in the preheated oven and bake for approximately 1 hour, or until the cake is done—until a toothpick comes out clean with no crumbs attached. Serve this moist molasses cake with vegan ice cream or soak it up with a shot of espresso—or do both!

Sage's Tiramisu

Serves 12

For the vanilla cake:
2½ cups all-purpose flour
1¾ cups evaporated cane juice
1 teaspoon sea salt
½ tablespoon vanilla extract
1 tablespoon vinegar
⅔ cup canola or safflower oil
2 cups water

For the mascarpone-style tofu cream:
7 ounces extra-firm silken tofu, drained
14 ounces soft tofu, drained
¾ cup sugar
½ cup canola or safflower oil
¼ cup bottled lemon juice
2 teaspoons vanilla extract
1 teaspoon sea salt

For the chocolate syrup:
1¼ cups cocoa powder
1 cup water
2 cups evaporated cane juice
Pinch sea salt
1 teaspoon vanilla extract

For the mocha-rum sauce:
¼ cup rum
½ cup chocolate syrup (recipe above)
½ cup liquid espresso

To assemble:
Ground cinnamon (garnish)

> **Tip:** You can make this cake the night before the day of serving.

For the vanilla cake: Preheat the oven to 350 degrees. Place parchment paper on the bottom of each of two 9 x 13 cake pans. Sift together all dry ingredients for vanilla cake. Whisk in all the wet ingredients for the cake. Portion out an equal amount of batter into each pan. Bake in the preheated oven for approximately 12 to 15 minutes or until the cake is light brown and a toothpick comes out clean.

For the mascarpone-style tofu cream: Add all ingredients to a blender and blend together until cream is uniform. Set aside and chill.

For the chocolate syrup: Add all ingredients to a blender and blend together until the syrup is uniform and sugar is dissolved, approximately 10 minutes.

For the mocha-rum sauce: Whisk together all the sauce ingredients until all ingredients are integrated.

To assemble: Remove vanilla cakes from their pans and peel off the parchment paper. Place 1 sheet of vanilla cake on a clean 9 x 13 pan. Soak it in ¾ cup of mocha rum sauce. Once the sauce is fully absorbed into the cake, scoop up one-third of the cream mixture and spread evenly across the cake. Follow that with another sheet of cake on top of the cream. Poke this layer with a fork to allow the sauce to infuse evenly. Slowly pour the rest of the mocha rum sauce over the top sheet of cake. When this has absorbed fully, spread the rest of the cream over the top evenly. Cover the cake carefully to protect it from picking up flavors from other items and place it in the fridge. Let the cake settle and firm for at least 8 hours. Score the cake into 12 servings—this will be 3 slices by 4 slices. Use a brownie server to properly pull these slices out of pan—the cake is fragile and is best taken from the pan with a server that is flat and is the same size as the piece you are taking out. Garnish each portion with chocolate syrup recipe and ground cinnamon.

Souley Vegan

OAKLAND, CA

301 Broadway
Oakland, CA 94607
(510) 922-1615

www.souleyvegan.com

The crew at Souley Vegan is passionate, honest, and fun-loving.

Tamearra Dyson, owner and chef

Is this your first restaurant?
Yes.

When did it open?
July 2009.

Do you want to have more than one restaurant?
We'll see . . . .

What's your favorite dish on the menu?
Our okra gumbo; it's okra, corn, peppers, stewed tomatoes, seaweed, onion, garlic, spices, and love.

What's your most popular appetizer?
Fried kale and Buffalo (seitan) wings.

What's the most popular entrée on the menu?
Southern fried tofu.

What's your most popular dessert?
The cheesecake—a tofu-based dessert with raw sugar and fresh fruit.

What do you feel is special about your restaurant?
My recipes aren't from a book; they're from my heart. Our customer service also sets us apart.

How often do you change your menu items? Do you have daily or weekly specials?

We do have daily specials: Our lunch specials are from 11 am to 3 pm, and we have happy hour from 3 pm to 6 pm. I usually don't take things off the menu since everything sells really well; however, I do enjoy adding crazy new things from time to time.

Do you have gluten-free, soy-free, and sugar-free options on your menu?

Yes, plenty.

What do you do to reduce your environmental impact?

We recycle as well as compost. Of course, that's in addition to our plant-based menu, which helps with the environment.

What are the most important lessons you've learned as owner or chef of this restaurant?

As an owner, I strive to make my business consistent. Our customers rely on the quality, texture, and flavor of the food as well as the customer service to be consistently good. I try to hire people who smile naturally so they'll be able to deliver genuine warmth to our customers at Souley Vegan.

Food is art, and people appreciate it as such. I'm grateful to be able to create food from my heart and see the community enjoy it. The impact we've had on the community is humbling. I've had people come in almost in tears because their loved ones are eating our food and loving it. It's amazing, actually. To be able to change people's minds through my self-expression is a beautiful thing.

What led you to want to open a vegan restaurant, and/or what led you to the vegan diet yourself?

I've been cooking vegan food since age eighteen. I felt I had something to offer the community, so I worked hard to bring Souley Vegan to life.

Since your restaurant first opened, has your view of what constitutes healthy or delicious foods changed? Have you changed the types of foods you offer?

Yes, definitely. Our customer base has developed into not only vegan and vegetarians but meat-eaters

that are interested in changing their diet to live a better quality of life. Young and old, people are becoming aware of their health and want to do better for themselves and their families.

I am always looking to get better and do better, which is why we have options for everyone, whether you eat gluten-free, soy-free, sugar-free, etc. I cook with fresh herbs and spices that I mix myself. That builds a strong flavor, but it also happens to be immune-building and blood-cleansing. And those ingredients help to build a superior quality of life. I never thought I would be making seitan, but the community asks for it, so we make our own in-house. I learned in the process that seitan has almost zero fat and almost zero carbs, and it's packed with even more protein than meat.

Where do you see the plant-based food movement going in coming years?

I see it developing and progressing. As we get more and more vegan food options, there will be no reason for people to revert back to eating death once they've had a taste of life. 🍲

Black-Eyed Pea Fritters

Makes 20 fritters

½   cup chopped green bell pepper
½   cup chopped red onion
1   tablespoon and 2 cups plus
    1 tablespoon olive oil
½   teaspoon sea salt
½   teaspoon black pepper
¼   teaspoon cayenne pepper
1   teaspoon minced garlic
2   cups cooked black-eyed peas
½   cup water, plus more as needed
1   cup brown rice flour

In a pan, sauté the bell peppers and red onions in 1 tablespoon olive oil. Sauté for about 2 minutes then add salt, pepper, cayenne, and minced garlic. Sauté for another 2 minutes and set aside.

Combine sautéed ingredients and cooked black-eyed peas in a blender with ½ cup water. (Note: If too thick for blender to blend, then add small amounts of water as needed. The mixture needs to blend like a slightly thick cream; too much water will make it too thin.)

Pour 2 cups olive oil into a pot and place it over medium heat.

Pour blended mixture in a medium bowl and add brown rice flour. Roll into 1" balls and place the balls carefully into 1 tablespoon hot oil. Fry until golden brown. Set fried balls on a paper towel to absorb excess oil. Serve while warm.

Gluten-Free Chocolate Pudding with Cinnamon-Glazed Apples

Serves 6

2   pounds firm tofu
3½ cups cocoa powder (or more if
    you like extra chocolate)
2   cups raw sugar
¼   teaspoon sea salt
Juice of ½ lemon
1   cup water
¼   teaspoon olive oil
1   cup diced apple
1   teaspoon ground cinnamon
¼   teaspoon raw sugar

In a large bowl combine tofu, cocoa powder, raw sugar, sea salt, and lemon juice and thoroughly mix together.

Transfer the tofu-chocolate mixture to a blender and blend, adding small amounts of water until mixture looks smooth and creamy. Remove and chill in the fridge for 30 minutes.

In small pan over medium heat, add the olive oil and diced apple. Carefully turn apple pieces in pan as not to mash them. Let the apples heat for 1 minute, then add cinnamon and raw sugar. Let simmer in its juices for 1 more minute, then set aside to cool.

Place the tofu pudding in a dessert bowl, top with glazed apples, and serve!

Stuff I Eat

INGLEWOOD, CA

114 N. Market St.
Inglewood, CA 90301
(310) 671-0115

www.stuffieat.com

> Stuff I Eat is a place where you walk in and feel at home.

Babette Davis, owner and chef

Is this your first restaurant?
Yes.

When did it open?
July 2008. We are coming up on our sixth anniversary now.

Do you want to have more than one restaurant?
Sure!

What's your favorite dish on the menu?
The Kilimanjaro Quesadilla, which is a quesadilla topped with vegan cheese sauce, wild and black rice, seasoned tofu, black beans, sautéed Portobello mushrooms, mock chicken salad, carrot un-tuna, salsa corn, diced BBQ tofu, guacamole, sautéed broccoli, chopped kale, and clover sprouts.

What's your most popular appetizer?
We don't have appetizers. We don't serve appetizers because appetizers are snacks served before a main course. Our portions are hearty and guests usually end up taking some home.

What's the most popular entrée on the menu?
Currently, it's our Soul Food Platter: yams, mac 'n' cheese, BBQ tofu, kale greens, black-eyed pea soup, corn bread muffin, and potato salad.

What's your most popular dessert?
Sweet potato pie.

What do you feel is special about your restaurant?
I think it's special because it's obvious that we love what we do and people taste that in the food.

How often do you change your menu items? Do you have daily or weekly specials?
We don't change our menu items that often. That said, we're getting ready to revamp our menu now and it's been about two-and-a-half years since we last changed it. We do offer daily specials.

Do you have gluten-free, soy-free, and sugar-free options on your menu?
Yes! Our customers are welcome to tell us they can't have tofu in their entrée. We also have gluten-free items. Our new menu will indicate which items are gluten-free.

What do you do to reduce your environmental impact?
We use compostable cups, containers, and utensils made from corn. We also use silverware and plates in the restaurant to reduce waste. And we encourage our customers not to waste food.

What are the most important lessons you've learned as owner or chef of this restaurant?
I've improved my organizational skills, and that's important in all areas. I love what I do more now. I've become much more conscientious about waste. I've learned to delegate my workload.

What led you to want to open a vegan restaurant, and/or what led you to the vegan diet yourself?
I have to give my husband Ron credit for that. We met in 1990 when he was transitioning to a vegetarian diet. He had read the book *Fit for Life* by Harvey and Marilyn Diamond, and he was into running. I hardly worked out and was still eating the Standard American Diet. I read *Fit for Life* and the light was switched on, and I never turned back. Then a few years later we both went completely vegan.

I was working as an airline stewardess at the time and was tired of it. Ron would make these delicious vegan tacos and other dishes, so when I came home from my trips, he would make me food and we started talking about catering and opening a restaurant, etc., just putting it out there in the universe. We started catering and our business caught on with some of the local churches.

During that time my husband and I went walking through downtown Inglewood, noticing the vacant storefronts. One was open and the landlord was inside. He let us lease the building with no money down! We couldn't believe it. We opened our doors in July of 2008. To this day, my husband always says, "Closed mouths don't get fed!" And he's right. The message here is follow your dreams.

In the time since your restaurant first opened, how has the plant-based food movement changed? Do you find more demand now for vegan food?
It's changed so much. You go to places now that have more vegan options. And people are looking for alternative ways to eat better and healthier. Everyone knows someone who isn't well, and usually it's diet-related. Our customers want to learn more about plant-based diets and how to transition.

Since your restaurant first opened, has your view of what constitutes healthy or delicious foods changed? Have you changed the types of foods you offer?
Yes. More and more, I'm striving to add live foods to my menu. For the last several months, we've been offering raw dishes that provide live enzymes and nutrients, more so than cooked foods. I'm also into juicing. The more live foods for me, the better. Our menu continues to evolve, and I'm working on having more live-food options, which is the healthiest choice.

Where do you see the plant-based food movement going in coming years?
With the news of climate change, and changes in our food production, I think people are becoming increasingly aware that what we put on our plate has a huge impact on our environment. I see more awareness, and people are yearning to change to a healthier lifestyle. I only see growth, which is great news for Stuff I Eat and other vegan establishments. The best has yet to come! 🐾

Enchilada Pie

Serves 8–10

For the red sauce:
- 16 ounces tomato paste
- 3 cups water
- 4 tomatoes
- 2 tablespoons Bragg Liquid Aminos
- 2 tablespoons cumin
- ¼ cup agave syrup

For the cream sauce:
- 2 12-ounce packages extra-firm silken tofu
- 2 cups water
- 1 tablespoon turmeric
- ¼ cup Bragg Liquid Aminos
- 1 tablespoon nutritional yeast

To assemble:
- 1 dozen corn tortillas
- 3 cups cooked yellow polenta
- 4 cups unsalted corn chips
- 2 cups corn
- 2 10-ounce packages Follow Your Heart Vegan Gourmet Cheddar, grated
- Pinch paprika (optional)

Add all red sauce ingredients except agave to a blender and blend on a high speed. Add the agave syrup to adjust the sweetness to taste. Set aside.

Add all cream sauce ingredients to a blender and blend on a high speed. The sauce should have a "cheesy" taste to it and a golden yellow color (due to the turmeric).

To assemble: Preheat the oven to 350 degrees. Take a 4-quart pan with a lid and begin to layer your ingredients. Start with 1 cup red sauce, then ¼ cup cream sauce. Then take 3 to 4 corn tortillas and dip them in your red sauce and lay in dish.

Next, add about a 1"-thick layer of polenta. Repeat with another cup of red sauce and ¼ cup cream sauce. Repeat with the 3 to 4 tortilla shells dipped in red sauce. Then add the corn chips and corn. Repeat with red sauce and cream sauce. Then add your final layer of tortillas dipped in red sauce and top with grated vegan cheese and sprinkle a little paprika on top, if using. Cover pan with a lid and bake in the preheated oven for approximately 30 to 40 minutes. Remove when the cheese is nice and melted on top.

Chocolate Bundt Cake

Makes 1 bundt cake

¾   cup agave syrup
½   cup cold-pressed, extra-virgin
     olive oil
2   cups almond milk
2   cups barley flour
1   teaspoon baking powder
½   teaspoon baking soda
1   teaspoon ground cinnamon
1   teaspoon vanilla powder
1   teaspoon sea salt

Preheat the oven to 300 degrees. Grease a bundt pan and set aside. Place the agave syrup, olive oil, and almond milk in a blender and blend on high speed until thoroughly mixed. Place barley flour, baking powder, baking soda, cinnamon, vanilla powder, and sea salt in a mixing bowl and whisk together. Add the wet mix to the dry using a whisk, stirring until smooth. Pour the cake mixture into the greased bundt pan. Place in the preheated oven and bake for 30 minutes. (Bake until a toothpick comes out clean with no crumbs attached.)

Remove the pan and let it cool. Serve alone or with fresh fruit.

Sublime

FORT LAUDERDALE, FL

1431 N. Federal Hwy.
Fort Lauderdale, FL 33304
(954) 615-1431

www.sublimerestaurant.com

Showing how "plant-based food can indeed be sublime," as the company's motto states, Fort Lauderdale–based Sublime Restaurant & Bar makes you feel extra-good about eating vegan because it donates one-hundred percent of its profits to animal welfare.

Nanci Alexander, owner

Is this your first restaurant?
Yes.

When did it open?
2003.

Do you want to have more than one restaurant?
Perhaps.

What's your favorite dish on the menu?
All, but especially the fire-roasted artichoke with panko and garlic "butter."

What's your most popular appetizer?
Frito Misto, with crispy cauliflower, sweet chili sauce, and sesame seed.

What's the most popular entrée on the menu?
Vegetable lasagna.

What's your most popular dessert?
The coconut cake.

What do you feel is special about your restaurant?
Sublime donates one-hundred percent of its profits to animal welfare.

How often do you change your menu items? Do you have daily or weekly specials?

We change our menu items regularly. We have specials based on the availability of ingredients from our garden.

Do you have gluten-free, soy-free, and sugar-free options on your menu?

Yes, we have gluten-free and soy-free items.

What do you do to reduce your environmental impact?

Sublime has an aggressive recycling program, serves water purified on site (instead of bottled water), and uses state-of-the-art energy-monitoring equipment.

What are the most important lessons you've learned as owner or chef of this restaurant?

Listen to guests, not salespeople.

What led you to want to open a vegan restaurant, and/or what led you to the vegan diet yourself?

Wanting people to have the opportunity to experience sublime vegan cuisine in a sublime

atmosphere. Animals raised and tortured for food suffer in great numbers every second, and humans can help to reduce the suffering. It's all about what people choose to eat.

In the time since your restaurant first opened, how has the plant-based food movement changed? Do you find more demand now for vegan food?

The plant-based food movement has changed, with a growing number of people becoming informed of the health benefits. Thus, more demand for vegan food.

Since your restaurant first opened, has your view of what constitutes healthy or delicious foods changed? Have you changed the types of foods you offer?

Although the menu changes, my view regarding healthy or delicious food has not changed.

Where do you see the plant-based food movement going in coming years?

Meat, dairy, and egg substitutes will continue to improve and become more Sublime. More establishments, such as arenas and cruise ships, will offer plant-based food because it is a good business decision. 🍃

This spicy Asian dish gives you a hint of the tropics with its inclusion of coconut milk in the sauce.

Thai Red Curry

Serves 4–6

For the red curry sauce:
1   14-ounce can coconut milk
2   tablespoons plus 1 teaspoon
     red curry paste
2   teaspoons lime juice
Pinch sea salt
Pinch white pepper

For the vegetables and rice:
¼   cup vegetable oil
1   cup broccoli florets
½   cup sliced celery
½   cup julienned carrots
½   cup sliced onions
½   cup julienned red peppers
½   cup sugar snap peas
¼   cup cilantro
¼   cup sliced scallions
½   cup sliced water chestnuts
½   cup bean sprouts
Drizzle sesame oil

To assemble:
2   cups jasmine rice (cooked or
     steamed according to package)
Cilantro and scallions (garnish)

Whisk all ingredients for the red curry sauce together until curry paste is well blended and set aside.

Heat the vegetable oil in a large sauté pan over a medium-high burner. Sauté all vegetables together, except water chestnuts and bean sprouts, for 5 to 7 minutes until they begin to crisp. When the other vegetables are crisp, toss in the water chestnuts and sprouts along with a drizzle of sesame oil. Sauté another minute. Add red curry sauce, stir together, and remove from heat.

To assemble: Place the rice in the center of dish, scoop vegetables on top of rice, and pour the curry sauce around the edge of the rice. Garnish with cilantro and scallions.

Sublime Apple Crumb Pie à la Mode (see photo on page 233)

Makes one 9" pie

For the pie dough:
1¼ cups unbleached all-purpose flour
¼ teaspoon salt
2 tablespoons vegan butter substitute
3 tablespoons shortening
½ cup ice water

For the oatmeal streusel:
2¼ tablespoons vegan butter substitute
2½ tablespoons sugar
3 tablespoons brown sugar
5 tablespoons all-purpose flour
2½ tablespoons oats
Pinch cinnamon

For the filling:
8 Granny Smith apples
1⅓ cups sugar
1 tablespoon ground cinnamon
5 tablespoons vegan butter substitute
½ cup currants
2 tablespoons cornstarch

For the pie dough: Mix together the flour and salt. Use dough cutter to cut butter and shortening into the flour until crumbles are about the size of quarters. Slowly add in ice water sparingly (amount may vary). Keep the dough floury and dry. Wrap and refrigerate while preparing streusel and filling.

For the oatmeal streusel: Add the vegan butter and sugar to a mixing bowl. Using a mixer, cream together the butter and sugar, mixing well. Combine the brown sugar, flour, oats, and cinnamon in a bowl and whisk together. Add the dry mixture to the butter mix and combine.

For the filling: Peel and core apples, cut into quarters, and then slice them into thin slices. Cook the apples in a large pot on the stovetop over medium heat with sugar, cinnamon, vegan butter, and currants until half cooked, al dente (cooked so as to be firm but not hard). Remove and drain the juices into a container. Place those drained juices into the pot and bring to a boil. Make a slurry by whisking water with cornstarch until you achieve a thin, muddy consistency, and then add the slurry to the pot of apple juices boiling on the stove. Bring to a boil for about 10 minutes while stirring carefully and cook the starch out. It will become a little thicker and not as light. Stir apples back into the cornstarch and apple reduction mix. Remove from the heat and set aside.

To assemble: Preheat the oven to 350 degrees. Roll the piecrust out on a floured surface and place it into a 9" greased pie pan. Fill the pie shell with the apple mixture. Top with about ¼" streusel. Place the pie pan into the heated oven and bake for about 30 to 40 minutes. Remove and let it cool before cutting. Serve with a scoop of your favorite vegan vanilla ice cream.

SunCafé Organic

LOS ANGELES, CA

3711 Cahuenga Blvd.
Studio City, CA 91604
(818) 308-7420

www.suncafe.com

SunCafé creates raw and cooked vegan food so tasty and full of flavor that no one ever goes away feeling deprived for eating healthy!

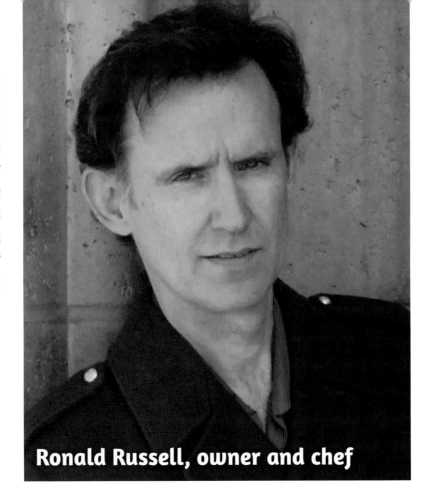

Ronald Russell, owner and chef

Is this your first restaurant?
Yes, but I have since added The Plum Café & Bakery in Sacramento.

When did SunCafé open?
May 2009.

Do you want to have more restaurants?
We are in the process of opening more SunCafés.

How many do you hope to have in the future?
Our goal is to have one or two cafés in most major cities.

What's your favorite dish on the menu?
Nachos with SunChorizo.

What's your most popular appetizer?
Lettuce Leaf Tacos, raw tacos with SunChorizo, avocado, and cashew cheese.

What's the most popular entrée on the menu?
Our award-winning, gluten-free mac and cheese.

What's your most popular dessert?
Chocolate almond-butter pie.

What do you feel is special about your restaurant?
The growth of our menu, developed by many chef contributors and the owners, who are total foodies; this gives us a wide variety of dish profiles. Also, our extensive raw food selection has been voted the best raw food in Los Angeles.

How often do you change your menu items? Do you have daily or weekly specials?
We have monthly specials, and we change our menu every six months to add new and seasonal choices.

Do you have gluten-free, soy-free, and sugar-free options on your menu?
We have a large selection of soy-, gluten-, and sugar-free options. All our desserts are gluten-free; all our sandwiches have three gluten-free bun options. We don't use sucrose in any dish made at the restaurant.

What do you do to reduce your environmental impact?
We use biodegradable to-go containers and recycled materials wherever possible. We also only buy organic produce.

What are the most important lessons you've learned as owner or chef of this restaurant?
One lesson we live by is an unflinching commitment to quality. In the beginning, we found it difficult to be consistent. We've come a long way.

What led you to want to open a vegan restaurant, and/or what led you to the vegan diet yourself?
I was a chef through college and couldn't stand the sight of meat on a grill after a while. I never ate meat or eggs again after that experience. I gave up all milk products about fifteen years ago.

In the time since your restaurant first opened, how has the plant-based food movement changed? Do you find more demand now for vegan food?
It's exciting to see an increasing number people turn toward a more natural, sustainable, healthy vegan diet. It's definitely a quickly growing trend.

Since your restaurant first opened, has your view of what constitutes healthy or delicious foods changed? Have you changed the types of foods you offer?
We are never satisfied with the quality of our food at SunCafé Organic. We've won close to a dozen food awards, but we always strive to be better, more innovative, and more exciting for our customers. Our goal is to shock people with how good raw food and cooked vegan food can be. We've had customers and critics compare SunCafé's food to three-Michelin-starred restaurants in Paris and such food institutions as Spago and Mastro's Steakhouse.

Where do you see the plant-based food movement going in coming years?
It continues to grow and I see no reason for that growth to slow down. We also have many customers that tell us they've overcome major health issues such as heart disease, diabetes, and even cancer through eating a raw, nutrient-dense diet. It's exciting to see people making transformations in the quality of their health and their life. 🍃

Moroccan Tajine

Serves 4

For the sauce:
½ cup sesame seeds
½ cup water
⅛ cup lemon juice
1½ teaspoons sea salt
½ teaspoon minced garlic
½ teaspoon paprika
½ teaspoon ground cinnamon
2 tablespoons extra-virgin olive oil

For the stew:
1 carrot, chopped
2 celery stalks, chopped
½ cup peas (fresh or frozen)
1 large zucchini, chopped
½ apple, chopped
¼ cup minced onion
¼ cup chopped green onion
2 tablespoons chopped fresh dill

For the date/cinnamon sauce:
½ cup whole dates
1 teaspoon ground cinnamon
Small pinch cayenne
2½ cups water

To assemble:
½ cup raisins (garnish)
Dill sprigs (garnish)

Preheat the oven to 300 degrees. Gather together the sauce ingredients in a blender. Mix on high until smooth. Next gather together the stew ingredients. Mix them with the sauce in a large bowl. Place on a baking tray and bake in the heated oven for 15 minutes. Set aside.

Combine all the date/cinnamon sauce ingredients in a blender. Blend on high until smooth. Set aside.

To assemble: Mold tajine in 3½" mold circles or use a 1-cup measuring cup. Drizzle date/cinnamon sauce over the top and around the plate. Garnish with raisins and dill sprigs, then serve.

True Bistro

SOMERVILLE, MA

1153 Broadway
Somerville, MA 02144
(617) 627-9000

www.truebistroboston.com

True Bistro serves extraordinary vegan cuisine created from the highest quality and freshest plant-based ingredients, providing an upscale vegan refuge for the Greater Boston area.

Stuart Reiter, co-owner and chef

Is this your first restaurant?
This is the first and only True Bistro.

When did it open?
November 2010.

Do you want to have more than one restaurant?
Not at this time.

What's your favorite dish on the menu?
The Vietnamese crepe: hon shimeji mushrooms, fried tofu, and mung sprouts, served with a spicy dipping sauce.

What's your most popular appetizer?
Our house-made ravioli with sweet potato and galangal filling and a citrus-infused coconut cream sauce.

What's the most popular entrée on the menu?
The blackened seitan with creamy grits and collard greens.

What's your most popular dessert?
The Death by Chocolate cake.

What do you feel is special about your restaurant?
Our ability to reach out to customers beyond the vegetarian community is what's special about True Bistro.

How often do you change your menu items? Do you have daily or weekly specials?
Seasonally. We do not have specials, but do offer prix-fixe menus on holidays.

Do you have gluten-free, soy-free, and sugar-free options on your menu?
We have several gluten-free options.

What do you do to reduce your environmental impact?
We compost our vegetable scraps. Our fry oil is collected and used as biodiesel by local companies. And we participate in our city's recycling program.

What are the most important lessons you've learned as owner or chef of this restaurant?
The most important lesson I've learned is to continue to be open to new ideas.

What led you to want to open a vegan restaurant, and/or what led you to the vegan diet yourself?
There was a need for an upscale vegan restaurant in the Boston area, which led to the decision to open True Bistro. I personally became vegan as part of my commitment to animal welfare.

In the time since your restaurant first opened, how has the plant-based food movement changed? Do you find more demand now for vegan food?
We are relatively new and have not gained this perspective yet.

Since your restaurant first opened, has your view of what constitutes healthy or delicious foods changed? Have you changed the types of foods you offer?
I try to put an emphasis on showcasing plants rather than replicating animal-based foods. This has been my view for a number of years, but I was unsure if others would be like-minded. I am grateful that the response to my approach has been positive.

Where do you see the plant-based food movement going in coming years?
I believe that the movement will slowly increase with time and that one day the variety of factors that draw people to this diet (animal welfare, environmentalism, health) will lead to a majority of people adopting a plant-based diet.

Phyllo Triangles with Sorrel Cream

Serves 4–6

For the stuffing:
4 yellow onions, sliced
8 cloves garlic, sliced
1 tablespoon sunflower oil
1 bunch red Swiss chard, stems removed
½ bunch fresh Italian parsley, leaves picked
8 stalks oregano, leaves picked
1 pound firm tofu, drained
1 tablespoon nutritional yeast
1½ teaspoons Champagne vinegar
1½ teaspoons sea salt
1 teaspoon ground black pepper
2 tablespoons tahini
2 tablespoons extra-virgin olive oil

For the sorrel cream:
½ cup sliced shallot
1 teaspoon extra-virgin olive oil
½ teaspoon sea salt
½ cup Sauvignon Blanc
¾ cup sorrel
2 tablespoons chervil
1 cup cashew cream (or other nondairy cream substitute)
1 teaspoon Dijon mustard
A few shavings nutmeg

To assemble:
1 1-pound package phyllo
¼ cup toasted almonds
¼ cup toasted and peeled hazelnuts
1 tablespoon extra-virgin olive oil, for brushing

To garnish (optional):
Toasted pine nuts
Blanched haricots verts
Chervil leaves

Combine the sliced yellow onions, garlic cloves, and sunflower oil in a heavy sauté pan. Cook over low heat, stirring frequently, until deep golden brown. Set aside to cool. Meanwhile, bring several quarts of water to a boil and put a bowl of ice water to the side of that. Salt the water and then plunge the Swiss chard, parsley, and oregano in to the boiling water. Cook the greens for half a minute and then move them to ice water. When the greens are cool, remove them from the ice water and press out as much water as possible, and then chop them finely. In a stand mixer combine all of the stuffing ingredients and mix well. Taste and adjust the seasoning to suit your palate. Set aside.

For the sorrel cream: In a pan over high heat, sweat the shallot in the olive oil with the sea salt. When the shallot is translucent, add the wine and reduce by half. Add the sorrel and chervil and cover the pot for 3 minutes. Stir in the cashew cream, mustard, and nutmeg, and gently bring the mixture to a simmer. Blend the sauce and return it to the pot and keep warm over very low heat. Taste and adjust the salt to your palate. Set aside.

To assemble: Preheat your oven to 350 degrees. Remove the phyllo dough from the fridge to thaw on the countertop. Place the almonds and hazelnuts in a food processor and grind them until they resemble a fine meal. Take the phyllo and remove a single layer. Cut the sheet in to a strip approximately 3 x 8. Brush the phyllo with a thin layer of olive oil and then sprinkle lightly with some of the crushed nuts. Place ¼ cup of the tofu stuffing at one end and then fold the phyllo to form triangles, in the manner of folding a flag. Brush the top of the triangle with more olive oil. Continue this process with the remaining tofu mixture. Place the

triangles on a baking tray and bake the phyllo in the oven until golden brown, approximately 10 minutes.

Spoon warm sorrel cream on a plate and stack 2 phyllo triangles on top. Top with one of the optional garnishes, if using.

Pumpkin Cheesecake with Bourbon-Brown Sugar Cream

Serves 12

For the crust:
5   dates, soaked in warm water
1½ cups pecans, lightly toasted
Pinch salt

For the filling:
3   cups cashew pieces, soaked 1 to
    2 hours
1¼ cups almond milk
¾   cup dark agave syrup
1   cup pumpkin puree
2   tablespoons lemon juice
1   teaspoon ground cinnamon
½   teaspoon ground ginger
¼   teaspoon ground cloves
¼   teaspoon ground nutmeg
¼   teaspoon allspice
¼   teaspoon sea salt
¾   cup plus 2 tablespoons
    coconut oil
2   tablespoons liquid lecithin

*For the bourbon–brown sugar
cream:*
4   tablespoons brown sugar
3   tablespoons bourbon
¾   cup almond milk
½   teaspoon agar powder
3   tablespoons almond oil

Drain the dates and peel off the skin and remove the seeds. Process the pecans with the dates and salt in a food processor until a fine meal is formed. Press the meal into the bottom of a 9" springform pan.

Add all filling ingredients to the blender, minus the coconut oil and the liquid lecithin, and blend until smooth, 2 to 3 minutes.

Add the coconut oil and lecithin to the blender and incorporate fully. Pour the contents of the blender in the springform pan containing the crust. Tap the pan on the counter several times to remove air bubbles and then smooth the top. Place in the freezer for 2 hours, then transfer to the fridge overnight to set.

In a saucepan, melt the sugar with the bourbon over low heat. Whisk in the almond milk and agar. Cook at a simmer for 5 minutes, then transfer to a pan to cool. When the mixture is cool and has set, stir in the almond oil. Use the cream as a plate garnish by placing the slices of the cheesecake atop it.

Vegetarian Haven

TORONTO, ON, CANADA

17 Baldwin St.
Toronto, ON M5T 1L1 Canada
(416) 621-3636

www.vegetarianhaven.com

A vegan bistro serving eclectic, wholesome Asian fusion cuisine in an elegantly casual dining atmosphere, Vegetarian Haven is in a historic downtown Toronto neighborhood.

Shing Tong, owner and chef

Is this your first restaurant?
No.

When did it open?
2003.

Do you want to have more than one restaurant?
Not a primary consideration at this time.

What's your favorite dish on the menu?
The chef's special, which changes every day.

What's your most popular appetizer?
Seared vegetable dumplings.

What's the most popular entrée on the menu?
Chef's special.

What's your most popular dessert?
Tofu cheesecake.

What do you feel is special about your restaurant?
The restaurant has a cozy, genuine atmosphere, which creates a sense of connectedness between our patrons and the restaurant.

How often do you change your menu items? Do you have daily or weekly specials?
We generally make small ingredient changes for summer and winter. We have a daily special that incorporates seasonal produce.

Do you have gluten-free, soy-free, and sugar-free options on your menu?
Yes.

What do you do to reduce your environmental impact?
We choose local seasonal produce over imported. We use recycled products. And we are retrofitted with energy-efficient lighting and low-flow faucets.

What are the most important lessons you've learned as owner or chef of this restaurant?
You can't please everybody, but always be kind.

What led you to want to open a vegan restaurant, and/or what led you to the vegan diet yourself?
One evening, my husband and I got lost on our way to my mother-in-law's birthday celebration. We drove into a shopping plaza and parked in front of a restaurant. I dashed in to ask for directions. To my surprise, it was a vegetarian restaurant. I didn't know we had vegetarian restaurants in Toronto.

(This was twenty-seven years ago.) From that point on, I returned there every chance I got to try various dishes. In later years, I explored vegetarian restaurants in other cities such as Los Angeles, New York, Houston, Vancouver, and Hong Kong. My catalog of vegetarian dishes slowly expanded. I am very thankful to these restaurants for showing me that vegetarian food can be varied and delicious. They inspired me to learn to cook vegetarian food—I realized that I wanted to provide the same inspiration to new vegetarians that they had provided me. (More of my story is available under "How It All Began" on www.vegetarianhaven.com.)

In the time since your restaurant first opened, how has the plant-based food movement changed? Do you find more demand now for vegan food?
There's a greater understanding now about the benefits of a plant-based diet. It has become more accepted. Demand for vegan food is definitely growing.

Since your restaurant first opened, has your view of what constitutes healthy or delicious foods changed? Have you changed the types of foods you offer?
My view of what kinds of food to offer is fundamentally the same, but it's also evolved as new information is discovered.

Where do you see the plant-based food movement going in coming years?
It will continue to grow exponentially. 🐚

The legend: Eighteen arhats (spiritual practitioners, destroyers of enemies, enlightened beings) were gathering to attend the Buddha's birthday celebration. They could not come to a consensus on what gift to bring. After a long discussion, they decided to each pick an ingredient and cook a dish for the Buddha. And the Buddha was delighted, hence this recipe's name.

There is an unspoken respect for this dish in that, if you order Buddha's Delight in any Chinese restaurant anywhere in the world, the chef understands that this is to be cooked without meat and worthy of the Buddha.

Buddha's Delight

Serves 4–6

6   dried shiitake mushrooms
4   dried red dates*
6   dried wood ear mushrooms*
6   dried cloud ear mushrooms*
10 dried lily flowers*
6   thumb-size pieces dried black moss
2   sticks dried bean curd
¼   cup uncooked glass noodles (mung bean noodles)
1   tablespoon minced fresh ginger
6   canned straw mushrooms, halved
10 fresh or canned water chestnuts
10 fresh or canned ginkgo nuts
10 baby carrots
10 fresh or canned bamboo shoots, cut into 2" slices
3   whole small bok choy heads cut into quarters
1   cup puffy seitan chunks*
8   leaves napa cabbage, halved
3   tablespoons sunflower oil
3   tablespoons light soy sauce
3   tablespoons dark soy sauce
2   tablespoons soy paste*
2   tablespoons sesame seed oil
Pinch sugar (optional)
1   tablespoon minced fresh ginger
2   cups vegetable stock
10 snow peas

* These ingredients can be found in an Asian food market.

Soak shiitake mushrooms, red dates, wood ear mushrooms, cloud ear mushrooms, lily flowers, black moss, bean curd sticks, and glass noodles in water for about 30 minutes to rehydrate them until soft. Cut the shiitake mushrooms and red dates into halves, and cut the glass noodles and bean curd sticks into 2" strips.

In a wok or saucepot, sauté the minced ginger and shiitake mushrooms over medium heat for 2 minutes. Add all the previously soaked ingredients except the glass noodles (they will dissolve if put in too early) plus straw mushrooms through sunflower oil and cook for another minute. Add all seasonings and vegetable stock to the wok or pot, cover, and cook in a slow simmer. Stir occasionally. Cook until sauce thickens, approximately 20 minutes. Toss in presoaked glass noodles and follow with the snow peas (adding them at the end to retain their bright green color and crunchy texture). Stir the noodles in the sauce, remove from heat, and serve.

This is a simple salad dressing that can be whipped up easily with a few ingredients and can be kept refrigerated for a week or two. It is refreshing and aromatic and is a great dressing for any salad.

Gluten-Free Ginger-Sesame Vinaigrette

Makes 1 cup

¼ cup minced fresh ginger*
¼ cup red rice vinegar
¼ cup sesame seed oil
¼ cup Bragg Liquid Aminos**
4 tablespoons sugar
1 teaspoon toasted black sesame seeds

* Make sure you use fresh ginger root, not ginger powder.

** If you don't need this dressing to be gluten-free, you can use soy sauce instead of Bragg Liquid Aminos.

Mix all ingredients in a bowl. Stir well until sugar is dissolved in the liquid.

Veggie Grill

MULTIPLE LOCATIONS

The Dome in Hollywood
6374-A Sunset Blvd.
Hollywood, CA 90028
(323) 962-3354

(Other locations in California, Oregon, and Washington)

www.veggiegrill.com

A healthy, vegan alternative to traditional burger-and-fries joints, Veggie Grill serves delicious, inexpensive, and approachable plant-based food in a friendly and convenient setting.

Ray White, cofounder

Is this your first restaurant?
No, I have owned and operated eight previous restaurants.

When did the first Veggie Grill open?
Our first Veggie Grill restaurant opened in 2006 at University Center in Irvine.

What's your favorite dish on the menu?
Without a doubt, it is the Bali Bliss, with blackened tempeh, grilled onions, jalapeños, avocado, lettuce, and tomato.

What's your most popular appetizer?
Our crispy "chicken" wings—Buffalo-style.

What's the most popular entrée on the menu?
Our All Hail Kale salad and Santa Fe Crispy Chickin' sandwich.

What's your most popular dessert?
Our carrot cake. People can't believe it contains no eggs, dairy, refined sugars, trans fats, or cholesterol.

What do you feel is special about your restaurant?
We make plant-based food that's surprisingly delicious and appealing for everyone.

How often do you change your menu items? Do you have daily or weekly specials?
Currently, we change our menu two times a year—in the spring and fall. We are not currently offering daily or weekly menu specials.

Do you have gluten-free, soy-free, and sugar-free options on your menu?

Yes. We have many gluten-free, soy-free, and sugar-free options available for guests. We also offer plenty of options free of specific allergens.

What do you do to reduce your environmental impact?

By offering a plant-based menu, we're automatically good for the planet, but we also provide recyclable packaging.

What are the most important lessons you've learned as owner or chef of this restaurant?

You must always stay the course no matter what outcomes develop. You must always believe in your passion.

What led you to want to open a vegan restaurant, and/or what led you to the vegan diet yourself?

It was a personal quest for me as I had lost family members due to heart disease. I wanted to develop a food culture of conscious eating to reduce cholesterol in your diet. This is my passion and my mission to change the world.

In the time since your restaurant first opened, how has the plant-based food movement changed?

Do you find more demand now for vegan food?

When I started twenty years ago, the plant-based movement was primarily made up of women, college students, and the gay community. Today, the stats have changed dramatically, with men and women being close to equal, and more and more of the African-American and Hispanic communities getting onboard. These inroads with mainstream America are an indication that the vegan culture is really starting to take off.

Since your restaurant first opened, has your view of what constitutes healthy or delicious foods changed? Have you changed the types of foods you offer?

Food fads come and go, but the fundamental building blocks of flavor, texture, and appearance are always important. I firmly believe in the adage "you are what you eat." The cleaner you eat, the cleaner your body wants you to eat; it is a fundamental law of nature. And so these fundamentals have not changed in our approach to food.

Where do you see the plant-based food movement going in coming years?

This movement is growing here in America. I believe an entire generation is making a conscious change to eat more mindfully. Enjoying a plant-based diet is no longer a fringe movement. 🌱

Crostini Italiano (pictured opposite)

Serves 4–6

1   package Field Roast Italian
    Sausage*
2   tablespoons olive oil
½   teaspoon crushed garlic
3   tablespoons chopped chives
Pinch salt
Pinch freshly ground pepper
1   French bread baguette, sliced
1   4-ounce jar of olive tapenade
1   8-ounce container Tofutti
    cream cheese, at room
    temperature

* Vegan, available at Whole Foods.

Remove casing from Field Roast Sausage. In a skillet over medium-high heat, warm 2 tablespoons of olive oil. Add the sausage and brown evenly on all sides, for approximately 5 minutes. Remove the sausage from skillet, pat it dry with a paper towel, and let it cool for 5 minutes. Chop it coarsely.

In separate bowl, combine crushed garlic and chives with the salt and pepper and mix thoroughly. Slice the baguette in ½"-thick rounds. Brown in toaster oven at 375 degrees (or under the broiler) for approximately 2 minutes.

To assemble: Take a toasted baguette round, top with 1 teaspoon of olive tapenade, 1 teaspoon of coarsely chopped sausage, and 1 dollop of vegan cream cheese. Repeat with the remaining slices of bread. Serve and enjoy.

Farr (Out) Yam

Serves 4–6

1   cup farro
5   medium-size yams
1   medium onion, diced
⅛   cup olive oil
2   cloves garlic, minced
2   cups shredded Brussels sprouts
1   8-ounce bag baby spinach
3   tablespoons balsamic vinegar
1   teaspoon Earth Balance butter
    substitute
Pinch salt and pinch freshly
    ground pepper, to taste

Preheat the oven to 375 degrees. Place the farro in a large pot and add water to cover. Bring to a boil. Lower heat and simmer 50 minutes. Remove from the heat and drain the farro in a colander. Bake the yams in the preheated oven for 30 minutes.

In the meantime, place the onion in a pan and sauté with olive oil over medium-high heat. When onion is translucent, add minced garlic. Cook for 1 minute. Add the Brussels sprouts, and cook for 2 minutes. Add spinach, cook for 1 minute, then mix together thoroughly. Stir in 3 tablespoons of balsamic vinegar. Remove from heat and cover.

To assemble: Split the yams open. Add Earth Balance butter substitute and approximately 3 tablespoons of farro to each. Top that with a generous serving of sautéed vegetables. Add salt and pepper to taste.

Cherry Royal

Serves 4–6

2 teaspoons powdered sugar

1 8-ounce container Tofutti cream cheese, at room temperature

¼ cup minced vegan maraschino cherries*

⅛ cup cherry juice (from maraschino cherries jar)

6 Newman-O's Original cream-filled chocolate cookies*

2 bananas, sliced in half

1 scoop soy chocolate cherry ice cream (or your favorite vegan ice cream)**

1 teaspoon vegan chocolate syrup (like Santa Cruz)

1 teaspoon ground flaxseed

4 vegan maraschino cherries (garnish)

* Available at Whole Foods.

** Available at Trader Joe's.

In a large bowl combine powdered sugar and cream cheese. Mix thoroughly. Combine the minced cherries and cherry juice with the cream cheese mixture.

To assemble, crumble 1 cookie in the bottom of an individual serving bowl, add a banana slice, 1 scoop of cherry ice cream, a drizzle of chocolate syrup, and a dollop of the sweetened cream cheese. Sprinkle with ground flaxseed. Place 1 cherry on top. Repeat with the other servings.

Veggies on Fire

THE HAGUE, NETHERLANDS

Beeklaan 385
The Hague, Netherlands 2562 AZ
+31-070-361-7406

www.veggiesonfire.nl

Veggies on Fire is a modern and welcoming restaurant that takes plant-based cuisine into the twenty-first century.

John and Carin Galstaun, chefs and owners

Is this your first restaurant?
Yes.

When did it open?
April 12, 2013.

Do you want to have more than one restaurant?
We have no definite plans.

What's your favorite dish on the menu?
The chocolate mousse, which is made with wonderful, rich, organic dark chocolate and maple syrup.

What's your most popular appetizer?
The Thai Tempeh Tempura; it's a delicately spiced Thai red-curry tempeh, fried in a light rice-flour batter and served with a homemade wasabi mayonnaise—all organic ingredients, of course.

What's the most popular entrée on the menu?
The chipotle burger, consisting of brown rice, three kinds of beans, oat flakes, and chipotle, jalapeño, poblano, and amarillo peppers, served on a homemade bun. Delicately flavored, spicy, and addictive. Every bite makes you want to eat more.

What's your most popular dessert?
The lemon cheesecake is definitely the most popular dessert. The combination of tangy lemon and naturally sweetened raspberry sauce is simply irresistible.

What do you feel is special about your restaurant?
The dishes and interior are timeless yet modern. The food is truly artisan with no processed ingredients, and we use local, organic seasonal vegetables.

How often do you change your menu items? Do you have daily or weekly specials?

We change our menu quarterly, adjusting the nature of the dishes according to the changes in climate. Our spring and summer menus will include more leafy veggies; we'll use lighter sauces and dressings, giving the dish an overall cooling character. When fall and winter come around, the dishes become more warming in nature (stews, baked items, etc.).

Do you have gluten-free, soy-free, and sugar-free options on your menu?

We have several gluten-free items on the menu, a real favorite being our shepherd's pie that contains potatoes, yams, and seasonal vegetables served with a fresh leafy salad with homemade low-fat orange-ginger dressing. But almost every item on the menu can be altered to suit gluten-free guests.

What do you do to reduce your environmental impact?

All our veggies are delivered in returnable crates, so there's no packaging material [waste]. We took great care in designing the restaurant using only environmentally safe paints. We used local wood in building the kitchen extension and the bar, sourced from forests no farther than twenty miles away from the Hague.

What are the most important lessons you've learned as owner or chef of this restaurant?

Not coming from the hospitality business at all, we discovered that restaurant work is extremely hard but ultimately gratifying. With all the preparations, we have a full day of work behind us already once we open our doors to the guests at 5 pm. And then we have a full night ahead of us. We weren't accustomed to that, but realizing you have fulfilled your dream and can now bring plant-based whole-food nutrition to the world, while at the same time reducing animal cruelty, makes it very satisfying.

What led you to want to open a vegan restaurant, and/or what led you to the vegan diet yourself?

When we met in 1994, we both decided to become vegetarian, and we both became vegan ten years ago.

We were one-hundred-percent motivated by all the animal cruelty going on, realizing that the meat and dairy industries were by far the largest contributors to all the suffering.

We were never satisfied by what was available in supermarkets or in restaurants, so we both delved into the culinary aspects of plant-based food. And then we decided to turn our lives around; we gave up our office jobs and started building this restaurant. When we lived in Florida, we were just around the corner from Sublime Restaurant; we've been going there since the third day it opened many years ago. It definitely served as a great example to us.

In the time since your restaurant first opened, how has the plant-based food movement changed? Do you find more demand now for vegan food?

We've noticed an increased demand for plant-based food. [This] is a great movement for people for whom mere vegetarian food does not suffice any longer. They have moved to the next level.

Since your restaurant first opened, has your view of what constitutes healthy or delicious foods changed? Have you changed the types of foods you offer?

Our view of what constitutes healthy and delicious food was firmly established a couple of years ago and has not really changed since we opened the restaurant, and I dare say, I don't think it'll change any time soon. Food should be pure, whole, and delicious. These three basic building blocks are unchangeable and fixed, while also providing you with infinite possibilities to produce the best-tasting, best-looking, and most nutritious dishes in the world.

Where do you see the plant-based food movement going in coming years?

We see it growing, definitely. It is so encouraging when we hear guests talking about books like *The China Study* as though it is a standard text. We'll learn more and more, and we'll refine the knowledge we gather; it'll be empowering and exciting. 🐖

Red Curry Tempeh Tempura

Serves 4

For the Thai red curry tempeh:
5   shallots, chopped
6   red chili peppers, chopped
4   cloves garlic, chopped
4   2" pieces galangal, chopped
Juice of 6 limes
2   tablespoons ground coriander
2   teaspoons salt
½   cup walnut oil (or other nut oil)
6" piece lemongrass, chopped
1   6-ounce block tempeh, cut into
    ⅓"-wide strips

For the tempura batter:
1   cup all-purpose flour
1   cup rice flour
1   teaspoon salt
1½ cups cold water

For the wasabi mayonnaise:
1   cup soy milk
Pinch salt
1   tablespoon mustard
3   tablespoons lemon juice
½   teaspoon wasabi paste
2   cups neutral vegetable oil
    (peanut or rice bran)

To assemble:
Vegetable oil, for frying
2½ cups arugula
12 cherry tomatoes, quartered
½   bell pepper, thinly sliced
1   tablespoon lemon juice

Add all red curry tempeh ingredients, minus the tempeh strips, to a bowl. Using an immersion blender, blend all the ingredients into a paste. Massage the paste carefully into the tempeh strips and let them marinate in the refrigerator for at least 1 hour.

To make the tempura batter, whisk together flours and salt in a small bowl. Just before use, add cold water and mix until it has the thickness of a heavy syrup.

Combine all wasabi mayonnaise ingredients, minus the oil, in a bowl and blend well with an immersion blender. Once the ingredients have combined, slowly drizzle in the oil while continuing to blend. Mixture should become nice and thick. Cool in refrigerator until ready for use.

To assemble: Add oil to a saucepan and heat over high heat. Dip the marinated strips of tempeh carefully into the tempura batter until fully coated. Fry the tempeh strips until golden brown, approximately 2½ minutes. Remove them from the pan and place them on a plate covered with a paper towel to soak up any excess oil. Repeat with the remaining tempeh strips.

To plate, place some arugula on the dish. Add pieces of tomato and bell pepper slices. Place the strips of fried tempeh carefully on the plate and drizzle with lemon juice. Serve with the wasabi mayonnaise.

Lemon Cheesecake with Raspberry Sauce

Serves 8

For the filling:
24 *ounces firm silken tofu*
½   *cup rice syrup*
⅓   *cup agave syrup*
¼   *teaspoon lemon bourbon*
Zest of 1 lemon
Juice of 1 lemon
1½ *tablespoons arrowroot*

For the piecrust:
½   *cup roasted hazelnuts*
1   *cup whole-wheat pastry flour*
¼   *teaspoon salt*
Zest of 1 lemon
¼   *cup canola oil*
3   *tablespoons maple syrup*
2   *tablespoons cold water*

For the sauce:
1   *cup raspberries*
¾   *cup water*
1   *tablespoon* kuzu *(kudzu),*
    dissolved in 1 tablespoon water
⅓   *cup agave syrup*

To garnish:
Lemon zest or toasted coconut
    flakes

Preheat the oven to 350 degrees. In a blender, combine all the filling ingredients and blend well. Set aside.

In a food processor, blend the hazelnuts until flourlike. In a bowl add the blended nuts to the pastry flour, salt, and zest. In another bowl, mix the oil, maple syrup, and water together. Add the wet ingredients to the dry, stirring together with a spoon until the mixture forms a crumbly dough. Press the dough into the bottom of a greased 9" pie pan.

Spoon filling into the piecrust. Bake in the preheated oven for 45 minutes. Remove the cheesecake from the oven and let cool for at least 3 hours before serving.

While the cheesecake is baking, prepare the sauce. In a saucepot, cook the raspberries with water and add the dissolved *kuzu* to the raspberries as they cook. Stir well for 2 or 3 minutes until the sauce thickens. Turn off the burner and stir in the agave syrup. Let the sauce cool.

To assemble: Serve the cheesecake with raspberry sauce on top and garnish with some lemon zest or toasted coconut flakes.

Wayward Café

SEATTLE, WA

5253 University Way NE
Seattle, WA 98105
(206) 524-0204

www.waywardvegancafe.com

Offering friendly service and a neighborhood feel, Wayward Café has a truly extensive menu of veganized versions of classic diner food.

Colin (pictured) **and Tami Blanchette, co-owners and chefs**

Interview with Tami Blanchette

Is this your first restaurant?
No. I previously owned Pizza Pi Vegan Pizzeria from December of 2007 until November of 2011.

When did Wayward Café open?
Wayward was a workers' collective before we purchased it in November of 2008. It was going out of business and we brought it back to life! It's no longer a collective, but we do like our employees to have a voice.

Do you want to have more than one restaurant?
It's always been a dream to have more locations, but we're so hands-on that we're just doing our best to keep up with how much we're expanding in our single location.

What's your favorite dish on the menu?
I'm a big fan of our lasagna and country fried "steak"—oh, and the "filet mignon" cannot be beat!

What's your most popular appetizer?
It's a tie between the fried "mozzarella" wedges and the smoky "bacon" fries!

What's the most popular entrée on the menu?
Probably the club sandwich, though it's tough to narrow it down to just one!

What's your most popular dessert?
Chocolate peanut butter cheesecake—house-made, of course!

What do you feel is special about your restaurant?
We're one-hundred-percent vegan; we're vegan owned and operated, and we make the food many people miss when going vegan.

How often do you change your menu items? Do you have daily or weekly specials?
We try to do a new menu every six to eight months. We have weekly specials that start every Saturday.

Do you have gluten-free, soy-free, and sugar-free options on your menu?
We have an extensive gluten-free menu, including gluten-free pancakes, French toast, club sandwich, and wraps, just to name a few items! We have a very limited soy-free selection, though it's definitely possible to eat soy-free at Wayward.

What do you do to reduce your environmental impact?
In addition to composting and recycling, we've installed a low-flow toilet in our restroom and we try very hard to minimize waste by making orders correctly the first time and paying attention to the cooking practices in our kitchen.

What are the most important lessons you've learned as owner or chef of this restaurant?
As an owner the lessons are numerous, quite different from the lessons I've learned as a chef. Most important, I've learned that you can't please everyone and not to take it personally. I've also learned that we're part of a community that wants to support us and will go to great lengths to do so.

What led you to want to open a vegan restaurant, and/or what led you to the vegan diet yourself?
I've worked in restaurants all my life so it seemed like a natural transition to own them. Going vegan is what really made it possible, though. I went vegan for my cats, honestly; I knew I would never eat them, so why would I eat any other animal?

In the time since your restaurant first opened, how has the plant-based food movement changed? Do you find more demand now for vegan food?
I think that the plant-based food movement has changed to include many more health-food vegans rather than ethics-based vegans. When we first opened both our pizzeria and then Wayward, it seemed like the climate was much more activist-centered rather than those who are primarily health-focused. I definitely think the demand has gone up in the last few years as is evident by our continued growth.

Since your restaurant first opened, has your view of what constitutes healthy or delicious foods changed? Have you changed the types of foods you offer?
Our food choices have not changed all that much since we first opened—but we've changed how many options we offer. We've included many more gluten-free choices since the beginning.

Where do you see the plant-based food movement going in coming years?
I see it expanding greatly, but unfortunately I think it will have less to do with the animals as time goes on and more to do with health issues. I feel like activism in my community has already started to die down, which is disheartening to me. After all, why do this if not for the lives we save? 🐾

Nutloaf

Serves 6

- 1   cup chopped walnuts
- 1   cup slivered almonds
- 1   large white onion, diced small
- 1   tablespoon ground flaxseed
- 1   12-ounce block medium-firm tofu
- ½   cup textured vegetable protein (TVP) granules
- ¼   cup nutritional yeast flakes
- ⅓   cup bread crumbs
- 1   tablespoon ground sage
- 1   tablespoon soy sauce
- ½   tablespoon vegan chicken broth powder
- 1   teaspoon dried thyme
- ½   teaspoon xanthan gum
- 2   tablespoons vegan margarine, softened
- 2   tablespoons minced garlic

Preheat the oven to 425 degrees. In a food processor grind the walnuts and almonds until they resemble a meal. Place all ingredients, including the processed nuts, in a large mixing bowl. Using clean hands, mash everything together into a paste. Mix very well. Spray a small cookie sheet with nonstick oil. Put the nutloaf dough onto the cookie sheet and spread evenly, filling all sides to the edge of the cookie sheet. Smooth the top to make sure the dough is level. Place the cookie sheet in the preheated oven for 45 minutes. Remove and allow to cool slightly before cutting.

Served as we do at our restaurant: either in a cold sandwich on toasted French bread with vegan mayonnaise, lettuce, and tomato, or in an open-faced hot sandwich on grilled sourdough topped with mushroom gravy and a side of garlic steamed kale.

ZenKitchen

OTTAWA, ON, CANADA

634 Somerset St. W.
Ottawa, ON K1R 5K4 Canada
(613) 233-6404

www.zenkitchen.ca

ZenKitchen is an award-winning, upscale, gourmet vegan restaurant serving artfully made, inventive, beautiful food.

Dave Loan, owner

Is this your first restaurant?
Yes.

When did it open?
July 2009.

Do you want to have more than one restaurant?
Good grief, no!

What's your favorite dish on the menu?
Our ravioli. Fresh, handmade, egg-free pasta stuffed with a blend of aged soy and bitter herbs, in a smoked tomato sauce.

What's your most popular appetizer?
Polenta fries! Crisp outside and creamy inside.

What's the most popular entrée on the menu?
Eggplant Parmesan. We make a Parmesan from *pepitas* (pumpkin seeds) and layer the eggplant with a vegan Mornay sauce.

What's your most popular dessert?
Mexican chocolate cake—rich, dark cake with a spicy chocolate sauce, served warm.

What do you feel is special about your restaurant?
We have a warm, inviting dining room and a friendly staff. Our food is beautifully presented and very flavorful. And we offer a full wine, beer, and cocktail list.

How often do you change your menu items? Do you have daily or weekly specials?

We have a chef's tasting menu that changes monthly. Other dishes change as produce becomes available through the seasons.

Do you have gluten-free, soy-free, and sugar-free options on your menu?

Diners requiring gluten-free meals have become a huge part of our customer base. Most of our menu is gluten-free and we take great care to prevent cross-contamination. We also address a wide range of food allergies and sensitivities, including soy, sugar, and everything else.

What do you do to reduce your environmental impact?

We rent a recycling bin for cardboard and recycling bins for cans and bottles. Our cooking oil is picked up and used for a biofuel project, saving us money and keeping the oil out of the landfill. Food scraps and leftovers—approximately sixty gallons each week—go to compost. We refuse to carry bottled water, preferring to filter and make our own sparkling water. And we purchase produce from local farmers as much as possible.

What led you to want to open a vegan restaurant, and/or what led you to the vegan diet yourself?

The root of our vegan restaurant came from three principles: We wanted a place anyone could come to and enjoy a good meal, without worrying about what was in it; we enjoyed the challenge of creating flavorful and beautiful dishes from plant-based foods; and we had a strong desire to have a business that's environmentally sustainable, healthful, and cruelty-free.

In the time since your restaurant first opened, how has the plant-based food movement changed? Do you find more demand now for vegan food?

We're seeing more demand for vegan food from non-vegans, in particular. In fact, about eighty percent of our customers are omnivores who just want a good meal. The message of introducing more plant-based

food into your diet seems to be resonating, and that's good for everyone.

Since your restaurant first opened, has your view of what constitutes healthy or delicious foods changed? Have you changed the types of foods you offer?

Global influences have continued to have an impact on vegan cuisine, both through the availability of ingredients that we didn't see ten years ago and through cooking techniques that are fairly recent developments. We do more molecular gastronomy now, including some very cool elements in many of our dishes. At the same time, we're building on very ancient techniques, such as the ones used in our cheese and tofu production.

Where do you see the plant-based food movement going in coming years?

The world is our oyster mushroom. Diners are becoming more health-conscious and aware of factory farming and other cruelty issues, while demanding more flavorful food. It's up to us to step up to the plate—the dinner plate—and offer our supporters the full dining experience while still respecting our values. 🍵

This is a complex but delicious salad that showcases beets in many different ways! We serve beets roasted, boiled, pickled, dehydrated, and even as a "paint" with ume vinegar. There are many different components to this dish, but don't be intimidated by it; if you truly enjoy food, you might just decide to keep some of these items on hand at all times anyway!

Tasting of Beets

Serves 4

For the pickled beets:
5   medium purple beets
1   cup red wine vinegar
½   cup red wine
½   cup water
1   tablespoon pickling salt
1   tablespoon granulated cane sugar
1   teaspoon pickling spices

For the ume-beet paint:
2   medium purple beets, boiled, peeled, and cut into chunks
1   tablespoon ume vinegar (Japanese pickled plum vinegar)
1   tablespoon and 1 teaspoon mirin (Japanese rice wine for cooking)

3   tablespoons unsweetened rice vinegar

For the roasted beets:
3   small chioggia beets
1   teaspoon grapeseed oil
Pinch kosher salt

For the boiled beets:
3   small golden beets
Water as needed, to cover
1   tablespoon kosher salt

For the dehydrated beet chips:
1   small chioggia beet, peeled
¼   cup water
2   tablespoons granulated cane sugar

For the black olive dust:
1   cup Kalamata olives

For the tofu feta:
4   cups water
2   tablespoons kosher salt
1   teaspoon herbes de Provence
1   16-ounce block firm tofu (vacuum-sealed, not water-packed)

For the toasted pecans:
1   cup pecan halves
1   tablespoon maple syrup
½   tablespoon grapeseed oil
Pinch kosher salt
Pinch ground black pepper

To assemble:
4   cups local, seasonal salad greens
1   tablespoon cold-pressed olive oil

For the pickled beets: Place the beets in a large pot and cover completely with water. Bring to a boil over high heat and allow them to cook fully, about 45 minutes. Check their doneness with a sharp paring knife by inserting it into the center of a beet. When you can pierce a beet with little resistance, they're done. Remove the beets from the water and allow them to cool until you can handle them comfortably. Remove the skins from the beets, then slice into bite-size wedges, and place them all in a clean container into which you can pour the pickling liquid without it overflowing. In a saucepan, bring the vinegar, wine, water, salt, sugar, and spices to a boil. Pour over the beets and allow them to sit until the liquid cools to room temperature. Place a cover on the beets and store in the fridge for up to 3 weeks. These beets can be eaten after 2 hours, but allowing them to rest in the pickling liquid for at least a day is recommended.

For the ume-beet paint: Place the cooked beets, ume vinegar, mirin, and rice vinegar in a blender and puree on high until it is completely smooth. Scrape down the sides of the blender as necessary. If your blender is not powerful enough to make it completely smooth, do your best and pass the mixture through a fine strainer with a ladle to get out as many chunks as possible. Refrigerate until ready for use.

For the roasted beets: Preheat the oven to 400 degrees. Toss the beets with the oil and salt. Create a small pouch out of tinfoil and place beets inside of it. Seal the pouch tightly, and place on a small tray in your preheated oven. Bake until the beats are cooked, approximately 45 minutes. Check with a sharp paring knife. If they are still a bit firm, place back in the oven at 10-minute intervals until they are done.

Remove from oven and allow to cool so that you can handle them. Remove the skins and slice the beets crosswise into half moons about ¼" thick. Reserve in the fridge until you need them. They can last for up to 3 days in the fridge.

For the boiled beets: Follow the same cooking method as for the pickled beets. Peel the beets when they are cool enough to handle, and cut them into ½" chunks. Reserve in the fridge until you need them. They can last for up to 3 days in the fridge.

For the dehydrated beet chips: Place the water and sugar in a small saucepot and

bring to a simmer. Allow it to cook until all of the sugar is dissolved. Cool the mixture down in the fridge. This simple syrup will keep for a month.

Slice the beet paper thin, being sure to slice it crosswise as to show off the beautiful pattern of it. (If you have a mandoline, this is a perfect use for it. If you do not have one, then use your sharpest knife.)

Toss all of the slices in a small bowl, and coat gently with the simple syrup.

Layer the beets on a small baking sheet lined with parchment paper (or a silicone baking liner if you have one) in a single layer, so they are not touching. Set the oven to 150 degrees. Place the baking sheet in the oven overnight (or at least 8 hours), until fully dried out. The following morning, carefully remove them from the tray and try not to break them. (They will be very fragile!) They should have a nice sheen on

recipe continued next page

the side that was facing down, thanks to the syrup.

Reserve at room temperature until you need them. These will keep for weeks if covered and left somewhere not too humid.

For the black olive dust: Remove the pits from the olives. If you have an olive pitter—perfect! But if you don't, simply crush the olives with the palm of your hand, a small pot, mallet, or side of your knife, then remove the pits.

Place the pitted olives in a single layer (with as little brine as possible) on a parchment paper–lined sheet tray. Heat the oven to 150 degrees. Place the tray in the oven overnight, until the olives are fully dried out.

The following morning, remove the tray and chop the dried olives with your knife until they resemble a dark powder. Do not use your food processor, as you might be tempted to, as the heat generated by the blade will turn the dried olives into a paste! Reserve the olive dust at room temperature, with a lid on. This will keep for a month easily.

For the tofu feta: Make a brine by mixing the water, salt, and herbes de Provence together. Cut the tofu into 4 even pieces and submerge it in the brine. Allow it to sit for at least 2 days, and up to 1 month in the fridge. Over the course of time, the outside of the tofu will turn slightly gray. This is normal and not hazardous. When ready to use, take a piece of the tofu and crumble it like you would a traditional feta cheese.

For the toasted pecans: Preheat the oven to 350 degrees. Toss all ingredients together in a bowl and lay out on a parchment paper–lined baking sheet. Place in the oven for 15 to 20 minutes, mixing every 5 minutes to ensure even cooking, until the pecans are fully toasted.

Remove the sheet from the oven, allow the nuts to cool, then store them in a closed container at room temperature until they are needed. They will keep for up to 3 weeks before they start to taste a bit stale.

To assemble: For each plate, use a brush or spoon to "paint" the ume-beet sauce onto the plate in a decorative fashion. Next, lay a few pieces of the pickled, roasted, and boiled beets on the bottom of the plate. Mix the greens with the olive oil and place on each plate, topping the first beets. Arrange the remaining pickled, roasted, and boiled beets on top of and around the greens, mixing the types up as you go to create a kaleidoscope of colors, textures, and flavors.

Crumble the tofu over top of the dish—it is salty, so you don't want to overdo it. Garnish the salad with a few pecans and a sprinkle of black olive dust. Carefully place 4 to 5 pieces of the beet chips around the salad, standing them up if you like, to add a nice final touch to the plate. Serve immediately, as you do not want the salad to wilt!

This is a very popular dish at ZenKitchen. One of its attractions is that you can use pretty much whatever fresh produce you want! It varies with the seasons, based on what is local and available: bright fresh leafy bok choy and carrots in the summer or root vegetables in winter. The curry sauce provides a range of flavors, from lemongrass and galangal to chilies and cilantro. Note that we cook the sauce and vegetables separately, to ensure the vegetables retain their texture and color. We serve the curry over jasmine rice infused with Kaffir lime leaf, and offer pickled red onion and mango chutney on the side.

Thai-Inspired Green Curry

Serves 4

For the curry sauce:
- 1   teaspoon cumin seeds
- 1   teaspoon coriander seeds
- 1   medium Spanish onion, coarsely chopped
- 6   cloves garlic, peeled
- 1   1½" piece galangal, peeled and coarsely chopped
- 3   stalks lemongrass, bruised and coarsely chopped
- 4   Thai chilies, stemmed
- ½   teaspoon ground black pepper
- 1   lime, peeled and minced
- 3   cups full-fat coconut milk

- 1   cup coconut cream
- ½   bunch cilantro, including stems
- ½   bunch Thai basil leaves
- ¼   cup lime juice
- 3   tablespoons agave syrup
- 1   tablespoon kosher salt

For the vegetables:
- 2   heirloom carrots, diced into ¾" cubes
- ½   head cauliflower, separated into bite-size florets
- 2   pieces Hakurei turnips, peeled and cut into 16 wedges
- ¼   cup grapeseed oil, as needed

Kosher salt, to taste
Ground black pepper, to taste
- 1   green zucchini, sliced lengthwise and then bias-cut (45-degree angle) ¼" thick
- ½   cup edamame, shelled and blanched
- 8   baby bok choy, halved

To assemble:
- 1½ cups jasmine rice
- 2   Kaffir lime leaves
- ½   cup crushed toasted cashews
- 1   tablespoon toasted sesame seeds

recipe continued next page

For the curry sauce: Put the cumin and coriander seeds in a hot, dry frying pan and stir until they begin to brown. Remove immediately. (They will burn quickly.) When cool, grind in a mortar and pestle or clean coffee grinder. Put the onion, garlic, galangal, lemongrass, chilies, black pepper, and minced lime in a food processor with the cumin and coriander. Pulse until the mixture breaks down into an even consistency and everything is mixed together. Scrape down the sides of the bowl as you go to ensure everything is being combined. Transfer the contents of the food processor to a heavy-bottomed saucepot. Add coconut milk and coconut cream and bring to a simmer; cook for 20 minutes. Remove from the heat and transfer to a blender.

Using a blender, puree the coconut curry mixture in batches with the cilantro and basil. After each batch has been blended completely and no large pieces of anything remain, pass it through a fine mesh strainer, using a ladle, into a clean bowl. Add the lime juice, agave syrup, and salt. Mix thoroughly with a whisk and taste. If the curry is too spicy, add a bit more agave syrup. Or, add more salt, lime juice, or chilies to taste. If not using the curry right away, cool it and store it in the fridge for up to a week, or in the freezer for up to 3 months.

For the vegetables: Preheat the oven to 375 degrees. Toss the carrots, cauliflower, and turnips lightly with grapeseed oil, salt, and pepper and place on a tray in the preheated oven. Roast until slightly colored but still remaining slightly firm in the center—approximately 20 minutes. Remove the tray from the oven and allow vegetables to cool to room temperature.

Get 4 dinner bowls ready.

Heat a deep-walled sauté pan or a wok over medium-high heat. Add grapeseed oil to coat the bottom of the pan, heat it up, then add the zucchini and sauté it for 1 minute to get some color on it. Next, add the carrots and turnips and sauté for 2 more minutes. Add the cauliflower and edamame and cook for 1 minute. Add the bok choy; 30 seconds later, add the curry sauce. Bring the sauce to a simmer and allow to cook, stirring occasionally for 5 minutes so that it reduces slightly and the vegetables will all be cooked through and hot.

To assemble: Rinse the jasmine rice in cold water and drain. Place the rice and Kaffir lime leaves in a heavy pot, and add 2¼ cups of cold water. Place the pot on a burner over high heat and bring it to a boil, then reduce the heat to a simmer and cover with a lid. Cook for about 12 minutes or until the water is absorbed. Remove the lime leaves before serving.

Transfer the rice to the center your bowls. Use a large spoon to scoop the vegetable mixture into the center of each bowl, on top of the rice. Try to divide the vegetables evenly among the bowls. Scatter some toasted cashews and sesame seeds on top. Serve immediately and enjoy!

Index

By Recipe

Avocado Apple Tatare with
Walnut Bonbons 152

Award-Winning Chickpea Fries 188

Beet Salad 32

Bistro Steak Sandwich 181

Black-Eyed Pea Fritters 224

Buddha Lentil Burger 38

Buddha's Delight 250

Butternut Gnocchi with Brussels Leaves,
Butternut Velouté, Pepitas, and
Pumpkin Seed Oil 200

Canelones de Seitan or Tempeh 170

Celery-Breaded Cutlet with Wild Rice
and Mixed Vegetables 70

Cherry Royal 258

Chia Pudding 160

Chicken Fried Tempeh 76

Chocolate Bundt Cake 230

Chocolate Raspberry Hazelnut Cake 108

Coconut-Squash Soup
with Garbanzo Bean Garnish 130

Coconut Tofu and Blacked Tempeh
with Grapefruit Yuzu 118

Crostini Italiano 256

Dijon-Glazed Tofu 48

Enchilada Pie 229

Fabulous Phở: Aulacese (Vietnamese)
Traditional Soup 140

Farr (Out) Yam 256

G'day Satay Pie 100

Gaia's Treasure 157

Gluten-Free Chocolate Pudding
with Cinnamon-Glazed Apples 224

Gluten-Free Coconut
Strawberry Shortcake Cupcakes 58

Gluten-Free Ginger-Sesame Vinaigrette . . 252

Granada Chai 88

Green Chili Polenta 146

Hayashi Rice 28

Kelly and Erinn's Carrot Cake 134

Key Lime Tarts 208

Kimchi Nori Maki Roll 212

Lemon Cheesecake with Raspberry Sauce . . 264

Lentil Curry Stew 95

Live Coconut Cacao Cheesecake 96

Moroccan Tajine 240

Nacho Pizza 33

Nutloaf 268

One-Pot Vegetables and Tofu
with Sesame Rice 214

Oyster Mushroom and Spinach Raclette . . . 24

Pasta with Pumpkin Curry Sauce 82

Peach Polenta and Vanilla Tomatoes 150

Peanut Butter Blondies 112

Peruvian Leftovers Pie 90

Phyllo Triangles with Sorrel Cream 244

Pistachio-Crusted Eggplant Napoleon . . . 165

Porcini-Crusted Tofu 53

Praline Brownies 114

Pumpkin Cheesecake with
Bourbon–Brown Sugar Cream 246

Pumpkin–Chocolate Chip Bread Pudding . . 84

Pumpkin Noodle Salad 23

Quinoa Patties 112

Quinoa Tabbouleh 60

Raw Brownie Bliss Bites 66

Raw Cacao and Coconut Truffles 106

Raw Lime Parfait 192

Raw Pumpkin Lasagna with Italian Pesto . . 176

Red Curry Tempeh Tempura 262

Roasted Spaghetti Squash, Cauliflower,
Garlic, and Mashed Potatoes with
Porcini Mushroom Gravy 186

Saffron Rice with Barberries with a
Pot of Flavorful Vegetables 72

Sage's Shiitake Escargot 218

Sage's Tiramisu 220

Seitan Marsala 47

Simran Burger 65

Skillet Cornbread 78

Spicy Cha Cha 142

Stuffed Shiitake Mushrooms
with Almond-Cinnamon Sauce. 126
Sublime Apple Crumb Pie à la Mode 236
Swiss Bircher Muesli 158
Tagliata ai Carciofi e Chardonnay. 174
Tasting of Beets 272
Tempeh Reuben 136
Thai Noodles. 17
Thai Red Curry 234
Thai-Inspired Green Curry 275

Tofu Omelet Sheets 77
Tofu Spinach Lasagna 41
Tofu with Broccoli in Spicy Garlic Sauce . . 124
Tricolored Vegetable Pasta with Sun-
Dried Marinara and Cashew Cheese . . 107
Vertical Diner's Shoofly Cake 219
Vertical Diner's Tofu Scramble 218
Wild Forest. 195
Zucchini Hummus 18
Zuchetti Pesto 206

By Location

United States

Arizona
Green New American Vegetarian Restaurant
(Phoenix, Tempe). 115
Lovin' Spoonfuls
(Tucson) 143

California
Evolution
(San Diego) 91
Millennium
(San Francisco) 161
Real Food Daily
(West Hollywood, Pasadena, Santa Monica) . 209
Souley Vegan
(Oakland) 221
Stuff I Eat
(Inglewood) 225
SunCafé Organic
(Los Angeles) 237

Connecticut
G-Zen
(Branford) 103

Florida
Choices Café
(Miami) 61

Mi Vida
(Miami) 167
Sublime
(Fort Lauderdale) 231

Massachusetts
True Bistro
(Somerville) 241

Illinois
Karyn's On Green
(Chicago) 127

New York
Café Blossom
(New York City). 43
Candle Café
(New York City). 49
Hangawi Restaurant
(New York City). 121
Peacefood Café
(New York City). 183

North Carolina
Luna's Living Kitchen
(Charlotte). 153
Plant
(Asheville) 189

Oregon

Cornbread Café
(Eugene) 73

Portobello
(Portland) 197

Pennsylvania

Blackbird Pizzeria
(Philadelphia) 29

Texas

Counter Culture
(Austin) 79

Loving Hut
(Houston) 137

Utah

Sage's Café and Vertical Diner
(Salt Lake City) 215

Washington

Chaco Canyon
(Seattle) 55

Wayward Café
(Seattle) 265

Multiple Locations

Native Foods Café 177

Veggie Grill 253

International

Australia

Funky Pies
(Sydney) 97

Canada

Green Cuisine
(Victoria) 109

Lettuce Love Café
(Burlington) 131

Rawlicious
(Toronto) 203

Vegetarian Haven
(Toronto) 247

ZenKitchen
(Ottawa) 269

Denmark

42°Raw
(Copenhagen) 13

England

222 Veggie Vegan
(London) 19

El Piano
(York) 85

Germany

Coox and Candy
(Stuttgart) 67

Lucky Leek
(Berlin) 147

Israel

Buddha Burgers
(Eilat, Haifa, Ra'anana, and Tel Aviv) . . . 35

Italy

Mudra Café
(Milan) 171

Japan

Ain Soph. Ginza
(Tokyo) 25

The Netherlands

Veggies on Fire
(The Hague) 259

Spain

El Piano
(Granada, Málaga) 85

Photo Credits, Translations, and Permissions

All photography unless otherwise noted was provided by the respective restaurant and its sources.

Ain Soph. Ginza Q&A translation on pages 26–27 by Hiroco Nakamura.

Candle Café "Porcini-Crusted Seitan" recipe photo on page 52 by Anne Duggan.

Coox and Candy translations by Tanja Segal.

Green New American photos by Gina Barile.

Millennium exterior and interior shots on pages 161–163 by Joan Linn Bekins.

Mi Vida "Canelones de Seitan or Tempeh" recipe photo on page 170 by Brian Ko.

Plant photos on pages 189, 190, and 193 by Vickie Burick. "Wild Forest" recipe photo on page 194 by Nathan Metcalf.

Real Food Daily chefs photo on page 210 by Rusty Dunn. "Kimchi Nori Maki Roll" recipe photo on page 213 by Tara Punzone. "One-Pot Vegetables and Tofu with Sesame Rice" recipe originally published in *Vegan Family Meals* by Andrews McMeel Publishing, LLC. Copyright © 2011 Ann Gentry.

Stuff I Eat photos by Steve Weltman, Absolute Network Solutions.

ZenKitchen photos by April Anne Hewens Photography.

Acknowledgments

As an international project, the *HappyCow Cookbook* required a good deal of effort from a host of contributors around the world.

First of all, we are indebted to our profiled owners and chefs from top-rated vegan restaurants all over the globe. We thank them for sharing with us not only their recipes, but also a lot of insight into the nature of their operations and the reasons they became pioneer vegan restaurateurs. They are the spirit of this book.

Thank you to Zel Allen of *Vegetarians in Paradise* (www.vegparadise.com) for the wise counsel and the tireless recipe testing.

Thank you to Tanja Segal for the expert translations from German.

And thank you to our senior editor, Maria Teresa Hart; our associate editors, Evelyn Hays and Christy Morgan; and our assistant editors, Jessika Rieck and Vy Tran.

A special thank you to the wonderful actress Emily Deschanel for kindly penning the foreword to this volume.

And finally, we couldn't have made this book without the fine team at BenBella Books, the company that is fast becoming America's premiere plant-based book publisher: Jennifer Canzoneri, Sarah Dombrowsky, Debbie Harmsen, Alicia Kania, Shannon Kelly, Adrienne Lang, Monica Lowry, Lindsay Marshall—and their fearless leader, Glenn Yeffeth.

—Eric Brent and Glen Merzer

About the Editors

Eric Brent has been a vegan for twenty-plus years and a world traveler who's visited more than fifty countries, living and working in many of them. He started HappyCow as a labor of love back in 1999 to make finding food while on-the-go easier for himself and everyone else.

Glen Merzer is co-author of various titles including *Better Than Vegan* with Chef Del Sroufe; *Food Over Medicine* with Pamela Popper; *Mad Cowboy* with Howard Lyman; *No More Bull!* with Howard Lyman and Joanna Samorow-Merzer; and *Unprocessed* with Chef AJ. A playwright and screenwriter living in Los Angeles, Glen has been a vegetarian for forty years and a vegan for the last twenty.

About HappyCow

Founded in 1999, HappyCow was created as a public service to help travelers and people everywhere find vegan, vegetarian, and healthy food. Today, our online community has grown to include members from around the world who are passionate about the vegetarian and vegan lifestyle as a healthy, compassionate, and environmentally sustainable way of living. More than simply a restaurant and health food store guide, HappyCow is an ever-evolving online hub that serves millions worldwide as a one-stop resource for everything VEG.